The search for political community

Cambridge Cultural Social Studies

General editors: JEFFREY C. ALEXANDER, *Department of Sociology, University of California, Los Angeles,* and STEVEN SEIDMAN, *Department of Sociology, State University of New York, Albany*

Editorial Board
JEAN COMAROFF, *Department of Anthropology, University of Chicago*
DONNA HARAWAY, *Department of the History of Consciousness, University of California, Santa Cruz*
MICHELE LAMONT, *Department of Sociology, Princeton University*
THOMAS LAQUEUR, *Department of History, University of California, Berkeley*

Cambridge Cultural Social Studies is a forum for the most original and thoughtful work in cultural social studies. This includes theoretical works focusing on conceptual strategies, empirical studies covering specific topics such as gender, sexuality, politics, economics, social movements, and crime, and studies that address broad themes such as the culture of modernity. While the perspectives of the individual studies will vary, they will all share the same innovative reach and scholarly quality.

Also in the series

ILANA FRIEDRICH SILBER, *Virtuosity, charisma, and social control* LINDA NICHOLSON and STEVEN SEIDMAN (eds.), *Social postmodernism*
WILLIAM BOGARD, *The simulation of surveillance*
SUZANNE R. KIRSCHNER, *The religious and Romantic origins of psychoanalysis*

The search for political community

American activists reinventing commitment

Paul Lichterman
Department of Sociology, University of Wisconsin, Madison

CAMBRIDGE
UNIVERSITY PRESS

Published by the Press Syndicate of the University of Cambridge
The Pitt Building, Trumpington Street, Cambridge CB2 1RP
40 West 20th Street, New York, NY 10011-4211, USA
10 Stamford Road, Oakleigh, Melbourne 3166, Australia

First published 1996

Printed in Great Britain at the University Press, Cambridge

A catalogue record for this book is available from the British Library

Library of Congress cataloguing in publication data

Lichterman, Paul.
    The search for political community: American activists reinventing
commitment / Paul Lichterman.
        p.   cm. – (Cambridge cultural social studies)
    Includes bibliographical references and index.
    ISBN 0 521 48286 0 (hardback). – ISBN 0 521 48343 3 (pbk.)
    1. Political participation – United States.   2. Political
activists – United States.   3. Individualism – United States.
4. Community.   5. Social contract.   6. Commitment (Psychology)
I. Title.   II. Series.
JK1764.L53   1996
323'.042'0973 – dc20   95–40498   CIP

ISBN 0 521 48286 0 hardback
ISBN 0 521 48343 3 paperback

KS

Contents

Acknowledgments

I often looked forward to this opportunity to say how much I appreciated the activists who let me observe and participate alongside them. I want to thank the members of the Ridge Greens, the Seaview Greens, Airdale Citizens for Environmental Sanity, and Hillviewers Against Toxics for welcoming me, and for teaching me about what political commitment means. These activists opened their meetings, and activities, and personal lives to me. I am grateful, and inspired, too. Laura, Carl, Hope, and Lester were especially helpful in sharing insights about their organizations with me.

I am very grateful for academic advice and support. The arguments in this book benefited much from conversations with Todd Gitlin, who contributed both keen insight and a resolute regard for the broader picture, along with steady encouragement. Ann Swidler helped me define the core of this project, encouraging me to sharpen my own contributions. I have learned much, too, from Robert Bellah, who gave generous attention to the themes in the study, suggested valuable readings, and provided wonderful support. I thank others who shared comments or explored ideas with me in earlier stages of the project, including Jerry Karabel, G. E. Swanson, Jack Potter, Robert Dunn, Ron Lembo, Kathy Oberdeck, and Alan Wolfe. I appreciate as well the lively discussions and support we shared in the "Culture Club" reading group at Berkeley, whose members included Lyn Spillman, Rich Kaplan, Marcy Darnovsky, Mark Saroyan, and Luisa Schein. I want to thank John Foran and Christian Joppke for generously making available their newsletter and clippings files. From independent field work supervised by Michael Burawoy and a seminar in qualitative research with Aaron Cicourel, I learned the value of meshing theory and close attention to everyday social settings. I want to thank Richard Flacks for detailed, helpful commentary on a later draft of the manuscript, and Richard Merelman and Carol Mueller for contributing their thoughts on portions of the study. Colleagues at the University of Wisconsin, Madison, have helped me think through my arguments; I would like to thank Gerry Marwell, Pam Oliver, and Richard Schoenherr in particular. The Sociology department at Madison provided a congenial setting for discussing this work. My series editor for Cambridge University Press, Steven Seidman, offered wonderfully detailed and useful commentaries on the manuscript. Anonymous reviewers for Cambridge provided helpful feedback. I appreciate the care that editor Catherine Max at the Press has put into this project; she fielded my many questions with good humor, and organized the work's transition from manuscript to book with finesse.

Financial assistance helped me meet some research expenses. I am grateful for a Phi Beta Kappa Dissertation Scholarship, a Graduate Dean's Research Grant, and several small grants from the Sociology department at Berkeley. The Sociology department at the University of Washington, Seattle, kindly offered hospitality and opportunities for trying out ideas during my stay there as a Visiting Scholar.

The early musings that became this project got spurred on with a challenge from Nina Eliasoph, who has lived the project with me. We discussed, criticized, pondered, and enjoyed the field work and the writing. Nina wrote marvelous comments on multiple drafts of chapters, indulged me with steady support, and refreshed my curiosity as we mulled over this study during our walks and bicycle rides and field work mornings-after. Nina's sense of public-spirited commitment has inspired this study from beginning to end; her sense of humor has graced the foibles and little victories and surprises in between.

1

Personalism and political commitment

Critics often say that too few Americans get politically involved. Active political commitment is declining, goes one familiar complaint, because people have become too concerned with their own personal fulfillment. Critics fear that the widespread emphasis on self-fulfillment is destroying traditional community ties that are necessary for active citizenship and the sacrifices that may accompany it. Calls to reestablish "a sense of community" continue to resound in academic criticism, political leaders' rhetoric, and everyday talk about what is wrong with contemporary US culture.[1]

This book addresses the complaint about self-fulfillment and political commitment by exploring how different environmental activists practice their commitments to activism. Critics of the self-fulfillment ethos would not question that people can and do enter the political arena to win attention for their personal needs. The question is whether the self-fulfillment ethos necessarily detracts from a public-spirited politics, a politics that aims to secure a common, public good such as a safer environment for a wide community of citizens. Critics of modern US culture have often assumed that it takes certain kinds of communal bonds between people to nurture public-spirited commitments: they have advocated the kinds of ties that Americans in the past developed in local or perhaps national communities with shared civic or religious traditions that obligated community members to one another. People who grow up within such ties would find it easier, more natural to commit themselves to the public good than those who don't. These critics argue that the self-fulfillment ethos has weakened these communal ties. Modern society needs to reestablish the kind of community that will produce citizens

1

with a sense of public obligation who stand up for standards and work for the common good.

Committed citizens have not completely disappeared, and some do belong to communities whose members share traditions and a sense of communal belonging. A good example is Mrs. Davis of Hillviewers Against Toxics.[2] Toxic hazards from industrial plants ringing Hillview menaced largely low-income neighborhoods like Mrs. Davis' with the threat – occasionally realized – of a toxic fire or a slow, poisonous leak. Mrs. Davis did not, however, join her toxics group out of simple self-interest: she did not express concern about her neighborhood property values, and had so far escaped the chronic health problems that plagued some Hillview residents. Davis was new to grassroots activism, and looking for an organization to join when she attended her first Hillviewers Against Toxics (HAT) meeting. Conversations with her neighbors and the HAT staffperson made the anti-toxics struggle compelling to her.

An African-American woman in her forties, Mrs. Davis drew on communal traditions, a sense of belonging to the black Hillview community and to a broader community of African-American Christians, when she "went public" as an activist. When she ran for city council three years after joining HAT, several of her endorsement speakers, including her pastor and a member of a religious broadcasters association, spoke at length about her virtues as a Christian woman. Mrs. Davis did not often articulate a religious basis for her activism, and she did not always define her work as service to a specifically black community; she did not need to. She could take for granted a local moral universe of Christian charity and African-American communal service in which public-spirited good deeds made sense, were worthwhile. Of course, her community did not always live up to the standards its spokespersons set for it. HAT's staffperson asserted several times that his organization did what local churches should have been doing, had they not been worried about endangering the occasional economic or political support they received from Petrox, Hillview's largest taxpayer and a major target of HAT's anti-toxics efforts. Neither did Mrs. Davis' community-minded dedication keep her from eventually voicing dissatisfactions with the level of individual involvement that the HAT leadership allowed for members. The point is that Mrs. Davis lived within the kind of community ties that many critics of American individualism see as essential for public-spirited commitment, and threatened by the widespread quest for personal fulfillment.

Compare Carl of the Ridge Greens, an activist organization based about a half hour's drive from Hillview. Carl, like Mrs. Davis, had little experience with activism before getting involved with his organization. He had thought seriously about environmental and political issues, though, to the point of quitting his well-paying job in genetic engineering because of qualms about its moral and political implications. Carl followed political issues in the news with a passion and did not like most of what he learned. He figured, in fact, that conventional electoral politics would probably never raise the fundamental questions about corporate interests and environmental priorities that he found at the root of so much policy-making. The movement organizations he was familiar with went about "putting out fires" with single-issue political campaigns. He envisioned a popular movement that would publicize the fundamental questions about environmental priorities and social justice that smoldered behind any single issue. He wanted to be part of a movement that would let ordinary citizens voice alternatives to the usual answers given by big interests and single-issue agitators. He became more and more involved in community educating and occasional protests with the small US Green movement in hopes that it would provide one of those alternative voices, and was one of the key organizers in the successful effort to get the fledgling California Green Party on to the ballot in 1991.

Carl did not tap into the kinds of communal tradition that sustained Mrs. Davis. A white man in his thirties, son of liberal-minded and non-churchgoing college instructors, he did not nurture his political commitments with the sense of obligation to a particular people, community, or faith that Mrs. Davis had. No ready answer came to mind when I asked Carl what made him committed to activism; he supposed, after mulling it over, that his parents' fight against a color bar at their college may have inspired him. Carl's practice of political commitment grew out of a very personalized sense of political responsibility. A man who quit his job over its larger political implications – and screened future opportunities with a critical, political imagination – was one who assumed that individuals could and should exercise a great deal of political commitment in their own lives. Grassroots politics for Carl meant a highly participatory politics in which individuals could realize themselves, actualize themselves, as personal agents of social change both in activist organizations and in everyday life. Carl would have agreed with a former member of the Ridge Greens who declared that he "couldn't just be a little bit involved." Activism had to be self-fulfilling. Carl did not ease himself into political involvement by talking to local neighbors or accepting the tutelage of an organization staffperson. He practiced a self-propelled sense of social responsibility.

The terms of complaint about self-fulfillment make it hard to understand someone like Carl. Cultural analysts and critics have often argued that a widespread emphasis on personal fulfillment is incompatible with public, political commitments. This study challenges that argument. Rather than always weakening commitment, the culture of self-fulfillment has made possible in some settings a form of public-spirited political commitment that Carl and many others like him have practiced in a personalized, self-expressive way. In other words, some people's individualism supports rather than sabotages their political commitments. A culture of self-fulfillment may well have encouraged some Americans to turn away from political engagement and toward apolitical self-exploration or consumerism. But a strain of this culture has also enabled some activists to practice political commitments that include a strong critique of selfishness and acquisitiveness. This study examines those activists' personalized form of commitment, and contrasts it with the more "community"-centered commitments that critics of individualism have upheld.

Critics are right that a culture of personal fulfillment has grown large, especially in the last thirty years. This culture is changing the very meaning and practice of "community" itself for many Americans. The trend represents a growing predicament for theories that find real political commitments only in traditional communities bound by a common faith or common sense of communal pride. This study shows why some Americans make personalized political commitments to begin with, why they cannot practice a more traditional kind of political responsibility that would emphasize community belonging and the communal will over individual expression. The personalized commitments we examine in this study both create and are sustained by a form of political community that emphasizes individual voice without sacrificing the common good for private needs.

My arguments arise out of a study of grassroots activism in the US in the late 1980s and early 1990s. I draw on four case studies of citizen environmentalist organizations, along with other research material described at the end of this chapter. Since complaints about the emphasis on personal expressiveness and self-fulfillment counterpose this trend to commitments anchored in traditional communities, I chose my cases so that I could compare commitments practiced in different kinds of communities. I contrast the forms of "community" that a variety of white and mostly middle-class activists have invoked with the "community" underlying organizing drives in the largely African-American Hillview locale of Mrs. Davis . And I compare the results of my own field research with studies of other recent social activists. There are limits on what kinds of public involvement and what kinds of political organizations the personalized kind of political commitment can sustain. Nevertheless, the study argues that a personalized form of political commitment underlies significant portions of numerous recent grassroots movements in the US.

Some academic observers would suggest that personalized politics is relatively new, a product of rapid social change and cultural ferment that ignited the movements of the 1960s and fueled movements thereafter. Other observers have been skeptical of claims to newness, pointing out the existence of seemingly similar movements from many decades ago. Vigorous debates about the putative "newness" of some recent movements have generated some useful – if limited – insights, a good deal of miscommunication, and relatively little attention to the question of commitment that is central in this study. We will examine and critique arguments about "newness" as they apply to grassroots environmentalism in the 1980s and 1990s. Chapter 6 will suggest that the culture of commitment examined in this study is no newcomer in the US political scene, but that its modern form developed and changed during the US civil rights movement and became routinized in the 1970s. The institutional context for grassroots activism has helped to shape a succession of movements whose cultures of commitment bear a strong family resemblance. But the empirical question of "newness" will be much less important than the theoretical question of whether we need some new conceptual tools for thinking about political commitment.

My goal at the outset is to bring theoretical questions about commitment in American culture to bear on observations from contemporary social movements. The resulting encounter will illuminate how, why, and with what consequences have some Americans turned a popular kind of individualism to public-spirited political action. The notion of activism for the broad public good may seem increasingly unrealistic or outdated for activists influenced by the self-fulfillment themes in the cultural mainstream, or the identity-based politics of the 1980s and 1990s. Rather than dismiss the notion we should re-work it to reflect the role that self-fulfillment as a cultural trend can play in a public-spirited grassroots politics.

PERSONALISM AS A CULTURAL TREND

Individualism is not a single ethos in US society. Various individualisms have grown as the US itself has developed from a largely rural society to a highly industrialized one. Easiest to recognize, perhaps, is the instrumental or "utilitarian" individualism that drives individuals to save money and build an affluent lifestyle through careful calculation. Anyone who shops carefully for bargains or strategizes for a successful career practices this kind of individualism in some situations. Through countless stories, teachings, and rules of thumb, popular culture tells Americans of the virtues, and sometimes the vices, of individual hard work and sacrifice in the service of "getting ahead." But a somewhat different individualism concerns this study. It is the individualism women and men practice when they seek self-fulfillment and individualized expression, "growth" in personal development rather than growth in purely material well-being. This is the individualism that some critics have interpreted as excessive self-centeredness or "narcissism," fearing its corrosive effects on commitment to the common good. I will call this kind of individualism "personalism."

In this study, "personalism" refers to ways of speaking or acting which highlight a unique, personal self. Personalism supposes that one's own individuality has inherent value, apart from one's material or social achievements, no matter what connections to specific communities or institutions the individual maintains.[3] Personalism upholds a personal self that lives with ambivalence towards, and often in tension with, the institutional or communal standards that surround it (Taylor 1991, 1989; Bellah *et al.* 1985; MacIntyre 1981; Rieff 1966). But we should not reduce personalism to its most selfish or privatizing manifestations: personalism does not necessarily deny the existence of communities surrounding and shaping the self, but it accentuates an individualized relationship to any such communities. In contrast with a political identity that is defined by membership in a local, national, or global polity, a traditional religious identity that gets realized in a fellowship of believers,[4] or a communal identity that develops in relation to a specific community, the personal self gets developed by reflecting on individual biography, by establishing one's own individuality amidst an array of cultural, religious, or political authorities.

It is easy to assume that personalism is simply human nature. Isn't it just natural to want to develop one's individuality? Hasn't the main achievement of modern culture been a freeing of this natural, universal inclination from the constraints of tradition? It is easy for many Americans to counterpose "natural" or "real" selves to social "constraints" outside the self because of a popular version of personalism that is widespread in the US cultural mainstream. Cross-cultural study makes clear that not all cultures place the emphasis on personal development and personalized initiative that many Americans now take for granted.[5] Personalism is not a simple reflection of nature, but a way of defining and presenting the self. Developing individuality depends on interaction. There are norms for "expressing oneself," for being an individualist who can converse with others about personal feelings and experiences. Individuality does not pre-exist culture; it is a cultural accomplishment. Personalism develops in a kind of community in fact, one in which people create and practice norms of highly individualized expression.

Personalism echoes in many popular understandings of self and society. If we say that no individual, organization, or tradition can "tell us how to think" because each person has to "let his own intuitions guide him" or "find her own meaning in life" then we are speaking from the broad personalist tradition. When self-help books counsel readers to "look within" to find the resources to make decisions about changing relationships or changing jobs, they are counselling a personalist morality. If a political organization insists on making decisions through a unanimous consensus because it assumes that each member has a unique, inviolable contribution to make, then that organization is practicing a personalized politics. In all of these instances, the assumption is that each individual carries a unique moral will that is "authentic" (Taylor 1991) or real for that individual and needs to be respected. Personal authenticity – being true to an individual vision – becomes the standard by which to decide and prioritize.

Varied currents of personalism have long run through the US cultural mainstream. One of the most powerful is the quest for self-discovery through psychological therapy. One hundred years ago some Americans were trying to "get in touch with their feelings" by reading popular self-help books with messages strikingly similar to, if less technically articulated than, their contemporary counterparts. From the "mind cure" tracts of the late nineteenth century (Lears 1981) to the contemporary profusion of best-selling psychotherapies with specialized vocabularies (Lichterman 1992), Americans have continued reading about, talking about, and occasionally reacting against the search for self-realization.[6] We cannot equate personalism as a culture with the history of psychotherapy, nor with the popular psychologies that have so influenced everyday thinking in the US. But recent trends in therapeutic experiences represent one relatively well-documented indicator of a growing personalism in the US cultural mainstream during the last thirty years.

Figures on psychological help-seeking are a good source of evidence of personalism in the cultural mainstream because they suggest an increasing openness to focusing on the individual self, bracketing off communal ties. Psychologists and other mental health professionals often invite their clients to talk about personal experience and feelings in a context removed from communal or institutional authorities. So becoming a psychologist's client often means, among other things, becoming an apprentice in the culture of personalism. According to one national survey (Kulka, Veroff, and Douvan 1979) between the mid-1950s and the mid-1970s the proportion of all professional guidance-seeking individuals that sought out psychological guidance nearly doubled. The total number of Americans seeking psychologically oriented help – as distinguished from purely medical or religious guidance – tripled. These figures do not necessarily mean that Americans were any less mentally healthy by the mid-1970s than they were in the 1950s; the figures do imply that Americans became more willing to talk about private feelings and accept psychotherapeutic guidance.

Americans not only became more open to therapeutic guidance, but more oriented to self-fulfillment in their everyday lives. Between the mid-1950s and mid-1970s, Americans had become increasingly likely to define well-being in terms of personal expression rather than in terms of success at complying with institutionalized roles (Veroff, Douvan, and Kulka 1981). A review of national surveys (Yankelovich 1981: 4–5) claimed that a "preoccupation with self" and "search for self-fulfillment" – confined largely to campus youth in the 1960s – diffused through broader socio-economic strata. The increasing orientation to self-fulfillment reflects not only in survey responses but in talk about what matters in life. In his national study, Daniel Yankelovich (1981) heard a lot of interviewees phrase their life priorities in terms of self-realization. Robert Bellah and his research team (1985) heard a lot of this same kind of talk during the lengthy interviews and field research that went into their own study of moral reasoning several years later. Richard Flacks (1988) argued similarly that Americans after the 1960s became increasingly attuned to self-exploration and experimentation even as, and perhaps in part because, economic opportunity contracted.

Personalism has become a big enough part of the US mainstream that millions of Americans now participate in personal support groups (Wuthnow 1994). Roughly 75 million Americans belong to some kind of "small group" that "provides caring and support for its members" (Wuthnow 1994: 4). Nearly half of the group members in this small groups study described their groups as Bible study or prayer fellowships, while roughly one- eighth of group members belonged to therapeutic self-help groups such as 12-step groups focused on addictions. What is striking, though, is how personalism has suffused church-based as well as more specifically self-help small groups. The great majority of specifically religious group members characterized their groups as places for getting "emotional support" and discussing personal problems (Wuthnow 1994: 66–69). They wanted not so much to fulfill religious *duty* as to make religious teachings *personally fulfilling*, to use them therapeutically.

This study of small groups highlights not only the continuing, widespread dedication to personal development in the 1990s but the fact that personal fulfillment is a *cultural* accomplishment, that it happens in group settings. Members of supportive groups must know how to talk about themselves, about their deeply personal feelings and experiences. As the small groups study relates, these groups have norms for talking and listening, and their members have expectations about what a good group will be like. Members of small supportive groups do not participate in raw individual spontaneity but in a culture, a learned, shared way of speaking and acting: the culture of personalism. Personalist ways of creating community have suffused not only religious and self-help but some grassroots political groups, too. Thirty years before Wuthnow's small groups study, a critic warned that the US was undergoing a cultural revolution – a widespread turn to psychological thinking and corresponding abandonment of morality and public virtue rightly understood (Rieff 1966). We might well consider the ascendance of personalism in the US cultural mainstream as a quiet "revolution" in morality. We need to look more closely now at the complaints about this cultural revolution.

This study concerns itself mainly with two very broad positions on the question of personalism and public, political commitment, one of which I will call "communitarian," and the other, "radical democratic." Elements of each position overlap in specific works; some specific authors have spanned both positions in their writings.[7] I am highlighting the differences between the positions in order to chart the limits of the debate. The two positions suggest quite different ways of interpreting the evidence on the growth of personalist culture. The following review does not treat either set of views exhaustively, nor does it exhaust the positions in the debate. It focuses on a few particularly important arguments by sociologically oriented thinkers about relations between personalism and commitments to the public good.

COMMUNITARIAN VIEWS

The seesaw model

The complaint about self-fulfillment has often been inspired by an image of community that is quite different from the kind of community many support group members seek. For scholarly critics of self-fulfillment, whom we can call communitarians, a "sense of community" does not mean the good personal feelings someone may get from joining an organization or moving to a friendly neighborhood. Rather, a sense of community is a sense of obligation. Communitarians focus less on what communities can do for individuals and more on what members do to maintain a community. Communities only cohere, according to this view, when their members practice traditional obligations – contained in religious teachings or notions of good citizenship for instance – that are larger than any individual. Members of such a community share a sense of producing their lives together, depending on one another as bearers of ongoing traditions that pre-exist and will outlast any individual member.

Certainly members of a community may be "personally" invested in it: their feelings are an important part of their sense of communal belonging. But to communitarians, the crucial feature of commitment is the interdependence, the sense of obligation to and contribution to a collective body, not the sense of personal empowerment or self-realization upon which one might act, "making a difference" as an individual. Communitarians fear that the kinds of community that make public-spirited, political commitment possible have increasingly been supplanted by communities based on lifestyle tastes more than a sense of obligation. These communities strike communitarians as weak bases for nurturing political commitments that have a broad public good at heart. If people join a community in order to discover or express their individuality, then how can they develop broad horizons, dedication to shared goods and shared struggles?

Communitarian scholars and critics have often argued that communities formed out of a convergence of personal preferences will amount only to a collection of individuals pursuing private ends, not a broad public good. Their members will only practice personal gratification, not political virtue. The basic communitarian argument imagines public, political commitment and individuality in terms of a seesaw: as self-expression and private life become more important they pull down morality, political dedication, and public virtue. This seesaw model was perhaps articulated most simply and starkly by culture scholar Philip Rieff, who feared that with the rising personalism in the culture, moral obligation would become simply another "personal experience" that one could take or leave, experimenting with it as with any other personal experience. Personalism would corrode any sense of obligation that emanates from outside the self. Rieff sadly envisioned Americans living lives consisting of one personal experience after another, "freed from communal purpose" (Rieff 1966: 22).

The image of a seesaw serves to highlight two basic features of communitarian thinking about commitment to the common good. One is that communitarians have assumed dichotomous distinctions between the communal and the individual when they conceive how good commitments work. Serious commitments infringe on individual freedom in the interests of some broader good. The image is that people are torn between personal gratification and service to communities, and must balance the two in some way. We choose between private interests or the broad public good, individuality or shared bonds. Communitarians do not all simply rail against private interests and personal needs as if these would or should disappear. As a recent manifesto of communitarianism puts it, Americans need to institute more mutual obligation into the structure of everyday life to counterbalance the dedication to self-interest and self-expression – the "me-istic forces" – already strong in the culture (Etzioni 1993: 26). The image is of a need for better balance, an adjustment of the seesaw.

The other important aspect of the metaphorical seesaw is its tilt: in most communitarian accounts the seesaw of commitment in the US has tilted historically toward the "personal" and away from the public, political, or communal. Communitarian writer Christopher Lasch, for instance, flatly contended in 1979 that "after the political turmoil of the sixties, Americans have retreated to purely personal preoccupations" (Lasch 1979: 29). Even broader historical claims framed Lasch's account of the rise of personalism in US culture: as large bureaucracies and an intrusive welfare state grew during the twentieth century, experts and state bureaucrats took over many of the functions the traditional family once performed, but they neglected to carry on the family's role in teaching morality. Bureaucratic human service agencies ended up encouraging a self-indulgent, dependent population, a malleable clientele of big children who, having had selfish needs met, would not challenge the bureaucratic powers that be. An older morality of self-sacrifice, hard work, and communal effort declined, public standards decayed, and personalism took their place – a culture that Lasch judged harshly as self-centered, or "narcissistic." A seesaw of moral decline and individual efflorescence characterizes other communitarian accounts too. Theorist and critic Daniel Bell (1976), for instance, criticized an individualistic "fun morality," encouraged by the rise of mass consumption in the 1920s. "By the 1950s, American culture had become primarily hedonistic, concerned with play, fun, display, pleasure" – or in other words, with personal exploration and expression (Bell 1976: 70). During a decades-long tilt of the seesaw, "traditional morality was replaced by psychology" (Bell 1976: 72).

Seesaw thinking colors the kinds of solutions communitarians offer for the perceived weak state of commitment. Communitarian arguments tend to invoke a time when the seesaw "riders" sat in different positions relative to one another, when communities of faith, ethnicity, or political membership were more numerous, and more people participated in the kinds of ties that supported anti-toxics activist Mrs. Davis. While communitarian arguments are not all simply stuck in "golden age" reverie, their rhetoric often compares the present unfavorably with some imagined past. Rieff saw a communal past as nearly irretrievable and resigned himself to sometimes bitter criticism of a world blinded by an inward-focused psychological imagination. Lasch advocated "communities of competence" to take back some of the power and authority of professional experts, and invoked "localism" as a basis for resisting the suffocating grip of a therapeutic, bureaucratic sort of Big Brother. Bell called for a "great instauration," a kind of moral reawakening that would inspire Americans to limit their profane self-indulgence and personal exploration and reestablish commitments to the public good.

The terms of debate limit the insights these accounts can offer. An argument that imagines public-spirited political commitment on a seesaw with personalism will have to see personalism as a counterweight at best, or as is more often the case, a looming threat at worst. From the start, accounts such as those of Rieff, Lasch, and Bell disallow the possibility that personalism plays some positive role in political commitment. Painting cultural trends with the broadest of strokes, these accounts suggest that a self-centered, hedonistic personalism has nearly taken over the culture. They make it easy to dismiss Carl of the Ridge Greens as morally adrift, and difficult to account for people such as Mrs. Davis of HAT at all. Even if we sympathize with concerns about community and political commitment, critiques such as Lasch's make it too easy to conclude in a general way that "things are bad" from the communal standpoint, and getting worse at an increasingly rapid rate. By fiat, these critiques cut short the inquiry into personalism and its political consequences.

Developments within the communitarian imagination

Some studies have gotten beyond broad, highly general critiques of moral deterioration while still strongly indebted to a communitarian imagination. They have asked how and to what degree communitarian sentiments and individualism might coexist. In their much-cited study of individualism and commitment in the US, Bellah *et al.* (1985) found both individualistic and traditional, community-oriented sentiments alive in the US cultural mainstream. The authors argued that Americans find it most comfortable talking about their family ties or their volunteer work in terms of the individual benefits and good feelings these commitments bring. Some also reasoned in a language of communal obligation, justifying their commitments in terms of the greater public good of a community, local or national. The research team found communal languages to be less-practiced components of the culture than individualist ones; some of the inteviewees who could talk in terms of communal obligation did so only haltingly, struggling to make sense out of commitments that strained the logic of individualist reasoning.

In a somewhat similar vein, Wuthnow (1991) interviewed volunteers to find out how they would explain why they gave their time to volunteer fire departments, literacy programs, or community fundraisers. Patterns took shape in the form of explanation volunteers gave; they tapped into a cultural pool of acceptable idioms for explaining their motives. Some of these idioms evinced the strong influence of personalism, such as the commonly heard rationale that volunteering would give the volunteer a sense of fulfillment. While Wuthnow's volunteers were engaging in activities conventionally considered less "political" than those of activists that challenge structural relationships or everyday social routines, the study is valuable in this discussion for offering a perspective on personalism and public-spirited pursuits.

Both studies avoided simple versions of historical seesaw thinking, finding a mix of individualism and communal expression in both individual lives and in the culture at large. In fact, Wuthnow started from what many observers might consider a paradox – that the US cultural mainstream is strongly individualistic, yet Americans contribute extensively to volunteer efforts. It turned out that many volunteers defined volunteering as an act of individual non-conformity, or one that resulted from purely personal opportunities, or one that highlighted for them their own self-sufficiency. They made volunteering tractable to an individualistic culture that is prone to dismiss people who perform caring acts as excessively self-righteous do-gooders.

These studies did not depart entirely from the seesaw model. The Bellah team suggested that if the activists and volunteers in their study could not define their commitments in terms of communal obligations, then those commitments would have a precarious basis, and might not last long. Personalism might justify impulsive protest – that of an activist who says he is politically involved because at the moment, that is "where I'm at" (Bellah *et al.* 1985: 133). But the risk is that such a political commitment would easily fade, only to reemerge in some other short-lived personal enthusiasm. How could others depend on someone who tied political commitments to personal preference instead of a sense of obligation? Personalism would not sustain a true community that shared a sense of obligation to a common good rather than simply a common enthusiasm for the same tastes or lifestyles. In the end, community-mindedness and self-expressiveness, public virtue and private gratification, opposed each other on a conceptual seesaw. Wuthnow's volunteers study accommodated itself more to the personalism in the US cultural mainstream. The volunteers' stress on self-fulfillment did not simply drain their commitment to volunteering. Rather, personalism and other individualisms helped volunteers define volunteering as a comfortably limited, "doable" commitment. Still, Wuthnow concluded that personalism limited the bonds of obligation volunteers could produce with those they helped, or with society in general. Practicing compassion because it feels good would not promote a strong sense of community, but more individualism (1991: 117, 292). If I cannot talk about my commitment to reducing hunger or poverty without relating these commitments back to my own personal needs, then how sturdy can my relationship to the hungry or poor be?

Personalism can produce a kind of social tie, then, but according to these studies this tie is a weak one, and perhaps an undependable one too. Both studies saw modern forms of individualism as inescapable realities rather than simply evils to bemoan or dismiss. The studies arrive at a crucial dilemma: where in a multicultural society would Americans find the inspiration for commitments that may once have been nurtured in traditional faith communities and local polities? The Bellah team raised the question with particular poignancy:

We thus face a profound impasse. Modern individualism seems to be producing a way of life that is neither individually nor socially viable, yet a return to traditional forms would be to return to intolerable discrimination and oppression. The question, then, is whether the older civic and biblical traditions have the capacity to reformulate themselves (1985: 144).

The answer is contained in the question. Communal tradition will revive public spirit. But the question remains whether there are kinds of political engagements that might depend upon and even accentuate individuality rather than only accommodate it or else rein it in. If some activists practice such engagements, we cannot clearly perceive them from communitarian terms of discussion. We cannot readily find a place for Carl, who practiced long-term political commitments but rarely drew on the terms of civic or biblical traditions.

The seesaw model offers some basic insight – it is not flatly wrong. Activists and volunteers do juggle the more communal and the more individualistically oriented languages of commitment, and the latter may well predominate for many groups in US society. The notion of a long historical transition from the communal to the individualistic itself has a distinguished history. Much sociological theorizing about community and commitment, from Ferdinand Toennies and Emile Durkheim to contemporary commentators, has invoked some notion of this transition, even if it is hard to demarcate its historical parameters clearly.

But we can still wonder whether the entire potential of personalism has been examined in communitarian sociological arguments of either polemical or carefully measured varieties. If ongoing social change has created increasing opportunities and affinities for self-direction and self-development,[8] then we ought to consider whether personalism may inspire public commitments beyond transitory impulse or self-centered notions of "helping" – let alone "hedonism" or "narcissism." The question is pressing for practical reasons, not just theoretical ones. In a nation of diverse cultural, religious, and political communities, considerable numbers of people will find limited appeal in the biblical and civic traditions to which the Bellah team referred. The political communities built around these traditions, even in their more modern formulations, have not always welcomed members of cultural minorities or women as full participants. Some degree of individualism in relation to these traditions may be necessary for achieving a fairer, more open, community of citizens.

Tilting the seesaw: the liberal reaction

The communitarian complaint was in fact countered by other critics in the 1980s and 1990s who wanted to valorize the individualisms that make communitarians wary. These critics, often called "liberals," have found a moralistic elitism in communitarian writing. The liberals have argued in effect that "everyone is entitled to some personal space."[9] Regarding personalism and politics, one influential argument (Clecak 1983) has it that a "quest for fulfillment" motivated much of the social unrest of the 1960s and 1970s. Women, African-Americans, and others demanded more economic opportunity so that ultimately they would have more means for pursuing personal growth in their private lives.[10]

This line of thinking does not leave the seesaw model so much as focus favorably on the "individualism" side of the seesaw while failing to examine the other side carefully. It may be true that some activists in

social justice movements of the 1960s and 1970s fought for fuller opportunities for their own self-development, among other motives. But
Clecak's argument ignores the communitarians' questions about the fate
of public-spirited commitments by assuming that the ultimate ends of
political activism are always private and individual. It is entirely reasonable to argue that individualistic people can join together for some kinds
of political action. But that does not answer the question of whether they
can act for a broad common interest, for a public good larger than self-
interest. Other voices in the debate about personalism and commitment
suggest more viable alternatives to communitarian arguments. Rather
than simply celebrating what communitarians condemn, they question
the seesaw dualities of self-fulfillment and public commitment.

RADICAL DEMOCRATIC VIEWS: A PLACE FOR
PERSONALIZED POLITICS

In an individualistic culture that counterposes the individual to the
community, it is easy to imagine political commitments as ongoing feats
of self-discipline or self-sacrifice. It is harder to imagine a kind of political commitment that complements self-realization and could even be
strengthened by it. A variety of views suggest this possibility, though, and
we can call them "radical democratic." They do not necessarily advocate
"radical" political ideologies, but they advocate a change in, an extension
of, democratic politics as conventionally practiced. These radical democratic views, like communitarian ones, reject a popular, individualistic
way of thinking that imagines all people have a "free" or "pure" self that
pre-exists social relationships. Rather, self-realization means fulfilling
individual potential in a social context, not finding a pre-social, pure self.

Radical democratic theorists depart from communitarians, however,
by advocating more questioning, critically reflective stances toward the
communal standards that anchor public commitment in communitarian
imagery. Radical democratic positions do not often take up the question
of personalism specifically, and so they do not provide direct answers to
the question of whether personalism can complement commitments to
the public good. But these positions accent individuality within their
notions of public-spirited commitment. They also question the ways the
communitarians pack the terms "public" and "private" onto the conceptual seesaw of public commitment and private gratification. So they offer
an alternative to the seesaw model, and they open up more room for
engaging rather than discounting a personalized politics.

Radical democratic theorists imagine a kind of political community whose members debate many of their own assumptions. Participants in this community could collectively change their priorities and their ways of defining their community as newly recognized groups or new claims become part of the community. They might even call into question the future of any one communal tradition. The communitarian imagination has lacked a vocabulary for describing a community that sustains this much self-redefinition and this much questioning. Working within the broad, radical democratic camp, Jürgen Habermas has theorized an ideal model of political community that depends on individuals who can criticize both themselves and other members without being held back by ideological blinders or by uncritically accepted traditions (1987: 77–111). Members committed to this kind of community increasingly realize their individual potentials as they replace unquestioned traditions or habits with open discussion between free and equal individuals about their community's priorities. Reasoning together, members of the ideal community that Habermas envisions could come to at least temporary consensus on issues and assumptions that divide them. Individuals in this kind of community would all carry highly individualized commitments rather like those of Carl, depicted at the start of this chapter; the community's notions of the public good would arise through deliberations between self-propelled, yet socially responsible individuals. Habermas imagines a collectivity in which an individual "can walk tall" (1986: 125) without walking away from commitments.

Other radical democratic theorists, with less faith in a universal reasonability than Habermas, also challenge the communitarians' understanding of public commitment. Much more than Habermas, Chantal Mouffe (1993, 1992a, 1992b) criticizes the communitarians for upholding a notion of the public good that depends on tradition shared across a society.[11] While adopting some of the communitarians' concerns, Mouffe has insisted on a fundamentally pluralist stance toward culture and tradition. She argues against communitarians for failing to acknowledge that there are always competing, incommensurable traditions of defining the public good. Mouffe, like Habermas, upholds a notion of public commitment beyond self-interest or self-gratification, and at the same time secures a place for individual autonomy in her image of a community of the committed. In contrast with Habermas, though, she argues that no normative model of a political community can apply universally; "democracy" will always be open to different interpretations. Neither should theorists appeal to a universal human capacity for reason as the means for reaching a consensus on the public good.

Mouffe and Habermas certainly represent the varied spectrum of positions among radical democracy theorists. Habermas looks foward to democratic political communities that substitute critical, reasoned debate in place of some of the traditions that communitarians have sought to reinvigorate. Mouffe envisions fluid, ever-changing political communities in which groups with different traditions and different kinds of "reason" commit themselves to a search for egalitarian ways of living together that respect individual autonomy. But in their own ways, both Habermas and Mouffe suggest a challenge to "seesaw" thinking that counterposes self-realization to public-spirited commitment. Both envision communities of the committed that, in different ways, allow a space for individuality that is hard to articulate within the terms of communitarian arguments.[12]

Criticisms of the notions of public and private themselves play important roles in radical democratic thinking about political commitment. Feminist theorists within the radical democratic arena have made crucial contributions here, with important implications for a personalized politics. The realm of public-spirited commitment that communitarians uphold has historically been one sustained by predominantly male forms of discussion and sociability – and the expectation that men, not women, would practice them. The "public good" has often been defined in ways that systematically privilege everyday knowledge and practices of men, while relegating knowledge and practices most often shared by women to a "private" sphere beyond communal debate. While some communitarian theorists note these historic patterns (for instance, Bellah *et al.* 1985), they do not systematically integrate this gender gradient into their treatment of the public good or the common interest. The trouble then arises that these images of commitment could too easily conjure up a self-sufficient (male) citizen debating in an abstract male style about issues that are salient to a culturally trained male imagination, while the (usually female) less-valued but necessary activities that free this citizen from domestic duties remain "private" and beyond critical scrutiny. Feminist theorists such as Fraser (1985), Mouffe (1993), Dietz (1992), Young (1987), and Benhabib and Cornell (1987) insist, then, that for a political community to be a fully democratic one in which all individuals realize rather than restrain their potentials, it must open up debate about any social relationships or traditions, especially ones distinguishing public from private, which result in subordinate positions for women.

The contemporary feminist movement in fact grew out of women's dissatisfactions with being relegated to private roles within the student new left of the 1960s (Evans 1979). Practicing the dictum "the personal is political," newly formed feminist consciousness-raising groups put words to women's individual, private experiences of subordination that had long gone unremarked. Embodying what would later become the articulated principles of radical democratic feminist theory, early women's movement activists practiced a kind of participatory democracy that emphasized individual expression and personal caring (Dietz 1992). Their organizations developed participatory forms of interaction that many activists, including some in this study, would later refer to as "feminist process." Among contemporary movements, the feminist movement has been perhaps the foremost conduit of a personalized politics that extends democratization into "personal" relations within movement organizations and "private" relations outside of them.

Radical democracy theorists' visions of political community have been engaged with not only contemporary feminist movements but a succession of social movements in the industrialized West. Given the different versions of a radical democracy ideal, it is not surprising that theorists such as Habermas and Mouffe have taken inspiration from different aspects of these movements and criticized different aspects as well. But they share the view that grassroots feminist, peace, youth, anti-nuclear, environmental, and other movements have tried to extend democracy itself as a public good.[13] These activists have tried to bring more egalitarian participation to decisions about environmental pollution, foreign policy, or women's opportunities that were previously closed behind corporate or state agency doors, or else relegated to a non-political "private" sphere beyond criticism. Theorists like Habermas and Mouffe, however, have contributed little empirical research on the *cultural forms* that radical democracy may take in these innovative political communities. In other words, what ways of speaking, thinking, and acting would characterize the radical democratic form of commitment for activists in the US? What kind of culture would enable a community to maintain both a shared commitment to the public good *and* a dedication to empower its members with a lot of individual autonomy?

I propose that personalism has sustained some contemporary political communities that roughly approximate the ideals that Habermas, Mouffe, and other radical democratic theorists articulate. These communities practice personalized politics. The culture of personalized politics prizes a kind of egalitarianism and individual empowerment that are in some ways congruent with Habermas' and Mouffe's visions of individualized, post-traditional, yet socially responsible commitments. At the same time, personalized politics is a specific culture with a specific history and affinities with specific social groups. It is certainly not a universal answer to the challenge of practicing public commitment in an individualistic society. It can be, as Mouffe would remind us, only a partial answer in a multicultural society. The field observations in the following chapters show that personalized politics as a culture limits activists in some ways, as does a more communitarian style of activism we will also examine. Bringing personalism to politics has ended up producing internal conflicts for activist groups since the 1960s. But that is very different from saying, as communitarians do, that personalism and public-spirited political commitment are incompatible. Instead, it turns out that communitarian-style culture is incompatible with the commitments that some activists nurture, given the political institutions and social opportunities surrounding them.

Communitarian and radical democratic positions cannot be parallel theoretical choices in a debate about political commitment. Communitarian theorists have named specific examples of political communities that practice the kind of commitment they advocate. Radical democracy theorists have not often specified the forms of commitment, the everyday practices that sustain the political community they favor. And besides, any specific forms of post-traditional, radical democratic community will be conflicted, or still evolving. That is true in Habermas' view because the process of subjecting traditional communal bonds to critical self-reflection continues apace in modern societies. It is true in Mouffe's view because a society would never arrive at a final consensus on the best way for its members to practice public commitment; definitions of the public good would always be contested in a democratic society. But these are not reason enough to conclude that communitarians have already identified all the potential models for political community – the traditional New England village, the ethnic enclave, or other traditional communities that are exemplars in their accounts.

In the concluding chapter I will return to the radical democratic theories with field research observations we can use to speak back to the varied positions I have introduced here. A close look at the personalized commitments of people like Carl will help us find some complementary ideals in the work of the rationalist Habermas and the cultural pluralist Mouffe, while pointing out theoretical blind spots in both. For now, we need to get beyond the blind spots in communitarian theories by conceptualizing "commitment" without the seesaw model.

STUDYING POLITICAL COMMITMENT

Commitment: political and public-spirited

The kind of commitment that theorists argue about in the above debates is both political and public-spirited; hence my use of the phrase "public, political commitment." It is a dedication to some public good partaken of in common by members of a community or society. The commitments that I have referred to as "public-spirited," like Mrs. Davis' and Carl's environmental activism, do not for the most part seek goods that individuals enjoy primarily as private citizens, such as income tax breaks. People may enter the political process as activists or voters to pursue such goods, but these will not count as "public-spirited" in this study. Rather, this study concerns commitments to a common interest such as clean air, or more democracy, that people *share* as a broad polity. Clean air or more democracy are "public goods" that people enjoy as members of a community that produces and protects them collectively. A single individual does not enjoy these goods on a separate basis the way she may enjoy a tax break; one cannot divide up the air for one's own benefit in order to avoid pollution from a neighboring chemical plant. The definition of public-spirited commitment in this study includes a sense of collective obligation similar to what communitarians uphold,[14] but with a crucial difference. The definition advanced here leaves open questions about *how* public, political commitments might get defined and practiced by groups or individuals. These questions get automatic answers if we adhere to the dualities of communitarian arguments: individual versus community, private gratification versus public virtue, personal transformation versus political change.

There are different kinds of "public" organizations. Some, though not all, service organizations and charity groups would qualify under my definition. "Public" here does not necessarily mean some organization or person that is widely known. My focus on political commitment in grass-roots social movements follows the suggestion in radical democratic theories that post-1960s social activists have been fashioning a personalized form of commitment. Communitarian theorists, too, have concerned themselves with the character of contemporary US social movements.[15] Some forms of activism fit my definition of public, political commitment more than others. Appendix I explains why the study focuses on recent environmental activism.

From commitment in the abstract to practices of commitment

There are varied ways to study political commitment, and this is a cultural study: it asks how activists define "commitment," and what assumptions they must share in order to practice commitment together. A cultural study of commitment needs to specify how it will approach "culture." Earlier communitarian theorists wrote their arguments in the form of sweeping, critical claims about cultural decline. In these accounts, commitment in general was in jeopardy because of a general preoccupation with self-exploration. These broad claims about large trends got sketchy historical substantiation at best, with little concrete detail from everyday life, save a few anecdotes. "Culture" in these works meant a broad ethos that permeates the arts, popular media, and everyday expression as well, slowly homogenizing the consciousness of an entire society. Though coming from different traditions,[16] Rieff, Lasch, and Bell all treated the modern culture they criticized as a general orientation which an astute observer might divine from a few "signs of the times." This level of generality fails to give a clear sense of what personalist culture is, how it shapes commitment in concrete situations, or where specifically we would look for it if we wanted to study it further. Vague and generalizing treatments of culture would make possible only vague, abstract accounts of personalism and commitment. These treatments enabled critics to damn an entire culture from a distance.

Wuthnow and the Bellah team sharpened their focus as culture analysts, leaving aside global critiques of art and popular media. What mattered about "culture" for them are the shared ways of speaking a culture provides its members. Studying communal or individualist "languages" of moral reasoning (Bellah *et al.*), or "vocabularies of motive" (Wuthnow), is a much more specific way of learning about commitment than is diagnosing a broad cultural ethos as earlier communitarians tried to do. *Talk* about commitment matters in these language-focused studies because talk reveals the categories and definitions that activists or volunteers have available for imagining how they can practice mutual responsibility, how they can build community. Commitment does not get practiced in a cultural vacuum; the physical acts of visiting the sick or helping low-income tenants fill out forms become ways of creating community ties depending on how people talk about, give meaning to, those physical acts.[17] The individualistic talk that these researchers heard during their studies led them to argue that many Americans' sense of obligation to others is limited; many Americans had a hard time seeing themselves as committed to others *for the sake of others* rather than for ultimately self-centered reasons. From interview talk, these studies extrapolated the future prospects for public-spirited commitments. The prospects seemed rather dim. But knowing how people talk about commitment in interviews is not the same as knowing how people practice political commitment in everyday settings.

Instead of making claims about a broad, general ethos, or focusing on patterns of talk about commitment in interviews, this book addresses commitment by examining how activists practice it in everyday settings. It finds out how personalism as a culture influences the ways that activists both talk about and practice commitments. Recent work in cultural theory (Bourdieu 1990, 1984, 1977) argues we should study "culture" as the patterns of speaking and acting that people practice in everyday situations. Like the language-centered approaches of Wuthnow and the Bellah team, this approach departs from the traditional socio-logical understanding of culture as end-goals or ultimate "values" that act as unseen, unmoved "movers" behind social acts (Swidler 1986). But this approach strongly highlights the ways language works in practice, in everyday contexts. It views "culture" as shared ways of doing things. Using this approach to culture, "commitment" is a shared way of talking about and practicing obligation in everyday settings. And "personalism" means shared ways of speaking or acting that emphasize the personal self rather than its relationships to specific communities or institutions (see also Lichterman 1995a).

It may sound contradictory to claim that personalist ways of doing things can be *shared* as a culture: doesn't personalism imply an emphasis on highly individualized expression rather than a shared activity? In fact, highly individualized expression follows very definite norms that get passed down through patterns of group socialization. Some activists like Carl in this study participated in organizations that highlighted a very personalized kind of politics and these organizations selected new recruits who could define and practice "activism" in the same personalized way. Personalism in everyday life is very much a "shared way of doing things," and not an individual invention from scratch. Hence, this study finds personalism in everyday settings – activist meetings, conferences, task groups, state-sponsored public hearings, and informal get-togethers. The shared ways of talking and acting in these sites are not just "effects" of a culture that really exists somewhere else; they *are* culture in everyday process.

Two kinds of commitment in practice

This study focuses on two patterns of activist commitment – two kinds of group bonds. Each kind of commitment both nurtured and reinforced a kind of activist identity that made those bonds meaningful. I found out what "commitment" meant by hearing the activists talk in their own everyday settings. I discovered the important reference points – prior social movements, historical events, local community groups, personal experiences – that activists used to anchor their commitments, to make "commitment" a meaningful thing to do. In other words, I discovered the *social identities*[18] that they created for themselves in the course of practicing commitment.

Some activists, such as Mrs. Davis, rooted their commitments in local communities. These activists presented themselves as "concerned members of the community" to neighbors, to health department bureaucrats, and to members of their own environmental groups. They linked their activism with prior, local community involvements and locally shared traditions. I have called this kind of commitment "communitarian" since in many ways it reflects the sense of obligation upheld in communitarian theorists' accounts.

Other activists such as Carl participated in bonds of commitment that highlighted the individual person as an important locus of political efficacy. A good "community" for them was one that could allow individual identities and political wills to resonate loudly within collective accomplishments. These activists talked not only about becoming involved in movement organizations but also about changing their entire personal lives in line with a politicized sense of which occupations and lifestyles are worthwhile. These activists spoke less "on behalf of the local community" and more as individual agents of social change who belonged to more geographically diffuse communities, including the community of participants in their movement, and beyond that a larger community of people who practiced a "progressive" or left-liberal politics by politicizing their everyday lives. These activists articulated diverse social identities: they traced their personalized radicalism to the "enlightening" effects of a particular college experience, perhaps, or a good book. I have called the culture of commitment they shared "personalized."

Personalized and communitarian commitments create different bonds of responsibility, and different senses of what constitutes "good" activism. If we reduce these differences to quantities – "more" or "less" commitment – as the dichotomies of communitarian thinking would suggest, then we preclude the possibility that communitarian theorists have overlooked a type of commitment that is supported rather than diminished by self-fulfillment. Few studies have addressed the debate about personalism and political commitment with observations from everyday life in social movements. Participant-observation research can open up access to practical understandings of "commitment" that activists themselves take for granted in group interaction. Systematic participating and observing showed me aspects of group culture that did not reveal themselves in interviews conducted outside of activists' own contexts. For that reason, participant-observation was the primary method in this study.

INTO THE FIELD

This study's arguments draw on intensive examination of four organizations, two from the US Green movement and two from the grassroots anti-toxics movement.

The US Greens

Like their counterparts in Germany and other countries, members of the US Green movement propose both political and cultural change as the answer to global and local environmental problems. Born in the mid-1980s, the US Green movement was not simply a counter-cultural leftover; members of the Green organizations in this study considered themselves seriously committed to social change over the long haul. Greens committed themselves to "Green values" that they culled from middle-class, left-of-center movements since the 1960s. Greens undertook varied projects in different regions – rainforest advocacy, genetic engineering protests, Green electoral party organizing – all in order to enter "Green values" into political debate, mostly at the local level.

A central if often implicit underpinning to the movement was the assumption that individual selves have political efficacy, and that individuals ought to participate intensively in forming collective political wills. The appeals to self-empowerment and individual responsibility that I heard at an early meeting I attended suggested that the Green movement would be an important test case for arguments about personalism and political commitment. I studied one local affiliate of the movement, the *Ridge Greens*,[19] and chose the *Seaview Greens* – of similar size and demographic characteristics – for a shorter period of study, as a hedge against potential idiosyncrasies of the Ridge group.

The Grassroots Movement for Environmental Justice

At the same time that activists were trying to develop a US counterpart to Green movements in other countries, residents of cities and towns across the country were forming local organizations to protest toxic waste disposal plans drawn up both by private companies and by the US Environmental Protection Agency. The highly publicized environmental poisoning at Love Canal, New York in the late 1970s brought Love Canal resident Lois Gibbs into a leadership role for a movement as yet without a name. The national organization she helped initiate, the Citizen's Clearinghouse on Hazardous Wastes (CCHW), became a resource center for new local anti-toxics organizations, whose numbers grew from a couple of thousand in the early 1980s to over 8,000 at the close of the decade. Eschewing centralized authority or ideological leadership, the CCHW remained a resource and advice center for a growing movement whose participants also networked with other national organizations. By the time of its second national grassroots convention in 1989, the CCHW-named "Grassroots Movement Against Toxics" was evolving an "environmental justice" ideology (Szasz 1994; Capek 1993), and national spokespeople renamed it the Grassroots Movement for Environmental Justice (GMEJ).

Local groups formed in a variety of urban and rural settings. With less of a culturally radical impetus than the Greens, and more of a mainstream constituency, anti-toxics activists have relied on a long-standing populism in the US,[20] and local residence itself as an initial basis for group identity. GMEJ literature emphasized the political efficacy of local communities, of "normal folks," rather than of empowered individuals with new values. I chose two local anti-toxics groups within a fifty-mile radius of the Ridge Greens. One, *Hillviewers Against Toxics* (HAT), was a largely African-American organization in a small industrial city. Its church-influenced, communitarian commitment style provided a wonderful contrast with the personalized politics of the Greens. The other organization, *Airdale Citizens for Environmental Sanity* (ACES), sustained a hybrid of communitarian and personalized commitment styles, one that I will show was particularly suited to a suburban locale. Between the largely white, largely middle-class suburban ACES and the African-American, lower-to-moderate income HAT, the study tapped both ends of the socioeconomic continuum in the GMEJ, and both ends of the personalist–communitarian continuum within the anti-toxics movement too.

None of these organizations formed as a temporary response to a single environmental problem. Each dedicated itself to citizen activism over a long haul, rather than to the solution of a single local issue. Three of the four local organizations formed in 1985 or 1986; the ACES started three years earlier. The organizations were comparable in size and stated dedication to public involvement. HAT and the Green groups all had organizational structures that members had not completely formalized (Staggenborg 1988) as official during the study. Each had several levels of decision-making, with HAT's arranged in the more conventional terms of an executive board and non-board members, while the Greens had a less conventional but no less complicated arrangement of rotating leadership councils and project groups. Four of the five had mailing lists of between 100 and 150 people; ACES' list doubled from roughly 200 during the study. During the study, each group was ironing out, or replacing, its by-laws or else deliberating on its own future as a group. Each group operated in roughly the same regional media market and had the opportunity to respond to at least some of the same news stories and events. As comparably-sized, grassroots movement organizations each in the midst of deciding its own future, these groups gave me a perhaps unique opportunity to compare how ordinary citizens committed themselves to building political communities in different cultural and social milieux.

Methods of study

During roughly twenty-four months, I participated and observed in the Ridge Greens, Airdale Citizens for Environmental Sanity (ACES), and Hillviewers Against Toxics (HAT), and I spent eight months in the Seaview Green comparison group. During the field work, I attended coordinating meetings and general meetings. In each organization, I attended numerous other meetings devoted to specific tasks, projects, or organizing drives. I volunteered to help get out mailings, staff information tables, set up meeting halls, and go petitioning. I attended at least ten public hearings and protests with each of the anti-toxics groups. I kept field notes on all of these experiences, and coded and analyzed them in categories relevant to the questions motivating the study. The details of gaining access to study these organizations are described in Appendix I.

I interviewed between six and eight core members of each organization, with the exception of the Seaview Green comparison group, adding up to twenty-five interviews. I also conducted formal and informal interviews with Greens from different parts of the US at the 1989 US Green conference. I interviewed leading former Greens, and also participants in the Earth First! environmental network who were familiar with Green activism. In all I conducted thirty-two interviews. I also conducted informal interviews with anti-toxics activists at a regional and a national conference. The formal interviews were semi-structured, and lasted between 1½ and 3 hours each.

To understand how social background interacts with different commitment styles, I carried out demographic surveys with a national sample of Greens and a national sample of anti-toxics activists, both taken from national conferences. I also surveyed core members of the local organizations, with the exception of the Seaview Green comparison group. I present and interpret results of the national surveys in Chapter 5. Appendix I explains my procedures for carrying out the surveys.

OVERVIEW OF THE BOOK

Communitarian theorists criticized personalism for weakening people's capacities to commit themselves in general, and for weakening community ties that might otherwise sustain commitment. Chapter 2 examines the personalized politics of the US Greens, showing that personalism sustains public, political commitments among people who do not share the same communal attachments. Chapter 3 uses a suburban community organization to show that personalism does not necessarily weaken community ties; in this case it strengthened suburban activists' willingness to take risks for the good of their local community as a whole. Chapter 4 presents the communitarian-style commitment culture in Hillviewers Against Toxics, contrasting it with the more personalized ones and pointing out its own weaknesses. The chapter illustrates how differences in commitment cultures may impede multicultural alliance-building even when activists agree on issues. Appendix I details my reasons for choosing the organizations examined in these chapters, and explains my research strategies. Appendix II shows why the answer to this study's question about commitment required participant-observation research.

Chapters 5 and 6 provide broader social contexts that help explain why some activists tend toward personalized political commitments while others commit themselves with a more communitarian style. Chapter 5 shows how personalized commitment builds on cultural skills that tend to be more available to the professional middle classes than other strata. These cultural skills by themselves do not cause activists to adopt personalized commitments, but they facilitate the personalized style for groups of activists that do not share a lot of the same sources of inspiration for activism. Personalized political commitment evolved between civil rights activism of the 1950s and student activism of the 1960s, and it has roots in the highly personal crusades of earlier activists as well. After a brief consideration of this history, Chapter 6 examines post-1960s grassroots movements, showing that personalism became a routine basis for political community in a succession of culturally radical movements that have challenged the boundaries of conventional political debate. Personalized politics and culturally radical ideologies have mutually reinforced each other, as these activists carry on their visions outside of institutionalized forums.

Chapter 7 develops the radical democratic position I introduced in this chapter, threading that position back through the case material. By discounting personalism, communitarian thinkers cut short their inquiry into political commitment, but they were right to raise the issue of commitment to begin with. A focus on commitment illuminates theoretical and practical issues regarding political community that radical democratic theories, and social movement theories more generally, need to consider. The culture of personalized politics facilitates activism in some ways and limits it in others. I suggest how a new metaphor of commitment might help activists themselves overcome some of their limitations by broadening the horizons of their political communities.

2

Personalized politics: the case of the US Greens

Advocates of public commitment would have found little to complain about at the general meetings of the Seaview Greens. At each general meeting, core Seaview Green members and new members deliberated on a topic of public interest that would enable participants to apply a "Green" perspective, and also decide Seaview policy on that topic. In the meeting sketched below, the Seaview Greens were deciding on endorsements of local candidates and ballot initiatives. The meeting displays a collective commitment to participation and debate that I observed throughout my two years of participant-observation in the US Green movement.

Few if any participants at this meeting would have opposed an environmental protection initiative that would impose strict limits on pesticides and off-shore oil drilling. The corporate-funded opposition had spent millions of dollars to defeat this initiative, while nearly every environmentalist group in the state supported it. Nevertheless, no one at the meeting seemed to think it a waste of time that one participant asked whether the complicated, costly initiative would not end up stalled in the courts were it to pass. The man mentioned that he himself supported the proposition but thought these cautions ought to be raised. The "facilitator," the person responsible for moderating the group discussion, listened attentively and agreed that this would be important to keep in mind.

Boosterism for "our side" had not overshadowed the group's dedication to discussion. Several participants noted this emphasis on discussion in their evaluation of the meeting. One, a newcomer in her early twenties, said she appreciated that "people were not rigid in their values – it

30

wasn't like talking to a brick wall." Another was glad that "Greens are not just telling people how to think." A third was "not intimidated" as she thought she would be by this political discussion.

In another discussion exercise common in Green groups, the participants broke into small discussion groups so that each individual would have a chance to participate. The conversation in the group I joined illustrated the primacy of discussion and "Green" principles over strategizing for immediate gain[1]:

> Maria was skeptical of candidate Condici: "He said he's for neighborhood councils, but what does that mean? We don't know if he has a Green perspective on neighborhoods ..." I threw in that maybe Seaview should set a goal of endorsing at least one or two candidates, so that the nascent Green Party would be able to have some relationship with a politician who might be able to return a favor.
>
> Newcomer in his mid-fifties: "Yeah, that's a good idea, it's crass, it's real politics."
>
> Maria: "We don't want to just support the lesser of two evils – that's why we're here."
>
> Barb (Seaview member): "I'd prefer a green candidate come from the Greens, from out of this room."
>
> Maria and Barb's reasoning carried the group; it presented to the meeting as a whole its conclusion that neither Condici nor the other candidates ought to be endorsed in this election.

Participants did not, however, divorce a "Green" perspective from strategic concerns. Maria, for instance, advocated several times to the meeting as a whole that a new electoral entity like the Seaview chapter of the Green Party, striving to establish a reputation, needed to be especially careful about whom it endorsed: "It could come back to haunt us later." Maria's skeptical approach prevailed, but only after more debate. Greens decided the meeting had been worthwhile not only because it produced Green group opinion through free discussion, but because of the public contact it brought. One Seaview Green, a man in his late thirties, summarized after the small group discussions, "the process itself was worth it – educating 30 or 40 people here tonight." Another added, "The candidates got an education too, we left literature on the Green movement with them."

The Greens' emphasis on discussion and participation reflects a kind of activism also noted in grassroots anti-nuclear, peace, and women's activism of the 1970s and 1980s, and some new left activism of the 1960s (Melucci 1989, 1988, 1985; Breines 1982; Habermas 1987, 1970; Touraine *et al.* 1983; Cohen 1985). This kind of activism has tried to broaden the definition of "political" action beyond instrumental maneuvering with allies and against adversaries. Activists like US Greens wanted to politicize previously taken-for-granted ways of life – including taken-for-granted ways of conducting politics. They wanted to ground political strategies in a larger, ongoing discussion of social priorities, such as the Green priorities by which they judged local candidates. It is a kind of discussion that these activists have seen lacking in conventional party and interest group politics.

Not more than forty miles away, Greens in Ridgeville were anticipating their own electoral organizing. And once the state Registrar of Voters had given final approval to the Greens' petition for ballot status, the new Ridge Green Party chapter got off to a promising start. Only three months old, the group was attracting twenty or more regular attendees at meetings. Armed with the newly won right to register voters for the Green Party of California, members were conducting weekend voter registration drives, contacting established environmental organizations to solicit support, and planning fundraising.

In contrast, only five or six core members were still showing up for business meetings of an older Green group in Ridgeville. The old "Ridge Greens" was dissolving. In its five years of existence it had supported local environmental and anti-nuclear protests, and organized its own protest and public education events. The old group had put much energy into position papers for a national Green movement platform. And in the past year, it had been drained of much energy for new projects by haggling over group by-laws. The new Ridge Green group had focused itself on the goal of registering at least 80,000 Green Party voters by the end of 1991, in order to qualify the new party to participate in the 1992 elections.

Yet, the new electoral organizing group was reproducing some of the old organization's difficulties. Having begun with a great deal of enthusiasm, the Green Party volunteers were spending much of these first meetings arguing over group structure. At one of the first meetings of the new Green Party group a long-time Green argued against setting up an interim board of coordinators. The motion to set up the board was not based on a group consensus, he pointed out. A non-consensual decision, even if meant as a stopgap one to keep a group afloat, could alienate individual members, the final arbiters of a good decision. But without the interim executive board, Ridge Green Party members risked confusing prospective members and alienating a frazzled party organizer who was now stuck without delegated volunteers to help him set local Green Party organizing in motion.

And Ridge Greens were not alone in the Green movement with their organizational difficulties. The Seaview group endured similar difficulties, though it cohered as an active organization throughout this study without disbanding and reforming as the Ridge group did. Around the same time that the old Ridge Green group was dying and the new one was struggling to be born, Green chapters in northern Oregon, New York City, and New England were wrestling with conflicts over organization and decision-making.[2]

Why would activists struggle over organizational form if they were as serious about public responsibility as the Greens were with their engaging, even inviting discussions of the political scene? Clues to this puzzle became evident at the last meeting of the old Ridge Green group. I was surprised that no one was talking about the strengths and weaknesses of the group in which they had spent so much time. Finally, expectantly, I asked why they had put so much work into a group they seemed happy enough to "put to rest."

Brian: "We were trying to build a Green movement ... we had tried and now we're going to try in another way."

I had a hard time reconciling Brian's professed commitment to a "Green movement" with what seemed to me a disregard for its organizational basis. Were these activists only interested in Green organizations as long as they "felt good" and let individuals express their impulses, as communitarians would have feared? That seemed unlikely, since Brian had prefaced several of his comments by declaring, "I want to further the Greens." Others expressed the same commitment.

I realized I was trying to solve the puzzle I set for myself with the terms of seesaw-model dichotomies. I realized that these activists could quite easily detach their "political commitment" from any particular Green organization, and yet still strive to build a movement, and new movement organizations too. The importance of any one such organization was less salient, and the value of individual voice was more salient, than I had assumed. But neither the old Ridge Green group nor its successor existed primarily as outlets for spontaneity or self-development, as imagined in communitarian theorists' accounts of recent protest politics. Members of the Ridge Green Party were practicing their commitments in the interest of unambiguously public and "political" work – registering voters for the new Green Party of California. And their commitments could produce results; California Greens won ballot status.

PERSONALIZED POLITICAL COMMITMENT

This chapter addresses the puzzle above by proposing that activists in social movements since the 1960s have been enacting a kind of commitment that differs from traditional images of self-sacrificing group devotion that the term "commitment" often calls forth. These activists have been practicing a kind of political commitment suggested in some radical democratic theory. This form of commitment, personalized politics, combines a concern for broad public issues with an insistence that each individual activist is a locus of political responsibility and efficacy, outside as well as inside activist organizations. It is a public commitment that, for many Greens, has shaped life outside of Green movement organizations as well as inside them. Organizations do matter in personalized politics, and organizations are not meant simply to be short-lived sites for self-development. But the individual activist's sense of commitment is highly portable; it can be carried from group to group, in concert with other activists and imagined communities of activists who validate personalized politics. A tenuous, consensus-governed group may seem to be avoiding "commitment," not practicing it. On the contrary, most Greens were not trying to free themselves from social or moral obligations, as would the "hedonists" described in some communitarian arguments, but were practicing obligations in a different way. Greens wanted to meld their personalized commitments into a movement that aimed for social change, not just personal transformation.

Creating group bonds

If this kind of activist acts more as an individual political agent than as a member of a well-established organization, then how can a group of these activists act together? How can they build solidarity out of their individual commitments? I will argue that Greens relied on personalism as their shared basis for building democratic movement organizations. These activists organized groups that highlighted personal will, the importance of personal feelings in collective action. Of course Greens would say that their common dedication to "Green values," to be described shortly, is what brought them together. But what matters more is the *way* Greens might carry and practice the values described in their pamphlets and recruitment materials. "Green values" by themselves did not tell Greens *how* to make commitments or create group bonds in political communities; there would be more than one way to build Green activist groups. Greens carried their values as personal agents of social change. Their group activity relied on the background knowledge that

Greens ought to relate to one another, and to their values, as individually empowered activists building participatory political communities. Whether they articulated it explicitly or not, most Greens operated from this practical background knowledge.

There are other ways to create participatory democracy. Members could treat each other as "citizens," or as "community members" instead of as personal selves. People acting as citizens or community members would assign each other different sorts of responsibilities, and create different bonds of obligation, than those that are available when people assume political agency resides in a personal self without strong institutional grounding. They would draw on different political cultures than that produced by personalism. Greens have produced participatory democracy by treating members as individual selves deserving recognition, and by speaking of them as such during crises.

Personalism gave Greens the basis for maintaining their commitments over a long period of time. In sharing a personalized approach to activism, Greens could respect and listen to each other as they discussed broad social and environmental priorities, entertaining viewpoints rarely heard in mainstream US political discourse. They could brook discussion on issues ranging from city council candidacies to forest preservation to the nature of spirituality, and plan protests, educational campaigns, and electoral initiatives on those issues. They aired broad moral and political questions that often get squeezed out of public debate. Personalism produced some considerable limits as well as opportunities for group bonds. On the one hand, organizational stability remained a tenuous accomplishment among activists highlighting personal empowerment, and this indeed frustrated the activists at times. On the other hand, personalism gave these activists the basis for remaining engaged in an ongoing arena of grassroots activism in which issues and even organizations shifted but commitments endured.

Personalized politics versus group therapy

Communitarians feared that as personalism entered public, political life, the commitment "seesaw" would tilt menacingly: self-expression would overcome dedication to the common good, a focus on the private would replace a sense of public responsibility, and indulgent spontaneity would undermine durable commitment. Personalism might produce lifestyle enclaves centered on shared private tastes rather than shared public responsibilities. Or at best, it might make social commitment a limited, tidy affair, pulling the reins in on an individual's sense of obligation. In

Table 2.1 *Two types of activism*

	Therapeutic activism	Personalized politics
commitment duration	unpredicatable, indefinite	long-term, continuous, indefinite
model of interaction	exchange of feelings and needs between individuals	egalitarian collective action
main goal of commitment	self-development	innovation in political culture/ expansion of political debate; policy change
conception of public	the sum of private, expressive selves	a polity of individually empowered members
case example		US Green movement
provisional examples[4]	some "New Age" activists; some youth counter-culture participants of the late 1960s–early 1970s	anti-nuclear activists of the 1970s–1980s; early 1970s US women's movement; cultural feminists; women's peace movement; US men's movement; Earth First!; animal rights activists of 1980s; Pledge of Resistance

the view of many communitarian scholars, personalism would probably turn activism into a kind of group therapy.

But this chapter will show that Greens had a self-expressive cultural *means* to pursuing the common good of their groups and of society at large. Their collective efforts did not depend on shared fun or spontaneity. Their commitments were expansive rather than limited, taking up a lot of the self, and aiming ambitiously for broad social change. And Chapter 5 will show how Greens politicized "private" life, making it a site for practicing public responsibility, not a refuge from it.

The sort of activist communitarian accounts imply, in contrast, could be called a "therapeutic activist,"[3] for whom activism means either launching spontaneous, effusive protests or else burrowing deep into private self-exploration on the notion that one can contribute to social change only by changing one's inner self. Table 2.1 details some of the differences between therapeutic activism and personalized politics. Communitarians have imagined a kind of activism that is inspired by personalism but they fail to recognize the other potentials of personalism in practice.

The following sections of this chapter introduce US Green ideology, and show how personalism shaped Green movement-building. The account draws on my field research in the Ridge and Seaview groups, regional conferences, and the US Green conference in 1989, along with internal documents and Green movement literature.[5] I will show how personalism, despite its limits, made sense as a shared basis for Green movement-building because Greens had diverse sources of activist identity. Personalized politics has been prominent in other contemporary grassroots movements and "alternative" organizations, as Chapters 6 and 7 will note. Individualized commitments and tenuous, conflicted groups have characterized these efforts at political and cultural change too. This chapter will compare the Greens' pattern of commitment and togetherness with that of grassroots anti-nuclear activism of the 1970s and 1980s. The last section of this chapter considers alternative explanations for the puzzle with which the chapter began – that activists would practice a strongly held sense of public responsibility in tenuous organizations.

THE US GREENS AS A CASE IN PERSONALIZED POLITICS

The Green project in the US context

US Greens adapted the originally European "Green" designation to a US context, and ended up producing a distinctive case of personalized politics. From the start, the sixty-two community activists who met in 1984 to draft principles for a "green" movement in the US[6] combined a very public-spirited commitment with a highly personalized way of articulating it. Many argued that the US Greens' primary concern ought to be with "redefining and deepening the very understanding of 'politics' and 'public life'."[7] And they articulated this concern with a spirit of exploration and personal sharing. Following what would become a familiar decision-making format in the Green movement, participants broke into groups of three to imagine what a "green society" might be like. Responses included "beyond left and right," "connectedness with the earth," "empowerment," and "roots," among others.

The convenors drafted a list of "Ten Key Values," each one of which they elaborated upon in a full paragraph of questions phrased to invite dialogue. New recruits to local Green organizations in 1989 and 1990 received a verbal introduction to these values – stated almost identically to the 1984 draft form, and received a sheet with the "thought questions" too. Greens regularly referred to the Ten Key Values in justifying or opposing decisions. The values constitute an extended definition of "Green" in the US context. They are:

1	ecological wisdom	6	respect for diversity
2	decentralization	7	post-patriarchal values
3	grassroots democracy	8	personal and social responsibility
4	community-based economics	9	non-violence
5	global responsibility	10	future focus

Favoring grassroots, "bottom-up" organizing the convenors chose for the US movement the collective name "Committees of Correspondence," later changed to Green Committees of Correspondence (GCoC), named after the loosely organized networks that fanned the American Revolution. Between the founding conference and the beginning of my field work in 1989, over 200 local chapters were started across the US. They emerged in states such as Texas, Florida, Kansas, and Arkansas, as well as in states more often associated with the cultural milieu of "post-material" values (Inglehart 1990, 1981), such as California, Oregon, and Massachusetts. The Seaview and Ridge Green local chapters in this study formed within a year of the founding conference.

Local groups initiated varying activities. Chapters in Wisconsin, Kansas, and other states entered the toxic waste fray. Some groups around the country worked on local ballot initiatives, and some fielded candidates for city, county, or state office – including a leading figure in the national Green coordinating council who ran for the state legislative assembly seat in her district. Members of the Seaview Greens took a leading role in the campaign to make Seaview City a nuclear-free zone. Groups in California and New York sponsored street protests against environmental practices of large corporations. Many if not most local Green groups sponsored talk series on some aspect of "Green" philosophy or movement-building. Some encouraged members' "personal" or "spiritual" development by maintaining spirituality study groups or celebrating Native American seasonal rites, though the extent of a group's participation in these activities has varied widely. And during this study Green organizations in a number of states initiated Green electoral party organizing, in hopes of qualifying officially identified Green Party candidates to run on state ballots.[8]

To understand the US Greens' version of a personalized politics, it is first important to note how the US political context differs in some ways from European contexts that have nurtured Green movements and Green parties. In the case of Germany, whose Green movement and

Green party strongly influenced US Greens' aspirations, electoral law made small political parties more viable than they could be in the US: parties gaining a minimum percentage of votes were guaranteed parliamentary representation, and were reimbursed for electoral campaign expenses. The very slow start and at best uncertain long-term prospects for a US Green political party must be attributed at least partly to a less welcoming structure of opportunity than that available at the same time in Germany. Of course there have been similarities between US and German Greens' ways of defining organizational issues: disagreements between ideological "fundamentalists" and pragmatic "realists" in German Green politics echoed in some US Green debates during the late 1980s and early 1990s, especially those regarding electoral organizing. For instance, some of the more "fundamentalist" US Greens feared that a Green Party would in time develop the entrenched hierarchy and distance from constituents that make other large parties unacceptable in their eyes. Other US Greens, granting that building a party would be a difficult, long-term process, insisted that a small Green movement without a party would be fated for no more than small accomplishments in the densely populated arena of environmentalist organizations. Yet, this debate played out in a context that makes the stakes quite different than for German or other Green activists in a different governmental system. In the German case, Greens interested in electoral strategies have had more incentives than their US counterparts to work at bridging ideological differences with other political forces – and abridging lengthy ideological discussion – in the interests of appealing to more voters.

At least some Greens in this study were cognizant of the difficulties facing a strongly "values"-based US Green activism of either electoral-oriented or "movement" form. Greens appreciated, and sometimes joined, the efforts of numerous other single-issue environmental organizations that tackled forest preservation, or toxic waste, or nuclear arms-testing. But they also wanted to carve out a niche separate from other environmentalists whose single-issue foci might amount to "putting out fires" without addressing the incendiary conditions that prepared the grounds for continual flare-ups. So Greens distinguished their movement from other environmentalist or community activist movements by emphasizing the links between separate issues, by debating broad social and moral priorities, and by framing their projects in terms of the "Ten Key Values." In the words of the founding meeting convenors, they would redefine and deepen the very understanding of politics and public life. Hoping to link specific issues with discussion of broad priorities and systemic social and environmental relations, Greens in effect made communication a large aspect of their commitment to public responsibility. Both Greens and their critics in the environmental movement would agree that Green politics has highlighted writing and talk.

US Greens took it as their responsibility to enrich political culture as much as to fight for specific policies. Ideological talking and writing have been central forms of Green "doing," along with specific, local projects and protests like those described above. The book *Green Politics*, whose two authors (Capra and Spretnak) were active in the US Green movement, developed a wide enough audience to remain on the "environment" shelf of bookstores throughout the US nearly a decade after its publication in 1984. During that time Green-identified writings began turning up in some college course curricula as well, including a course that strongly influenced one of the Ridge Greens. Many Green locals across the US sponsored speaker series or community forums on environmental or broadly philosophical topics. And some Greens defined early Green electoral candidacies as opportunities to broaden the spectrum of political debate with new issues as much as opportunities to win local power. One candidate for a California seat in the House of Representatives, who was active in the 1989 national Green gathering described later on, included in a campaign statement that "she has some name recognition, she has a chance. Even if she does not win the race, we will have forced discussion on a number of important issues."

Some environmentalists criticized Greens for their emphasis on talk. Certainly Greens in this study evinced a dedication to ideological discussion, and to discussing their group dynamics. They complained at points that they spent too much time talking, and toward the end of the study some Greens began arguing for less participation-intensive organizations in the interests of party organizing. But it is a trap to write off talk as "non-political," or as not "action." If "action" includes only direct confrontations with state or corporate "powers that be," or recruitment campaigns, then much of what the activists in all the groups in this study did – attending meetings, carrying out administrative tasks, deciding on issues, publicizing identities – is not action. As many students of social movements argue, political issues do not come ready-made: defining new issues for debate and defining new identities ("Green") for political actors is an ongoing part of political action, especially for uninstitutionalized actors trying to broaden the limits of public discussion.[9] For Greens, ideological talk mattered within a long-term project of political and cultural change that included local action to reform politics and, for some Green groups, political party initiatives. Encouraging political talk was a "political" act in a public arena that some observers see as dominated by state bureaucrats who prefer to limit discussion of the basic social or moral priorities behind, say, forest harvesting policies or urban redevelopment.[10] An open discussion forum that values talk, even if the forum is a small one, might encourage individuals like the somewhat timid young women in this chapter's opening scenario toward more active engagement as citizens or as activists.

With their self-selected niche on the political map, many US Greens in effect committed themselves to a long and sometimes lonely road toward cultural and political change. Insisting on profound social change in line with the Ten Key Values meant investing themselves less in local, short-term projects or professionalized campaigns led by well-established organizations – though Greens did not simply ignore these. Greens had to be able to sustain themselves as highly committed individuals no matter how unwelcoming the activist arena or the broader public might be to what they offered. Later chapters will show that not all personalized politics has gotten practiced with the degree of individualized commitment that Green activism ended up requiring. The US Greens result as a particularly "pure" instance of personalized politics, one that will bring out the tensions and challenges of this culture in particularly high relief.

The individual as political agent in Green ideology

Green political ideologies have emphasized individualized commitment and individual efficacy apart from established communities or movements. A few examples will suffice.

In 1988, Petra Kelly, a leader in the German Green movement, closed her speech to an international Green congress with the following declaration:

Respecting each individual, his and her talents and individuality – without coercion, without mistrust and without committees and bureaucracies to control and watch over – that is also part of Green politics. Living our values is what Green politics is all about! (Kelly 1988: 6–7)

Delivered in Stockholm, the speech found an appreciative American audience; the movement newsletter which ran Kelly's speech printed the above passage as a pull quote in bold. In a similar vein, a draft of the Ridge Greens Handbook (1989) for new members quotes approvingly from the British Ecology Party's program on the place of individuals in a "new politics":

A new politics is emerging which does not seek the power of traditional politics (to gain domination over others and over the earth) but the creative power which comes from understanding the real value of each individual, and of the earth itself.

US Green movement publicist and activist Brian Tokar sums up his vision of a "participatory" Green movement organization thus:

Open process, attention to the personal needs of groups' members and avoidance of traditional leadership hierarchies. (Tokar 1989)

The US Greens' 1989 national platform statement on movement-building was a virtual manifesto of the powers – and responsibilities – of politicized individuals. It proposed that "all Greens are leaders. Green organizing must recognize and develop each person's unique leadership qualities." Organizing within the US Green movement "must help empower individual members of grassroots local groups."

We need to ask why US Greens wanted to emphasize individual expression, and what "individual expression" means in practice. It is wrong to assume that since Green ideology opposes narrow instrumentalist definitions of politics, Greens naturally gravitate to a personalized, expressive politics instead. Students of grassroots politics since the 1960s (for instance, Melucci 1989, 1988, 1985; Breines 1982) have tended to assume that anti-instrumentalist ideologies would produce personalized politics in practice. But there are many ways to "deepen the very understanding of 'politics' and 'public life'," as the US Green founders had put it. There are different ways to put ideologies like the Ten Key Values into practice. Even the Key Value of "personal and social responsibility" could be practiced in a faith-based or local civic community as much as by communities of personally empowered individuals. For instance, Greens received the *idea* of a communally based kind of activism with enthusiasm when delivered by community-action proponent Harry Boyte (Spretnak 1986). And while most grassroots movements talk of "empowering" people, they might empower people as a "community" rather than as a set of individuals.

Only some kinds of people would want or be able to participate in a movement that combines a great deal of talk about ideals with an emphasis on personalized initiative. They were people whose political identities developed from diverse radicalization experiences, rather than through political socialization in the same, established institutions.

BECOMING A GREEN

We can understand the individualized practice of commitment in the Green movement in light of Greens' political and cultural backgrounds.

During my time with the Ridge Greens,[11] the twelve core members were aged 22–50ish. Eight out of twelve were under 35, with no direct experience in 1960s movements. Most had at least one college degree. Early into this study, the Ridge Greens invited me to a "Green storytelling" dinner. Attended by nine of the twelve core members, the dinner was supposed to be an opportunity for members to tell each other about how they had gotten involved with the Greens. It was up to each individual to decide whether "getting involved with the Greens" meant getting involved in Green "politics," or becoming a kind of "environmentalist," or becoming an "activist" as opposed to a non-activist. Stories like these show us how an individual constructs an identity in relation to communal or cultural reference points. The narrative form of the story itself would say much about what "doing activism" means to the story-teller, what social obligation means and how one should practice it.[12] In telling this kind of story, each member would be constructing a social identity as an activist.

Chart 2.1 summarizes each member's story. Especially relevant information is italicized. In almost every case, becoming a Green developed through understanding oneself as culturally dislocated or radicalized.

Chart 2.1: Creating activist identities in the Ridge Greens

Brian told us he attended what he called a *"subversive" Unitarian church* when he was growing up, and said he thought his activism had to do with this church experience.

Heather went to a *"women's college,"* and had *"an instructor who introduced (her) to literature about the world Green movement."* She told us she had read radical feminist Shulamith Firestone's *The Dialectic of Sex*, which had a big effect on her.

Donald was an observant *Quaker* (member of the Society of Friends). He quickly glossed over Quaker tenets: "You know, bear witness, act against a wrong ..." apparently assuming we would be familiar with these teachings and understand their relevance to his decisions. He had worked in *Greenpeace* and *Citizens for a Better Environment*, and then "burned out" on environmentalism. Having heard about the Greens and their ideas a few months earlier, he decided he would try getting involved again.

George had seen *racial conflicts* erupt in high school. This *made him feel especially "different"* with his Middle Eastern background. Having entered college in the early 1970s, he *"thought the 1960s would keep happening"* on campus, but it didn't. He described himself later on as "looking for something to get involved with" and tried out a group that advocated *world government*. Not entirely satisfied with them, he read Capra and Spretnak's *Green Politics*, was very impressed, and went to one of the first Green conferences in northern California. He had been involved ever since.

Carl "didn't do activism" before joining the Greens. Before becoming a Green, he was *studying genetic engineering "because it was neat,"* he said self-disparagingly, now distancing himself from an academic curiosity he once pursued without worrying about the possible moral or environmental consequences. (A few years before, Carl had quit a lucrative computer specialist job in Massachusetts with a company heavily involved in engineering with military applications. A graduate student before taking the job, he had returned to school after quitting it).

Linda *"found out I was a pantheist* when I was eight years old." She told us of her special affection for trees, and her idea that trees were beings deserving reverence. She added that *long after leaving college she had gone back* (and now made a living as a part-time midwife).

Mike described himself as *"different"* both in terms of cultural background and family history. He grew up going to an *Armenian church while living in a suburban tract* that was largely Protestant and non-observant. As a child he watched the hillsides around his home in northern New Jersey being "destroyed" and turned into "shelves" with houses on them – *poking ironic fun at the suburban aesthetic*. He had always been told he was "very smart," but he never liked school much. He liked learning itself, though, and was not afraid to tell his teachers they were wrong – and bring the right book to school to prove it. "I was supposed to be the scholar," he said, but he had dropped out of college for the time being.

Joe had had a long-term interest in *"humanistic psychology."* He said he "got into the Greens because of *personal issues,"* without elaborating. But he wanted to pursue the Green cause for its *potential as a political party*, and not for personal reasons alone – *he wanted to combine both*. He *wasn't always interested in environmental issues*. He had a history in political activity; he had been involved in the *civil rights movement* (and later, I found out, in Democratic electoral politics too).

Larry was "a child of the 50s." He had done a *paper for school on African socialism*, and had thought the *Cuban revolution was a good idea*. Later on, he went to Southeast Asia as a *Peace Corps* volunteer.

When he returned, he *practiced meditation for twelve years.* He then got *involved in local political activity,* and for a while was a "block captain" for his neighborhood during elections. But he *"wanted to do something more."* Away at a retreat in the countryside one weekend, he heard someone mention the Greens, and thought they were just the kind of group he wanted to be involved in.

Nearly all Greens created identities for themselves as individual cultural émigrés, as people who bore culturally radical ideas on their own more than as members of established collectivities. George and Mike had a heightened sense of their cultural background as different from those around them. Brian and Heather defined their activism in terms of people or books that were culturally radicalizing. Larry enveloped himself in cultural difference with the Peace Corps in Borneo, while Carl chose to reject a conventional technological career by leaving his job on principle. Linda learned she could valorize the "pantheism" she claims to have discovered as a child. Joe was the only one who made experience in a long-established social movement part of his story. But he located his present desire to be a Green in his project to combine psychological development and political aims – a cultural radicalism *par excellence.* Only Donald spoke of becoming a Green in terms of maintaining a cultural orientation rather than loosening, changing or reacting to one. And in the US Quakerism has long been associated with dissent that highlights individual moral agency.

The Greens' stories of cultural dissent resulted in a group with diverse reference points for activist identity, with relatively few shared in common. Ridge Greens did not peg their identities on one shared political tradition – socialism, anarchism, or feminism, or the Democratic Party – or on one shared communal or civic entity. Neither was commitment to "environmentalism" a major part of these stories. Donald was also the only member who saw himself setting out to fight specific environmental causes, and still he mentioned his "Quakerism" ahead of environmentalism. Linda emphasized a kind of environmentalism as the primary basis of her commitment to the Greens, but her environmentalism grew out of spiritual commitments rather than interest in specific environmental issues.[13] Of course environmentalism was a primary ideological concern for Greens, and no anti-environmentalist could have lasted in the movement. But environmentalism alone is not what inspired potential activists to join the Green movement over the Sierra Club or any other organization.

What Greens did share was a highly individualized way of relating to the cultural reference points in their accounts. Becoming a Green did not mean being radicalized *into* established traditions and organizations – a political party or a religious community – so much as being individually jarred *out* of taken-for-granted cultural pathways. For instance, Heather worded her story in terms of an instructor who personally introduced her to Green literature. Her account suggested that the college was salient to her because it helped individuate her politically. She could have worded her college experience as making her "feel part of a women's community," but she did not. George and Mike spoke of their ethnic backgrounds not as sources of traditions that would inspire them but as sources of *difference* from a cultural mainstream. The Greens' stories were created on the assumption that practicing activism meant carrying a sense of being an enlightened or culturally radical *individual* more than an initiate or an ongoing member in a particular community.

The individual story-telling format itself, common to Green meetings, says much about the Greens' definition of activist identity. It tells us how they related their efforts to those of other activists and to society at large. The Greens' lengthy personal narratives represented the shared norm that Greens carry their commitments as empowered individual agents more than as adherents to a common tradition or as participants in an established institution. "Go-arounds" like the one above stressed an evolving activist biography, an engagement of the whole person in political commitment. They reproduced the culture of personalized politics. Greens rarely created short, sketchy self-accounts in these sessions; doing so produced hesitant glances beckoning the speaker to say more.

The Greens' norm of togetherness brooked some individual preferences more easily than others. Ridge Greens sincerely respected Donald's sense of duty, but Donald's relatively "strict" style did not get generalized as part of the Ridge Green routine. "New age" spirituality made greater inroads in the group than Donald's duty-bound sense of discipline and responsibility, even though new age precepts and those of the Society of Friends both ride on the broad personalist current in US culture. The difference is that the diffuse new age spirituality did not privilege any specific reference point outside the self, while Donald's style presupposed a sense of allegiance nurtured within a religious denomination, albeit one emphasizing a highly personalized sense of commitment. In short, a diffuse spirituality complemented the Greens' form of togetherness more than would a religiously informed sense of duty for a group of individuals who did not share the same religion.

Greens could work together while honoring individual differences because they shared personalism as a group norm. Together, they spoke and acted on the assumption that political commitment wells up from deep within one's own biography – that individual inspiration matters more than the specific communities or institutions that may have nurtured it. Activists with diverse sources of social identity and individualized understandings of radicalization would not create the kind of mutual bonds that characterize traditional civic or religious communities. Communitarians' notions of political commitment speak past the cultural predicament of activists such as the Ridge Greens. There were times when the Greens' solicitousness of individuals did allow them to engage in personal exploration that few political organizations would sponsor on their time. For instance, Ridge Greens honored the individual preferences of a few by beginning some meetings with new age-style rituals that included personal sharing, even though some members did not actively advocate for these rituals and others chafed at new age philosophy in general. All the same, communitarian arguments would miss that personalism as a shared norm gave Greens a basis for practicing activism together, not simply a license for group therapy or spiritual self-discovery.

THE USES OF PERSONALISM

The culture of personalism is a common coin that Greens shared and implicitly recognized as legitimate. Personalism enabled Greens to practice public responsibility together, insisting on the value of each individual's contribution. Greens did not always talk explicitly about self and feelings at meetings. And usually, the assumptions about individual commitment and efficacy stood without elaboration. Occasionally Greens did explicitly articulate the background knowledge underlying participation and decision-making in their groups. The following scenario from the 1989 national conference illustrates the principle of personalism underlying this and many other Green movement meetings I attended.

Personalized democracy in action

Much of the activity at the conference centered on working groups divided into ten areas. Along with roughly thirty others, I attended the sessions on "internal organizing" within the Green movement. A woman who was to become the national Green Clearinghouse coordinator "facilitated" these sessions. Our session began with participants calling out all of the issues they hoped to see covered in this working group. The facilitator instructed us to call these items out without fear of being "judged" on the relevance or importance of our items. After this "brain-storming" period, each individual participant was invited to contribute an item if she had not already done so. Altogether, we had brainstormed nearly forty items, ranging from "coalition-building," "people of color," and "fundraising," to "can everyone be Green?", to "preventing burnout" and "emotional literacy."

Each individual contributed to decision-making in the session. In all, the first of the two planned three-hour sessions produced a shorter list drawn from the original forty items, which eventually became themes for deliberation in smaller working groups at the next session. A lot of the group's common effort went into whittling down the individual contributions. Responding to a question about the group's final decisions, one participant exclaimed, "Decision! I'm overwhelmed at how much we're going to love each other by the end ... and that's *all*!" Later on she added, "I wish I didn't enjoy the process so much!" A regional leader at the session confided to me about the final product, "You or I could whip up something in three hours." But the norm of personal participation mattered more than the time that may have been saved if fewer or more "experienced" people had shepherded the process. The regional leader affirmed, "It's all about individual empowerment."

Greens hoped that their group efforts would be "fun" at least some of the time, and as the woman quoted above implied, some Greens saw the fun as potentially in tension with collective ends. But Greens did not intend their group togetherness to *depend* on shared fun. As we will see below, Greens committed themselves to working through group problems in meetings that were not necessarily enjoyable. The Greens also aimed to accomplish more at this conference than to increase feelings of individual "empowerment." They did in fact draft a national movement platform made up of position statements like those hammered out in the internal organizing working group. The roughly 250 activists in attendance would need a common repertoire of background knowledge to be able to take each other as legitimate participants. Activists like the Ridge Greens would not necessarily share a lot; a keynote speaker at the conference suggested that conference participants may have traveled diverse personal pathways to activism. Personalism provided a shared basis for these activists to work together. Without this shared cultural basis, the diverse gathering of activists could probably not have taken place, much less produce agreement on a preliminary movement platform.

Some of the conference delegates, particularly the "anti-capitalists" associated with the "Left Green Network" (LGN), looked askance at the self-expressive tone of much of the conference. Some people at an LGN caucus meeting complained that little had been accomplished at their working groups. One said there needed to be more "discipline." Yet, the Left Green faction as a whole did not make the style of participation an issue for debate at the conference, though it could have done so through the daily conference newsletter or numerous announcement periods. At the end of the conference, a leading member of the LGN, a man in his late twenties, said (appreciatively) that he thought the conference represented a "convergence of the new left and the 'new age'." While sharply contrasting his own "new left"-inspired way of thinking with the spiritual individualism and transcendentalism of "new age" philosophy, he figured that "treating people with respect" had not been "very high on the new left's agenda at the time of the Weather Underground." So activists who would carry on the new left tradition could learn from the new agers. This "convergence" on the rights of persons is not far from the personalist rationale for participation that other delegates upheld – the normative condition for action in common.

Newsletter reports and statements at a regional meeting of California Green locals gave glowing accounts of the 1989 conference. Even some Left Greens weighed in with an assessment that much had been accomplished. They were especially impressed that activists unschooled in the critique of capitalism had spent hours late into the night in dialogue with them, learning about and sometimes agreeing with the Left Greens' terms of debate.

Greens relied on personalistic notions of participation not just to make participation happen, but to increase it. For instance, we saw the Seaview Greens above trying to write by-laws that would bring individual and working group projects back under a strengthened Green umbrella. Seaviewers wanted to attract more people to the Green movement:

Ryan suggested that Seaview needed more of a "focus as a whole group." "We need to be networking with other groups and bringing in new people."

Imagining how to get group priorities met while enticing new members, Greens alighted upon personalistic definitions of participation:

Hope was disturbed that people did not appear involved in the last general meeting – they "looked down at their laps." She proposed that the meeting begin with each person saying something about themselves and why they were there. "We need to have something personal at the very beginning so that people can connect with us."

Other members did not reject the idea itself but balked at the amount of time this would take. Seaview Greens wanted to get things done as a group in which individual voices would resonate; the point was not for these voices to ring out for their own sake. As a compromise, Hope suggested that people who had not participated by a certain time be asked if they would like to introduce themselves and have their say on some point. "I want everyone to feel like they can participate," she affirmed. Hope maintained a personalistic definition of "participation" in tandem with her concern, articulated above, for the group's viability as a whole.

Other Seaviewers maintained a similar working definition of participation. For instance, Seaviewers planned a roughly hour-long discussion of their new introductory pamphlet as a way to get participants talking about what the Green movement should be saying and doing. But what if some participants were new and had little idea what the Greens were about? Leonard answered that "each can say 'what Green means to me'." Seaviewers assumed that individuals new to the Greens could offer up impressions about Green activism, and that Greens would respect these contributions, even if they did not make their way into the final pamphlet. Their assumptions may well have fit their constituency: recall that new participants at the candidates' forum strongly praised the Seaview organization for making political discussion more inviting, less intimidating.

Enlarging the network of personalized politics

The idea of a participant as a personal agent of social change also influenced Green recruiting efforts. Prospective members of the Ridge Greens in effect got introduced to the norm of personalized participation at orientation meetings. For their part, the orientation leaders assumed that Green activists would be self-starters rather than initiates in need of convincing by an authoritative Green voice. Laying out a broad field of "Green" thought and practice, orientation leaders would help prospective members "plug in" to some project that interested them, or encourage them to start their own. Ridge Green orientations began with a short history of Greens in Europe, and a shorter history of the Greens in the US. The two people "facilitating" the orientation would take turns going over the Ten Key Values, and then make announcements about projects currently under way. Prospective members heard little if any "selling" of the organization. Carl, one of the orientation facilitators, said that people interested in particular projects should use the project leaders' phone numbers on the newsletter, or else stick around to talk more about their interests after the meeting. Mike, with some concern in his voice, asked me after one orientation whether I thought that one of the project leaders had come on too strong; this was to be avoided at Green orientations. Core members would discuss afterwards whether a lot of people had participated or not in the meeting. They deemed the first orientation I attended a particular success because many of the twenty or so people who came had spoken up at least once.

Greens assumed some very broad ideological similarities between themselves and prospective members. At the orientation pictured above, for instance, people new to the Greens were supposed to jump right in and participate in a discussion of post-industrial and leftist "values." The discussion showed that participants were already familiar with left-oriented beliefs about politics and the environment. But more striking, they *related to* those beliefs in a similar, personalized way. Being a good progressive or leftist depended less on fighting for some particular ideological position – socialism, for instance – and more on carrying personal "values" that characterize how one should conduct one's life. This became especially clear in the words people used to describe the "values" they associated with the political left, values with which they apparently identified themselves:

People yelled out answers in a pretty articulate way. No one associated the "left" with "socialism," or economic well-being, or social justice, but with "creativity," "collectivity," "open-mindedness" and "anti-authoritarianism" – all ways of doing things. Some people disagreed with the latter term, and Carl, the other facilitator, cautioned that he knew some pretty authoritarian leftists. A couple of people quipped that we could summarize all this by saying that "left" values were "good" and "right" values were "bad."

Similarly, Green party organizers addressed themselves to a prospective voter who was already oriented to personalized cultural dissent. They presupposed a supporter who did not need sustained Green tutelage. This combination of assumptions shows through in the following discussion of voter registration at an early Seaview Green Party meeting:

New Green voter: "What if people ask who we are running? ... People are simple-minded – they want to vote for a person, for a personality."
New party volunteer: "You can tell them to register for the party that best represents their values."
New Green voter: "But there aren't many people like that!"
Seaview member: "Oh – I think that's starting to change."
New Green voter: "Yeah, you can find that at the College, but on Maple and 21st it ain't gonna get anybody. I know – I live there!"
Man from Abalone Alliance: "She's got a good point."

Another Seaview Green added that "there will be some salesmanship involved; conversion," with the tone of a man trying to imagine hypothetical events in an impending war. Responding to the question above about attracting voters outside of a college milieu, he offered conscientiously that "that's an important point; we haven't figured it out." The "average voter" posited in this conversation votes for a person with whom he can identify, not for "values" to which he has committed himself, and especially not for the non-mainstream values that Greens self-consciously put forward. Green activists were used to imagining prospective Greens as people who had already picked up a culturally alternative outlook: "register for the party that best represents their values." Or as one Green said about distributing the Ridge newsletter for recruitment purposes: "We should put them where we think people have our values, and they will be like us."

For Greens, the personalized way of articulating their ideology was even more of a common ground than the specific ideologies themselves. Greens expected prospective Greens to share only a vaguely defined, left-of-center stance represented in the Ten Key Values, one that highlights environmental issues in the context of broad political and cultural change. And they assumed predilections for particular environmental issues would be personal and unpredictable. For instance, I asked Larry why the Ridge Greens didn't choose a single project for new members, telling them that the project would be primary and "working group" activity secondary. He replied curtly, "That's a very nice idea but why don't you come to some orientations?" His experiences had taught him that "you can't tell people" what to get involved in. Instead, the Greens had to entice them with a "big menu" of issues so that lots of prospective members would find something that attracted them under the broad framework of the Ten Key Values. George also told me there had to be "interesting working groups" to attract people, and that is how they would join the Greens. Or as Mike said,

"We have to be tackling issues that appeal on a visceral level ... I know black males in jail is really important, but I really don't know what to do about it." But he *did* have lots of ideas about land use in Ridgeville.

Larry, George, and Mike were reacting to a very real dilemma in post-1960s movement-building: in a multi-issue activist milieu without ties to a political party or an established institution that could provide strategic direction, a small movement such as the US Greens would have little success "telling people what to do," especially if those people already carried their own ideas about how to effect social change. The Greens' predilection for personally empowered activists developed in the context of this broader organizational arena that Chapter 6 describes in more detail. The Ridge Greens thought they had to conceive recruitment in terms of a "visceral," personal attachment to issues, but at the same time wanted a Green movement organization with a common focus.

Greens tried to resolve the dilemma by giving prospective members the opportunity to develop underneath a Green aegis particular projects, such as Larry's campaign against widening a freeway or Mike's project to uncover and restore underground urban creeks. A group of people pursuing their political attachments in their own way might afford new members the chance to broaden their grasp of the Green-oriented issues or ideologies. Mike, for instance, claimed to have widened his political purview through Green activism:

"Since I've been in the Greens, I've become a feminist, and know a lot more about economics ... it's broadened my horizons – I joined as an environmentalist."

At general meetings such as the Seaview meeting described at the start of this chapter, members could broaden their horizons by hearing about projects and campaigns that other individuals and working groups were carrying out – campaigning for a nuclear-free zone, supporting a forest preservation ballot initiative, contributing to a community police watch, among others. The Green movement at the national level similarly attempted to integrate Greens' varied local projects and concerns into a common thrust toward a society slowly approaching one envisioned by the Ten Key Values. Finding the right organizational structure for this diversity-within-unity remained a great challenge.

ORGANIZING PERSONALIZED POLITICS

The meaning of "grassroots"

During this study, Seaview and Ridge Greens were trying to create an organizational structure that would maximize individual input while allowing individuals to fashion a group will. Seaview and the two Ridge groups all had in common a structure consisting of two levels: on the first level was an indefinite number of activity groups, formed by participants at will, and at the second level, a coordinating committee responsible for maintaining some overall direction for the organization. Seaview and Ridge Green groups also shared a consensus model of decision-making, the goal of which was to produce decisions that members agreed to unanimously after each had gotten a chance to contribute to the discussion.

The appeal of these practices for Greens depended in part on what "grassroots" meant for them.

Seaview Greens agreed that a "grassroots" Green group was one that propagated Green ideologies by welcoming the participation of diverse individuals who make different kinds of contributions. They shared the assumption that "grassroots" meant intensive participation by all individual members. During a by-laws meeting, Seaview stalwart Leonard contrasted this vision of the Seaview organization with a "vertical style of organization, with a president, vice-president, appointed people ... a pyramid structure." He wanted instead a "horizontal" structure in which

"individual people get involved and find a common purpose one way or another ... we're trying to form a new politic ... People from Fritjof Capra on down have been talking about finding a new way of doing things."

Leonard added that the Seaview group was trying to find this "new politic" by "backing into it." Wondering whether the Seaview group had simply rediscovered 1960s-style anti-authoritarianism, I asked Hope after the meeting about Seaview's goals:

I asked whether it was possible to combine some of the qualities of hierarchical organization with those of a decentralized group run on consensus. Wouldn't that free up some time for pursuing issues? Hope said she thought that was in fact what the by-laws group was trying to do. Using a "windshield wiper" metaphor, she embarked on an extended explanation of how people who joined the Greens "want to get away from hierarchical structures," but that the windshield wiper had swung too far in the other direction. Now the task was to come back to a middle point – all of which she explained with her arm in the air, gesturing the imaginary wiper. This was what Leonard's "new politic" was all about.

The Seaview Greens wanted to create a kind of group structure that would give more backbone to their organization while avoiding the conventional flow-chart of positions Leonard had described. No one was proposing to abolish authority; they were groping around for a new way of organizing it to maximize individual input without dissipating collective will. The old Ridge Green group had pursued a similar quest for the same kind of organization. They did not complete the quest to members' satisfaction, and as described below, continued the quest in the form of a new organization. The Seaview Greens worked hard on organizing their "new politic" and were rewarded with a structure that could make meetings like the one pictured at the start of this chapter both enjoyable and productive.

Centrifugal tendencies

The biggest challenge Seaview and Ridge Greens faced was to imbue their bi-level structures with a strong enough sense of collective purpose to keep the activity groups active and the coordinating committee coordinated with the groups. They wanted a more specific common purpose than their common commitment to the Ten Key Values. The group bonds they created seemed thinner than they had imagined for their "grassroots" movement. With an indefinite number of activity groups and only a broad mandate, it was difficult for Seaview Greens to legitimately prioritize some activities over others. All were valuable; none seemed absolutely essential. Group bonds would have to be flexible enough to accommodate a great deal of innovation. This was all the more the case since at least some Seaview Greens were ambivalent about specifying the long-term direction of the Green movement because in their vision of "grassroots" democracy, activists needed a lot of leeway for changing the course of the movement.

The working definition of "grassroots" sometimes led to tensions when individual Greens expected Green sponsorship for their projects even if others did not join them. Working group "loneliness" came up for discussion at several coordinating committee meetings. At one, Seaviewers dealt with complaints from the Nuclear-Free Zone working group that it did not receive enough support from the coordinating committee. At another, Steve responded to Randy's complaints of not receiving enough support for his efforts to expose a cult-like group using the Green name:

Steve: "I'm doing solid waste with a little help, and Leonard is doing the newsletter, and Barb is doing toxics alone after begging for money for months ... Randy must derive some standing from being part of the US Green movement. He wouldn't have gotten in [name of weekly newsmagazine] if he was just Randy Williams instead of a member of the Greens."

Leonard corrected Steve that he did get help from Neil and from Melinda. But in Hope's assessment, "We're all basically doing solo gigs here."

In the Ridge Greens, too, members complained of lacking a center. Carl once told me that the group should be able to get "fifty people called up on a phone tree to pack a city council meeting." This kind of action would have benefited Larry, whose working group on local transportation issues – largely a "solo gig" – had helped sway the city council of Flatburg to vote against a freeway extension plan. In fact, Larry was upset with some members of the Ridge coordinating council who insisted on approving any letter he wrote to the city council members thanking them for their vote. Ridge had tried to overcome its centrifugal tendencies with a "unifying project" for the organization – participation in Ridge county's nuclear-free zone campaign. The project was "not very unifying" as George recalled – only eight Greens had gotten involved when project coordinators had hoped for fifty or sixty.

Greens wanted to work together on common projects and not only pursue individual interests. Building an organization based on a great deal of personalized initiative was not the same as allowing individuals to pursue pet interests in a selfish way. Randy, for instance, had spoken with great conviction about his project's value for the Seaview Greens as a group. Neither did Greens simply want to drop organizational affiliations or detach from coordinating committees as soon as personal relationships became frustrating. On the contrary, Greens committed themselves to working together even when they found some members cantankerous. Hope explained to me, for instance, that she was learning to work with a difficult member of the Seaview organization; Ridge Greens similarly felt committed to keeping individual members included even if the interpersonal dynamics were trying. These organizations did not, then, make their togetherness depend on personal friendship. They aimed to be accessible public organizations, not personal clubs or cliques, and they spent considerable time working through organizational difficulties. Their group culture created strong challenges for centralized planning and organizational stability, but it also enabled participants with personalized commitments to regroup relatively easily and take some of the weight of their ambitious, long-term Green project off a particular organization.

CRISIS, DECLINE, AND REBIRTH IN THE RIDGE GREENS

Centrifugal tendencies widened some of the Green organizations' most threatening divisions. Individuals who made the extra commitment of time to join the coordinating committees found themselves doing work that Greens agreed was necessary but also difficult to valorize within their vision of good "grassroots" activism. Without a clearly articulated basis for their extra power and responsibility, these individuals could too easily appear illegitimate to other members. As a result, some of these seriously committed people would "burn-out" and feel underappreciated while others, just as serious, would feel abused or neglected. Both the Ridge and Seaview Green groups endured crises created by the centrifugal tendency, though the outcomes of these crises were different. These were not crises of selfishness or apathy, but they represented the most severe limitations in the Greens' personalized culture of commitment.

The Ridge Greens tried to reverse the trend toward overwork at the center and dissipation in the fringes. The following scenarios trace their efforts closely. A personalized form of togetherness did not save the Ridge Green group from disintegrating. But it did keep individual activists going in the public arena: it allowed activists to detach their overriding commitments from particular organizations such that some of the old Ridge Green members could quickly regroup as the Ridge Green Party, an organization with a clearer political mission.

Group responsibility and "personal process"

Four months into this study, it was becoming clear that no one was entirely happy with the way the old Ridge group was functioning. Donald complained there was too little sense of "group responsibility." He called a crisis meeting. At the meeting, Carl pointed to the meeting agenda as a prime example of Donald's complaints. As usual, most of the items on the sheet had been submitted by George, the informal group leader. A grassroots democracy as the Greens envisioned it was not supposed to work that way. In their eyes, George did too much directing – reminding or cajoling them to have literature ready for the Eco-cities conference, or to carry out their preparations for the Earth Day fair booth. George had his own view on the group dynamic:

George told us that members' "attitude" was "wrong," that they seemed to go to coordinating council meetings with a "reactive" attitude. Ridge members should have been happy about new developments in local environmental politics, he said, instead of seeing each new opportunity to sponsor an event as a "chore."

Other people at this meeting articulated the Ridge group's problems differently. Heidi said she wanted a long stretch of the meeting to be devoted to "personal process." Mike seconded Heidi's suggestion, though as we will see, he also spoke up strongly for the importance of "common values." Carl wanted to bring up "group responsibility," using the terms Donald had used. The seven members went back and forth trying to decide whether to talk about "personal process" or "group responsibility." We started discussing "personal process."

Heidi and Linda thought that bad "personal process" was the answer to Ridge's unequal distribution of power and responsibility and the resulting frustrations. The coordinating committee reminded Heidi of a "dysfunctional family," and she recommended that the group get an outside consultant; Linda quickly suggested one who used a bestselling author's televised material on family dynamics. Heidi added that she now understood how "personal process" and "group responsibility" could be connected: "Well, if you clear up the personal process, then group responsibility takes care of itself; you don't need to have someone [tell you what to do]." If members were better attuned to each other as persons, then group responsibility – the issue Donald thought was central – would develop naturally. But when Heidi and Linda talked about "process" they were not implying that the collective should serve mainly to enhance self-development. Linda, for instance, complained that the Ridge Greens weren't "doing anything" as a group – a complaint she would repeat several times before the group folded.

Mike and Carl wanted the Ridge Greens to create more of a space for political dialogue at meetings. Mike said that he had energy to devote to political causes but had a hard time seeing how to plug it into the Ridge Greens, and added "there are lots of political organizations in the area," implying that he would be tempted to break away and join one. He insisted that the group needed to talk about its "common values" in order to figure out what a common goal for the Ridge Greens might be. In the same breath, he said he felt like he was "being nickled and dimed to death" with routine tasks of group maintenance. Responsibility was always something that was "given out," not something he could take on his own initiative; George's *de facto* leadership seemed illegitimate.

"Politically" oriented Mike and Carl and "process" oriented Heidi and Linda seemed to disagree on Ridge's core problem, but they all upheld the prerogatives of personalized politics. They all shared a desire to have their individual autonomy respected: Heidi disparaged "having someone tell you what to do," and Mike wanted to take his own initiative. All Ridge Greens could understand a highly individual-oriented perspective on the group's problems, even though Mike, Carl, Donald, and Linda also spoke up for "group responsiblity." Thus Donald's original complaint about "leadership" and "responsibility" got translated into a language of "process," one with both benefits and disadvantages for group togetherness.

The strengths and weaknesses of process talk

Women and men in the Ridge Greens agreed that their organization was in trouble and needed to have more projects to do. But men talked more in terms of "politics" and "responsibility" while women gravitated more to the terms of personal expression. In this way they are similar to many post-1960s movement groups whose disagreements over organizational style split along gender lines. Chapter 6 will examine one such movement whose members, like Linda and Heidi above, wanted to practice activism in a psychologically sophisticated, "process"-conscious milieu. A personalist language of process bridges the gender divide in organizations like the Ridge Greens while other cultures of commitment might not. But it obscures one root of gender inequities in these organizations.

The norm of personalism acted as a sort of equalizer which both women and men in the Ridge Greens could accept as legitimate. In an ostensibly egalitarian organization, Ridge women had reason for grievances with some Ridge men. Women were accurate to point out that women more than men tended to drop out of groups like the coordinating committee. The centrifugal dynamic I have described exacerbated gender inequities which the larger society may have engendered in members of the Ridge Greens.[14] So in practice, a personalist principle gave women a basis for challenging the interactional dynamics that put men in agenda-setting roles. While Carl and Brian approached the Ridge Greens' problems differently from Heidi, they could not legitimately contest her own way of assessing the organization in terms of "process" rather than "leadership" or "group responsibility."

Psychological language bridged a gender divide, but it also made it difficult to discuss an organizational dynamic apart from gendered psychological differences. In a centrifugal organization whose *de facto* leaders got separated from other members, and thus delegitimated, any man who took a leading role could very easily look like he was trying to dominate the group. Without a way to talk about organizational responsibility apart from individual psychologies, women could easily see males' initiatives in terms of the male psychological need to dominate, whether or not the men in question were trying to grab power. Within their organization, gender differences would keep reappearing in exaggerated form unless the Ridge Greens could stop their centrifugal cycle. But this would take a forthright discussion about leadership itself, and no one in the Ridge Greens was supposed to be a formal leader. For women in the Ridge Greens, the personalist principle bought a powerful means for raising legitimate grievances, but ended up costing them opportunities for acquiring more leading roles. The more women identified themselves as essentially expressive and "personal," the more they distanced themselves from any positions of public prominence or authority. It became too easy to devalue the roles that men took, rather than finding ways to make more women into Green leaders. But this, again, would necessitate less of a psychological imagination and more of an organizational one.

In activist circles, attending to members' feelings and to patterns of interaction has been called "feminist process." The self-expressive style corresponds to notions of women's relationality and intuitive sense. It makes sense, then, that some feminist women have sought to enhance their own status in male-dominated organizations by valorizing "women's qualities." "Feminist process" is a misleading term, though, because it collapses an ideology of human relations (feminism) with one specific means for putting that ideology into practice (a kind of personalism). By advancing women's claims to participation through expressive selfhood, Ridge women found a way to challenge inequities in an individualistic language that men in the group understood. Ironically, this kind of challenge obscured one cause of the grievances – the organizational dynamic itself.[15] Both women and men[16] in the Ridge Greens called on their psychological imaginations as they tried to make the group both more participatory and more effective.

The Ridge Greens did meet with a group dynamics consultant for two sessions. After these "process sessions," there followed many more conversations about the group's troubles. During a task group meeting, I asked Carl and Suzanne why there was not more of a set procedure for dealing with perceived imbalances of power in this democratic, participation-oriented group.

Carl: "OK, do you (to me) or you (to Suzanne) want to be the one ... ?"
Suzanne: "See it's all of us ... if we're not willing to take responsibility it's our fault too ... I think it's psychological" (sounding definitive). She would make this comment again during the evening, and suggest that we "devote a whole meeting some time to talk about psychology, and how we work."
PL: "You mean everyone in the group has a psychological problem?"
Carl: "Everyone in the country has a psychological problem" (facetiously).
PL: "OK, then you can't use that as a reason, if everyone ..."
Carl: (cutting in) "It's personal power! We all have been trained that we can't do anything."

It is striking here that even Carl, a Ridge member who pushed for more cooperative projects with other activist groups, was using a language of psychology. He also concluded the group's problem was "deeper than" psychological dynamics. Carl's comment about personal power is not just a plea for more self-expressiveness as an end in itself; it sounds like a social critique. Carl had often spoken about expanding political participation as a goal of Green activism – fighting widespread powerlessness in society. In the context of the dialogue above, the safest interpretation is that he is both "thinking" a social critique, and articulating it in an idiom of "personal power" that complements a politics of personally empowered individuals.

Suzanne, while smirking a bit, suggested that using "status-quo techniques" might help the Greens attract more members. She referred to a newsletter article suggesting Greens ought to try "direct mail" the way political interest groups do. Catching the dubious look on Suzanne's face, Carl said that many Greens would look askance at this conventional kind of organizing. And Suzanne herself said she preferred to learn from spiritual-feminist author Starhawk[17] about how to have good "process" at meetings. The Ridge Greens remained poised uncomfortably between the procedures they thought stifled participation, and their own sometimes frustrating attempts at participatory democracy.

Portable commitments

Along with two newer members, Carl, Mike, and Donald dropped out of the Ridge Greens within six months of the "process" sessions. Mike became involved in local electoral politics, Donald began a professional master's program, and Carl split his time between his own graduate school career and the nascent Green political party effort in which he would come to play a major role later that same year. George threatened to take an extended leave of absence, though he did not do so, hoping that the new Green Party would reinvigorate Green activism in the area. Linda, one of the strongest proponents of working on group "process," claimed that the sessions with the outside facilitator had helped. When I asked how, she said that she now felt free to call on another Ridge member to hash out some upset with him. She could communicate, self to self. But she also continued to complain the Ridge group was "not doing anything," and in the next year she got involved in city politics and participated in a mass demonstration against corporate lumber-harvesting practices. In members' lived experience, "burn-out," frustration over perceived abuses of power, and lack of a focus caused them to quit the old Ridge Green group, an organization that had lasted over five years. Yet all the Ridge Greens expressed a strong commitment to remain activists. Much as personalism limited their organizations, it also made their ongoing activism possible to begin with.

Half of the core Ridge Greens eagerly re-formed themselves as the new Ridge Green Party. Others looked on with interest, waiting to see how the new organization would shape up. The new Ridge group continued trying to build an organization that would express Greens' individualized commitments. The Ridge Green Party established itself securely enough to contribute mightily to the California Green Party's successful bid for ballot status in 1991. It also revisited some of the challenges faced by the earlier Ridge group, as in the debate pictured near the start of this chapter over an interim coordinating board. At this and other meetings, Greens continued searching for an organizational structure that suited a "grassroots" group – meaning one in which activists' individually empowered voices would resonate within the common will. Organizing this kind of togetherness remained one of the most difficult parts of the Green project.

WERE THE RIDGE GREENS JUST PECULIAR? COMPARISONS

Ridge and Seaview Greens faced similar organizational dilemmas but the Seaview Greens did not express the same amount of frustration with group dynamics as did the Ridge group. But the Seaview group, too, solicited outside consultation in hopes of improving their group, right around the time that the California Green Party had won the right to register voters. Seaview's consultants outlined ground rules for discussions that the activists were supposed to conduct as personal selves. The consultants insisted on "full participation," meaning that people should "be out there as much as you can – say what feels comfortable to say." Below I list quotes representing the spectrum of statements Greens made about their mission and vision.[18]

"There is a split between lifestyle and electoral politics. This divisive thing is suicidal because the Greens is [sic] both."
"There's an environmental crisis. I want energy to go to expedite goals, getting work done."
"Our purpose is to have an impact. How do you do that when you're formless and mushy?"
"If politics weren't personal, I'd have no interest."
"We have gone from non-activism to total activism. We need a balance between political and internal."

While it is dangerous to interpret these statements out of context, the language suggests that many Seaviewers were concerned about the public mission of the group, and not just individuals' gratification alone. Seaview maintained a healthy existence as a group throughout this study, and continued to attract potential members to its orientation meetings. It also continued to exhibit the same pattern of overwork at the center and dissipation at the fringes. Like the Ridge group, Seaview was in search of a new language and format for egalitarian, intensive participation. It invoked a personalist principle, using outside "facilitators" to explore its organizational problems.

Is all this attention to group dynamics purely a "California" phenomenon? My observations at the 1989 national conference indicate otherwise. One illustration emerged from my talk with Sherry, a Green prominent at the national movement level and a leader in her local group in a midwestern state – one not known as a hotbed of personalist culture. She complained about decision-making at the conference, derided the term "Green process" as a "California term," and explained that "structure" is often the root problem in decision-making difficulties. But "structure," it turned out, amounted to the same thing as "process" with a different name. Sherry's explanation of "structure" started with the observation that "reality" is a tension between opposites, male and female. She insisted that while "society is destroying itself" because of its emphasis on "male" qualities, "in the Green movement, we've gone too far the other way." She had in mind the slow decision-making that had dogged the session on organization-building that we had both attended. The working group needed a structure that would enable people to take more initiative, to use their "male" side, instead of going around in circles of individual participation leading nowhere. She quipped to me that it was all very "Zen" to be coming out this way. I resolved that from then on I would be skeptical of people using "California" as an adjective to describe what is in fact a widespread mode of psychological thinking that comes in varied idioms.

With her combination of popular gender psychology and eastern spiritualism, Sherry had put her finger on the same kinds of decision-making bottlenecks I observed in the Ridge and Seaview Greens. Like the Seaview and Ridge Greens, Sherry's local group wanted to enhance individual participation without losing a common purpose. And like her "California" compatriots, Sherry needed a new language for talking about political participation, one that could describe individualized participation without neglecting a group's desire to create a common will. The language of "male enery" and "female energy" accomplished this task for her.

Radical feminists (Freeman 1975, 1972–3) and anti-nuclear activists before the Greens experienced the same kinds of organizational difficulties. For instance, anti-nuclear movement groups of the late 1970s and 1980s were severely stressed, and sometimes fragmented, by disagreements over decision-making processes (Barkan 1979; Vogel 1980; Epstein 1991). Rejecting elected or appointed leadership, anti-nuclear activists structured their movement and its protest activities around small, autonomous "affinity groups" of like-minded protesters, and councils of affinity-group spokespersons committed to reaching decisions by consensus rather than majority vote. A frustrating pattern emerged: "[W]hoever stays the longest, puts in the most hours and is the most persuasive, effectively becomes leadership. What follows is a self-appointed group of leaders" (Vogel 1980).

In its first six years, the US Green movement also favored decision-making by consensus, along with a loose affinity-group structure. Compare the above description of anti-nuclear movement leadership with this description of national Green movement organizing ten years later:

Most of the work sustaining the [platform writing] process, planning and staging the conference was done by a handful of people ... [We have been] delegating responsibility by the default method: we empower whoever is willing to do the job and then abandon them – a guaranteed recipe for burnout, resentment (Solnit 1990).

The recent history of anti-nuclear movement organizations was not so distant that Greens would repeat it out of ignorance. A leading activist in the major west coast anti-nuclear network of the early 1980s attended the first meeting of the Seaview Greens' own electoral organizing group. He cautioned them about the consensus decision-making procedures they were using:

"We [the Abalone Alliance] had 100,000 members, offices in every city ... it all fell apart." He said there had developed a leading elite that was quite separate from everyone else. Still he had not given up on the consensus decision-making process altogether, and hoped that computerized "bulletin boards" might ease the process.

It is striking that even after his cautionary tale, the anti-nuclear activist did not reject "alternative"-style organization. Neither did Greens take his cautions as a red light for their incipient efforts. It would be difficult to invent a new priniciple of group togetherness from scratch, one that would bring together a collection of activists radicalized in diverse ways.

PERSONALISM, PUBLIC COMMITMENT, AND THE GREENS

Reinventing commitment has been a difficult project for activists who try to act for the public good with a great deal of individual autonomy. Scenes of organizational difficulty in the Ridge Greens and other movement groups may suggest that the project is doomed to group in-fighting and dissipation. But this assessment begs the question of what other basis for political community is available to activists like US Greens who have taken varied routes to radicalization. Neither should we assume that other forms of political community avoid dilemmas of leadership; Chapter 4 will show that a much more communitarian culture of commitment produces leadership dilemmas in a different form. Greens did not anchor their commitments in the established, civic institutions that communitarians have imagined as the infrastructure of public virtue in the US – the town hall, the ethnic mutual aid society, the church-based public service effort. Greens had disparate sources of social identity as activists, and needed a basis for practicing political commitment together that would accommodate them. The Greens' shared personalism provided that basis. In the final chapter, I will suggest that activists could avoid some of the troubles Greens experienced, while still enjoying the benefits of personalism in politics, if they replaced some of the popular psychological talk with a new idiom that would bond individuals' commitments more explicitly to a broad political community.

Communitarians like Boyte (1989) have argued a different alternative – that activists need to speak traditional languages of citizenship or communal loyalty because doing so will make them more publicly responsible. In a similar vein, the communitarian theories examined in Chapter 1 assumed that public virtue would wither if not informed by traditional notions of good citizenship, religious faith, or both. Yet, in stark contrast to these arguments, personalism *enabled* Greens to set up forums like that described at the beginning of this chapter, forums for the kind of broad discussion that would exemplify public virtue for Bellah, Bell, Lasch, or Rieff. It enabled Greens to sustain local activist projects, to talk broadly about the political world in a society accustomed to public cynicism, and to begin electoral organizing, however fitfully, at the local level. It gave women in the movement a means for enunciating grievances as rightfully equal participants. Personalism enabled Greens to nurture their commitments, carrying them individually, from one organizational setting to another.

Greens' commitments were stronger than the organizations they built. Organizational efforts continued to frustrate them throughout this study. But we would obscure rather than illuminate the Greens' sense of public responsibility if we conclude from their experience with organizations that they were simply selfish, or interested only in "personal growth." By creating an alternative identity as "Green," we could say they sent a message to the wider society (Melucci 1989, 1985) about the interrelation of environmental and social problems. But they not only created a new identity, they practiced a sense of obligation that they hoped, over a long haul, would produce change in the spectrum of public debate and eventually in policy outcomes.

The organizational difficulties that Greens endured point to the cultural predicament for committed people who do not share the same affiliations with common institutions or cultural authorities. Communitarian arguments about political commitment have offered too few tools for addressing this predicament, in seeming hope that people of good will might discover, or rediscover, traditions that support steadfast commitment to a cause. Not all activists, however, can readily identify with these traditions. Not all happen to have been born into a religious, civic-minded, or labor unionist household. We need other images of political commitment, then, than those most salient in communitarian arguments. Rather than judge Greens according to communitarian models of commitment, we might evaluate them instead by the goal they implicitly set for themselves: to sustain commitment and togetherness among people with individualized, diverse radicalization experiences. In this light, Greens met with mixed success in creating a commitment style to suit their cultural predicament.

The Greens' style of movement-building reflects a widespread predicament for grassroots politicization in the post-1960s US. In the past thirty years, many thousands of activists and potential activists may have developed personalized commitments to the public good by reading a "radical" book, being inspired by a particular teacher or youth group counselor, or critically reconstructing their own cultural identity, rather than by receiving formalized political socialization in a party, labor union, or civic organization. Personalized politics would make cultural sense for these activists as well. Chapter 6 will show in more detail how the personalized commitment style does in fact run through other grassroots movements since the 1960s.

ALTERNATIVE ACCOUNTS

I want to consider briefly two other possible explanations for the puzzle that began this chapter – the puzzle of seemingly serious activists enduring a frustrating group dynamic that emphasizes members' individuality. These two accounts would pay less attention than I have to the question of public-spirited commitment. But they are worth addressing because some academic writings, "common sense," or both would find them plausible.

One account would hold that the Greens had a problem with political issues: they focused on either too many or too few. Environmentalism itself encompasses many different issues. The Green movement was especially diffuse in embracing such a wide variety of environmental and social issues under the aegis of the Ten Key Values. Any movement group that allows individual members to pursue so many specific issues and general interests under one movement umbrella would be strained. Practicing personalized politics does not necessarily mean fitting the difficult political niche that Greens carved out for themselves as a small, multi-issue movement amidst much larger and much better publicized single-issue organizations. At least part of the Greens' difficulties in sustaining the kind of togetherness they wanted may be a result, then, of remaining open to such a wide variety of issues without establishing a sharper focus on just a few.

A diffuse issue focus is a reasonable factor in explaining the Greens' centrifugal tendencies, but it is not sufficient in itself. It is worth keeping in mind the example of anti-nuclear organizations that developed a similar dynamic to that of the Greens, with a much more specific issue focus. A variation on this approach would hold that Greens could not identify enough truly pressing issues to create organizations as strong as their individual commitments. Maybe Greens were too privileged to have to confront concrete environmental issues "in their backyards" the way other activists have. But this approach would assume that "issues" are self-evidently important. Social movement research has emphasized, in contrast, that issues must be "framed" (Snow *et al.* 1986; Snow and Benford 1988), frames do not necessarily represent "reality," and that different framings appeal to different constituencies. Ridge and Seaview Greens acknowledged awareness of numerous issues that they themselves did not pursue in their own groups.

Not only issues and ideologies, but "activism" itself must be defined through different notions of political commitment. Greens defined "good" activism as a way of life, not a concerted effort to organize around one local issue. Greens addressed their activism to the broader social and cultural relations in industrial society that produce the conditions for specific issues such as toxic hazards. In this way, a Green Party, even if a long-shot effort, made more sense to Greens than joining one of the already existing single-issue environmental organizations, because it offered the possibility of addressing root causes of single social and environmental problems in a way that established interest groups and single-issue organizations did not.

Further, even if we take certain well-publicized environmental hazards as obvious, available issues for all the organizations in this study, it is not clear that the Greens were less "affected" by them than anti-toxics activists. Some Greens lived closer to publicized environmental hazards in Ridgeville than some anti-toxics activists in this study did to hazards in their own locales.[19] At the same time, Greens did take up toxics issues associated with a military contractor an hour's drive away. Personal proximity to "issues" did not cause the Greens to adopt the commitment and organizational styles that characterized them. The trouble with using issue focus to explain Green group dynamics is that this approach begs the question of why the Greens organized their focus on issues as they did.

A different account would explain the personalized commitment style as a political exercise in itself, a sign of discontent with bureaucratic, technocratic powers that be. This account would place the Green movement in a category of "new social movements" (NSMs) that have arisen since the 1960s. The NSM category arose out of European scholars' attempts to understand collective political identities and styles of activism – especially in the youth, women's, peace, anti-nuclear, and environmental movements – which struck them as "new" in relation to the "old" labor activism before the 1960s.[20] Rather than mount battles against capitalists and managers, these "new" movements contested post-war state bureaucracies for the undemocratic way in which they administered everyday life concerns such as the environment or nuclear energy, while citizens stood by disempowered. In contrast to faith in industrial technology or bureaucratic efficiency, these movements promoted new values emphasizing quality of life and self-realization. "Participation in collective action is seen to have no value unless it provides a direct response to personal needs" (Melucci 1989: 49). NSMs have created "temporary and ad hoc organizational structures" (Melucci 1985: 800–801) as a way of sending a message to society at large about their discontent with an instrumental "politics as usual" that disregards broader questions about values. The description of an NSM does seem to fit the US Greens: the group dynamic pictured in this chapter might make sense, then, as an unintended consequence of an activism whose overriding goal is to launch personal protests that will awaken an overly technocratic society to its shortcomings.

But a category as heterogeneous as the NSM one cannot successfully explain the dynamics of Green activism. Personalized politics is not coextensive with NSMs. NSM research has assumed that post-material values, including a desire for individual autonomy (Melucci 1989), the appearance of youth, women, and ecologists as social movement actors, and new organizational practices come all of a piece. But how do these values, practices, and actors relate to one another? In the US context, relatively new forms of movement organizing, such as "affinity groups" and rotating leadership, do not accompany all environmentalism: antitoxics activists like those examined in this study have often practiced more "conventional" styles of activism, yet they too are responses to the inadequacies of state regulation and the excesses of faith in industrial technology, so they too can be designated as members of a "new social movement."

It should be said that NSM arguments have benefited social movement scholarship by focusing on collective identities. Contemporary movements have spent much time elaborating identities as "radical women" or "ecologists," for instance, in order to call attention to their dissatisfactions with taken-for-granted ways of life in contemporary industrial societies. To NSM researchers, collective identity seemed a much more problematic accomplishment for these activists than for groups carrying on the decades-long tradition of working-class struggle. Focusing on collective identity represented a new departure from earlier research that took collective identities for granted as simply given by social "reality." NSM arguments led to the insight that all movements must construct collective identities as they define their grievances and their opposition (Gamson 1992; Hunt, Benford, and Snow 1994).

With its focus on collective identity, on movements as living "signposts" of discontent, this line of inquiry has said only little about commitment – about the sense of obligation with which activists carry those signposts. The Greens' frustrations as well as their satisfactions suggest that they meant to do more than announce their discontents to society at large. Why would they have bothered spending time trying to re-energize faltering organizations if they acted mainly as "signs," like brilliant fireworks meant only to arouse an audience briefly with colorful illumination? One answer is that activists derive a lot of satisfaction from their "expressive solidarity" in small, personalized groups (Melucci 1989). But as we saw in the case of the Greens, these groups are not always personally satisfying. Attempts to aright faltering groups got defined in terms of strengthening the group potential for collective projects more than in terms of repairing unsatisfying personal relationships as an end in itself. These activists wanted to enact commitments over a long haul, and relied on a shared personalism since they lacked a shared sense of cultural authority and community that supported "old" movements. A cultural perspective on commitment increases our understanding of what activists mean by "activism" itself. Green activists wanted both to announce a new collective identity and to find ways to enter it into public, political forums.

The Greens' personalism worked as a logic of unity amidst diverse social identities and cultural allegiances. The next chapter shows how personalism similarly provided a basis for togetherness among a group of suburban activists less culturally radical than most of the Greens. These activists shared a greater sense of local community belonging than did the Greens. In contrast to what communitarian arguments would suggest, personalism did not weaken an attachment to community among them. In fact, it helped them take some big risks on behalf of a locale that did not always appreciate them.

3

Speaking out in suburbia

TAKING RISKS

The Greens put on public education campaigns and attended demonstrations without worrying about whether they were sullying their reputations as respectable citizens. Going public was not nearly so easy for members of Airdale Citizens for Environmental Sanity (ACES). ACES had dedicated itself to sparking a critical public debate about environmental safety at a local firm, Microtechnologies Ltd. ("Microtech," or ML). The firm was a frequent military contractor, and secured a number of contracts for work related to upgrading US weapons systems. Work at Microtech resulted in highly toxic wastes, some of which had seeped into local groundwater, and the firm proposed to build an incinerator for disposing of them. A group of roughly six core members of the Airdale Citizens for Environmental Sanity (ACES) started a campaign to alert Airdale about the hazards of burning the wastes in the proposed incinerator. Most of Airdale did not care to listen, let alone debate the issue.

For ACES members, going public meant braving the withering stare of public opinion in Airdale, a small town of suburban-style neighborhoods about an hour's drive north of Ridgeville. The activists liked to tell newcomers the story of how someone at a public hearing on the incinerator had remarked, "There goes that crazy lady again," as the group's leading spokesperson, Laura, walked up to the microphone. Laura's son feared Laura would get arrested for her activism, leading to embarrassing consequences for him: "I have to go to school in this town." Other members thought they had paid with their local reputations for their association with ACES. One got dismissed by a neighboring city council as a mere anti-military "faddist" when he spoke on the incinerator issue. Another discovered that a few of her friendships may not survive her involvement in ACES. Another, finding herself on a dark street after an evening of door-to-door petitioning, flashed through her head spooky images of industry "whistle-blowers" who get stalked by company henchmen.

The chilly civic climate of suburban Airdale made activism feel risky if not scary for ACES members. As the largest single employer of Airdale residents, the Microtech plant helped keep criticism of its policies on ice. Yet with a core of seven members and a mailing list of other volunteers and supporters, ACES broke through the chill and became the regularly quoted local voice of dissent regarding Microtech policies. Environmentalists and local media too regarded them as a significant force behind the contractor's eventual decision to shelve plans for its proposed incinerator. The group moved on to confront other environmental hazards related to Microtech, and had existed for seven years by the end of my field research with them. How did these activists sustain their group and their commitment to the cause in a risky civic climate? Part of the answer involves understanding how personalism can sustain political commitment.

The culture of commitment in ACES was a hybrid of personalism and more communitarian practices and idioms, making ACES an important comparison case in this study. Personalism, especially through the leader's strong influence, shaped the ways ACES organized itself and reached out to Airdale. At the same time ACES members rooted themselves in their local community milieu and defined their activism as in the "community interest," even when other Airdalers showed little interest in their project. Greens carried their commitments as individual political agents applying general Green principles to their locales and to national politics. ACES members situated themselves more in a specific community to begin with. Greens addressed cultural radicals in their locales, while ACES members addressed Airdale residents in general. Most members of ACES did not practice their commitments as highly individualized responsibilities. They acted much more *as group members* than as individual political actors who apply the precepts of a loose, national movement to their locale.

ACES members "belonged" to their local community in a way that Greens did not, but like Greens, they had different cultural reference points. They did not discuss these much; in Airdale, "polite" people kept their religious faith and controversial political opinions to themselves. Personalism in ACES allowed members who shared few cultural reference points to risk activism together. While the case of the Greens showed that personalism can sustain public-spirited commitments, the case of ACES shows that personalism does not necessarily weaken a sense of community responsibility, as communitarian arguments have often assumed. It may in fact strengthen action in the communal interest when community members share little else in a privatized suburban locale.

Suburbs are the modal place of residence for Americans (Baumgartner 1988: 6). The civic cultures of suburban locales may strongly influence how grassroots politicization happens for many US citizens. While there are different suburban cultures, peopled by different class and ethnic groups, this chapter takes advantage of convincing field research findings (Baumgartner 1988) that corroborate a frequently recited criticism: everyday norms in highly residential suburbs with low-density housing squelch a vibrant civic life. A shared personalism may provide suburbanites one of the only means for breaking through suburban taboos on public controversy. Before pursuing this argument, we need to understand how ACES challenged some of the everyday routines in Airdale while maintaining a sense of belonging in Airdale.

FROM AFFINITY GROUP TO COMMUNITY ORGANIZATION

The crucial characteristic that the original ACES members shared was a willingness to discuss controversial issues raised by work at the contractor. The original core of five members who first met in 1983 were the only Airdale residents to step into the public – and imported – debate about the contractor. In the early 1980s the Anti-Militarism Network (AMN), a metropolitan group with a personalized political style, held regularly scheduled protests at Microtech to protest its military-related work. These mobilizations included legal protest marches and non-violent civil disobedience. The mobilizations reinforced local opinion that criticism of the contractor came only from outsiders, from the youthful, casually dressed "protesters" immortalized in countless televised accounts of dissent in the past twenty-five years. Laura and three other ACES members recalled wondering if they were the only Airdale residents who also questioned the politics and morality of high-technology work with military applications. Having signed a mailing list at one of AMN's demonstrations, they and another local resident decided to form a local "affinity group" to affiliate with other affinity groups under the AMN umbrella. Thus began ACES as a "peace group" dedicated to pressuring Microtech to take only peaceful and socially constructive research contracts.

An early newsletter reveals ACES shared some of the broad cultural radicalism of the Greens. While its goal statement was much shorter than the page-long, small-print Ten Key Values sheet that Greens gave prospective members, it enunciated the same endorsement of broadly defined values in individual and collective life:

As a peace group, we work toward peace, nonviolence, and justice on all levels; personal, social and political . . . Are these issues – life, peace, and justice – interrelated? Reflect for a moment. We believe that they are. Thus, we are committed to working toward . . . disarmament, demilitarization, and nonintervention, equitable distribution of wealth in and among nations, and action for ecological balance.[1]

The early goal statement also included a brief paragraph which, similar to the Green movement ideology, stressed the value of individual participation:

We use a process called consensus and strive for a non-sexist, non-racist, non-hierarchical structure. We are dedicated to maintaining a democratic environment wherein each person's opinions and concerns are valued.

But ACES departed from the organizational pattern characteristic of personalized politics as described in the last chapter: ACES continued from its start in 1983 with the original core membership largely intact. The AMN, in contrast, had largely disbanded by 1986 as members carried their diffuse commitments on to other causes. Laura recounted with a fresh sense of bewilderment how she figured out the AMN had dissolved only because she found herself and another ACES member to be the sole "public" at a public hearing on water and air contamination from the contractor. Late in 1986, an AMN member in Ridgeville had called the ACES "spokesperson," or representative to AMN's coordinating committee, to see if she would attend the hearing. When she and Laura went, they found "no Greenpeace, no protesting students, no AMN people."

Laura's comment underscores the tutelage relationship between ACES and activists from a metropolitan center relatively far from Airdale. Another core member, Barb, elaborated on this relationship, recalling that in their first few years, ACES was "looking for things to do ... piggy-backing onto other conferences." Laura and Sam, another core member, concurred on this, noting that it never occurred to ACES to sponsor its own conferences. In Laura's half-facetious account, it would take ACES three full meetings to put on a community showing of a film about the horrors of war: "We would agree to show the movie. We would agree at one meeting. Then the next meeting we would work on getting out the press release. Then the next meeting we would show the movie." To accompany the film they would invite a speaker from an established group, perhaps American Friends Service Committee. They did not consider being speakers themselves.

Beginning with the 1986 hearing, a sequence of events thrust ACES out of an "affinity group" mode of operation and nudged it toward the status of a more community-directed group, giving as often as receiving tutelage. While researching toxics for the public hearing that AMN had alerted them to, ACES discovered discrepancies between reports from the contractor, available from the state, and the contractor's official Environmental Impact Report (EIR), and asked state environmental regulators about them. An official misunderstood their question, answering that a particular experimental site at the ML facility "had already been referred to the state attorney general for investigation." Two local newspapers' reporters were present to hear this unintended information leak. ACES had in effect created the first publicized alert about specific environmental dangers at ML.

From then on, ACES was no longer a "peace group" but a "peace and environmental group." Still dedicated to "peace, nonviolence, and justice" on "personal, social, and political" levels, as well as to the consensus decision-making process, ACES had found one of what would turn out to be a number of issues around which to organize Airdale residents. The resulting tension between its earlier affinity group style and its increasing community presence and clout brought ACES to an important crossroads during this study. Slowly, ACES was becoming a forum not just for the few members[2] who regularly attended its meetings, but for Airdale residents who might have had contact with the group by receiving its newsletter, or by talking to one of its petition drive volunteers outside of a supermarket, or by hearing one of its members speak at a public hearing.

ACES came to focus much of its efforts on intervening in state-sponsored public hearings and environmental policy-making. During my 1½ years of field work, ACES was monitoring the Superfund clean-up program for groundwater tainted by contractor activities, pursuing a lawsuit over the above-mentioned deficiencies in Microtech's EIR, and leading a petition drive against the proposed incinerator mentioned earlier. It also prepared displays for community events, trying to mobilize Airdale residents to attend and speak out at public hearings on the contractor's hazardous waste disposal practices.

It would be easy to conclude that ACES changed its affinity group style when it "found" some issues around which to mobilize people. But it would be misleading to assume that new issues gave ACES a self-evident constituency and a self-evident need to mobilize that constituency. Why did ACES interpret the discrepancies in environmental impact reports as an opportunity to organize Airdale? Why did ACES members want to mobilize Airdale in general around these issues, rather than targeting the neighborhoods most likely to be affected by toxic leaks from Microtech? There is no natural progression from issues to strategies to constituencies. While the old Ridge Green group was dissipating, toxic hazards in an industrial part of Ridgeville no more than two miles from the Ridge Green office had been publicized, and a local group had formed to organize around these and potential toxic threats. Yet, the Ridge Greens did not seize on these toxic threats "in their backyard" as an opportunity to revive their sputtering group. While commitment for Ridge and Seaview Greens implied action directed to cultural dissenters, and ultimately to society at large, commitment for ACES members meant action directed to Airdale.

PUBLIC-SPIRITED COMMITMENT IN AIRDALE

Like the Greens, ACES promoted public discussion of political and moral issues apart from winning particular policy victories, though it saw both goals as intertwined. ACES was not a "NIMBY" group. The "not-in-my-backyard" tag has appealed to toxics-producing industries and some governmental officials (Szasz 1994) signifying that anti-toxics groups reject social responsibilities for waste disposal and care only about their property values or local aesthetics. In contrast, ACES wanted to "deepen the very understanding of politics and public life," to use the language of the US Greens' founding conference. But instead of creating an alternative forum situated mostly within a small but nationwide social movement network as the Greens were doing, ACES wanted to speak mainly to Airdale as an end in itself. It wanted to make the debate inviting to local residents. It patiently waited for its "town meetings" and other events to spark a critical awareness in local residents. More than one member referred to ACES as the "community conscience."

ACES as an organization aimed at much more than preserving property values or stopping one incinerator. Some ACES participants became active mainly out of their opposition to the incinerator, and receded from the local debate once ACES had won the incinerator issue. But the core members dedicated themselves to convincing Microtech's managers not only to reduce its highly toxic discharges but to contract only for environmentally safe, peacetime-oriented production. While situating their efforts in Airdale, ACES members' stance took them outside of their "backyard," to federal and state hearings on changes in toxic waste disposal policy, and to peace pickets and anti-militarism rallies. As with the incinerator struggle in Airdale, the activists' main goal in other actions was to raise the issue of participation itself – to demand more of a role for public scrutiny in waste disposal policy-making. One ACES core member summed up, "we're in it for the long haul."

ACES valued public participation both as a good in itself and as a strategy, but placed less emphasis on debate over general statements of values than the Greens. When the half-dozen original members first decided to meet as a group, Barb emphasized, "we wanted to see if there was something that could be *done*." She recalled that in the early days of ACES it was difficult to attract attendance with a movie or general discussion about peace issues. Sam recalled that at some meetings only two people showed up. In contrast, some of the Ridge and Seaview Greens' most well-attended events were talks given by notable ideologists from the culturally radical wing of peace and environmental activism in the US: Fritjof Capra, Joanna Macy, and Starhawk. But even Laura, who enunciated the group's founding principles far more often than other members, disclaimed interest in long theoretical discussions:

Laura asked me what I thought about the first meeting of the new Anti-Toxic Coalition of California. She said she was glad they didn't have a long discussion about their principles of unity, "as long as they were close enough."

ACES wanted to get Airdale residents to talk openly about, or hear discussion about, the environmental risks of military production. Just like Greens, core ACES members agreed that talk mattered. When ACES was invited to apply for a large foundation grant with the stipulation that money be used to "put pressure on military contractors," core members all suggested funding a "town meeting" in which scientists would make presentations and take questions on the effects of environmental hazards. While a televised "day of protest" at military production sites around the nation might have produced more "pressure" at least in the short run, ACES members wanted uninvolved residents to share in producing a new "public opinion" on weapons production. ACES members had judged their last "town meeting" a success, largely because it had *happened* in a town where not long before ACES members were stigmatized as "crazies" or "faddists." The title of the grant proposal Laura wrote summed up ACES' goal: "Speak Out, Airdale!"

Participation in public hearings was a major form of activity for ACES in 1989 and 1990. In fact, hearings on waste policy and on environmental impact assessments provided a framework for ACES to structure its organizing and educating work in Airdale. ACES used the hearings both as opportunities to change concrete policy and as sites for socializing the public to the value of participation. ACES members, from the leader to the newest participants, had begun going to ACES meetings thinking that "activists" were people who marched, jumped fences, or blocked roads – people unlike them. They were not alone. A man once approached Laura in a photocopy shop and informed her that "my wife will lie down in the street with you now," meaning that she had become critical of Microtech, had crossed over the great divide, and was geared up to do what she thought all activists do. Yet during their first seven years together, no member of ACES ever engaged in direct action protest. Speaking at state-sponsored hearings and other public events represented enough of a challenge for most ACES members.

GOING PUBLIC IN AIRDALE

While personalism did help keep ACES members talking to one another and to a wider public, most of the members did not personalize their politics to the great extent that Greens did. The ACES did not have a "storytelling" session during my field work with them, the way the Greens did. Personal storytelling makes sense for activists who see themselves as bearing their own, highly personalized commitments. Some members of ACES did have activist histories, and each at some point related a story or two about past experiences that were relevant to their work in ACES. Laura and a couple of others would have appreciated more time spent on relating their individual stories of commitment. The fact they did not have group sessions for telling these individual stories shows how their group culture differed from the Greens'.

Chart 3.1 introduces the core participants in ACES (the first seven names) and six other members who attended two or more of the monthly general meetings during the time of my study. Of varying age, all but one were white. All but two lived in Airdale. Three did part-time work in Airdale, seven commuted to jobs in other cities, and three were retired, two from Microtech. I have abstracted from everyday conversations the typical ways that participants in ACES talked about themselves in relation to the group, to activism more generally, and to communal institutions, political philosophies or identities that might have grounded their commitment to activism. Especially pertinent material is italicized.

Chart 3.1 Creating activist identities in ACES

Laura, original member and informal leader, was a single mother in her late 30s. She spoke several times of how it was *"exciting to be in a movement in which people's own commitments guided them without any need for leaders."* She had said she wanted ACES to be more *open to members' talking about their feelings* about environmental risks in Airdale. She herself said such an organization was good for *"sharing with like-minded individuals ... the community of it."*

John, an original member, was a retiree, civic volunteer, long-time union organizer and one-time mayoral candidate in his late 70s. John brought his philosophy about *"capitalism"* and *"greed"* to nearly every ACES meeting and public hearing that he attended. On more than one occasion, he insisted that group members talk about what they thought about capitalism and the way the weapons contractor was propelled by an unceasing quest for profit. John also presented himself as working to *convince local churches to come out with a position*, preferably an anti-capitalist one, on Microtech.

Barb, an original member in her mid-30s, was a former worker in a home for the elderly, and an accountant with a medical insurance company. She rarely referred to her own participation in the group or her reasons for it. Barb administered the group's finances and paperwork. She presented herself as a soft-spoken, facts-oriented person doing her bit for the good of the group and for other people in general. In ACES, she was known as having the technical knowledge to critique plans drawn up by the weapons contractor for treating toxic discharges.

Sam, an original member, was a Chinese-American father in his 40s who managed a customized metalwork business. Like Barb, Sam did a lot of work "behind the scenes"; his craftsmanship skills were evident in ACES' displays at fairs and public events. During my field work with the ACES, Sam did not talk much about his own participation in the group. He said he *thought Laura put things into words much better than he.*

Carrie, a part-time worker in her 40s, was an original member. She thought *Airdale was a "good place to raise kids,"* but *"liked taking them to Ridgeville" to "expose them."* She made a point of telling us at an ACES meeting that one of her sons had accompanied her to a grassroots anti-toxics activists conference in Washington, D.C. She was glad he had seen a homeless shelter while he was there. Another son ran for city council at age 18. ACES members also knew her *as*

a member of her church's "church and society" committee, and she
brought committee newsletters to ACES meetings.

Clement, a retired chemist, was a helpful "friend" but not a "member"
of ACES and *usually referred to the group as "them," not as "we."*
He shared his extensive technical knowledge with the group, giving
concise and down-to-earth descriptions of the nature of complicated
chemical reactions, for instance. Maintaining a bearing as a
reasoned, detached judge of the risks from environmental contamination, he encouraged ACES members to listen to contractor
spokespersons' arguments when he thought they were sound. While
not hesitating to identify what he thought were risky procedures at
ML, he presented himself as speaking from a scientific, not political,
standpoint. *"Get the documentation whenever you can,"* he advocated, instead of relying on someone else's interpretation of technical
information about the contractor.

Liz was a self-employed bookkeeper in her late 40s. *"I'm not ready to get
arrested yet"* she told the group several times in good humor. She
got involved in ACES as a concerned citizen who has the right to do
things like petitioning or marching in an orderly picket. Speaking of
a pro-peace picket she had gone to recently, she *described her fellow
picketers as "really a nice bunch of people"* and said it was good to
get together with *"like-minded citizens."*

Jack, Liz's husband, was much less involved with ACES than his wife.
He attended a few meetings, including the two held at his house.
"I'm here to make sure my wife doesn't get arrested" he quipped on
several occasions.

Margo, a part-time secretary in her late 40s, *considered herself "radical"
for supporting Greenpeace and favoring the right to an abortion.* She
was new to activism.

Rochelle, teacher and wife of a contractor employee, went to a couple of
meetings and offered herself as someone whose writing skills could
assist people writing letters to newspaper editors. She would introduce herself to ACES members as *"an ML scientist's wife who got
involved."* She was *apprehensive of the contractor's tendency to see
people like ACES members as "the nut fringe."*

Mrs. Starkey, recently retired contractor employee in her early 60s, went
to several meetings. She said she was *"still getting educated"* when
asked if she was willing to volunteer for any tasks, and during an
interview spoke of her involvement in ACES as a chance to be
educated as a member of the public.

Stacy, a student and entrepreneur in her 30s, went to several meetings and organized an Earth Day 1990 fair for Airdale. Stacy said she thought the number and complexity of issues related to the contractor was sometimes overwhelming, and that sometimes she needed to *"meditate to release the energy"* generated inside her by all the technical information. She described for the group her experience at a weapons test site demonstration as an *"empowering"* one that affected her personally and spiritually.

Sandy, an activist-lawyer in her late 30s, attended most of the meetings in an advisory capacity. She was a *longtime activist* who had been involved in early 1980s protests at military-related sites. She worked in a legal aid center that assisted ACES in challenging the contractor's waste disposal policy. More than any of the regular meeting attendees, Sandy brought news of protests in other locales, and occasionally, other countries. Sandy contrasted the ability of people in some other countries to draw strength from their culture with her sentiments about her own culture: *"I and most of the people I know are culturally alienated – from capitalism, greed."*

The majority of ACES members went public in ways different from those of Greens. A few like Stacy, Sandy, and Laura presented themselves as cultural radicals. Stacy in fact used some of the spiritualist and metaphysical imagery favored in highly individualistic "new age" circles. But the other ACES members did not carry a strong sense of being culturally "different." Unlike the Greens, there were no self-proclaimed radical feminists, pantheists, or people who spoke of their ethnic background or religion as making them feel "different." In contrast to some of the Greens' stories of radicalization, only Laura ever mentioned a book that had had an influence on her political thinking.[3] One member, John, spoke often about "capitalism" and "greed" as part of the popular socialism he espoused – without naming it as such. But he was not advocating that anyone in ACES leave the cultural mainstream for cultural radicalism or innovation; John did not present himself like Larry of the Ridge Greens, who was intrigued by "African socialism" in his youth and had embarked on a moral search that lead him to Eastern spirituality. John was a retired trade-unionist, and a practicing Catholic who referred to papal encyclicals on occasion as support for his stands on capitalism and militarism.

The way ACES members presented themselves to fellow members, activism was not a fruition of personal biography as Greens had constructed it. Apart from Stacy and Laura, the core ACES members had rules of thumb about the value of getting publicly involved, but did

not talk about themselves as "radicalized" individuals whose politicization was deeply enmeshed in their identities. They did not discuss their
activism as a product of personal inculcation. In contrast, recall Ridge
Greens who found sources of their activism from inspiration by a radical
college instructor, or a consciousness-raising book, a "subversive" church
youth group, or a deep spiritual awakening. Someone could join ACES
without a heavily personalized sense of political identity. ACES was even
open to Jack, a man who "followed his wife." Of course, Greens could
bring spouses and friends to meetings too. Other Green activists would
welcome them, and expect them to produce an individual stance and
contribute as "empowered" individuals to the meeting. Few would go for
long at Green meetings playing a subordinate role like Jack's.

Most ACES members shared an ambivalence about being politically
outspoken and this came through in the way they talked about their
activism too. Apart from Laura and longtime union organizer John,
ACES regulars[4] either maintained a "behind the scenes" stance in the
group, like Sam, Clement, or Barb – who once compared public speaking
with unpleasant medical procedures – or else presented themselves as
stepping tentatively, warily into public life. Liz was "not ready to get
arrested yet" – and her husband was not about to let her. Carrie
"exposed" her kids to sites of public controversy. Margo was brave to
voice "radical" positions that would have been *de rigueur* and unremarkable to Greens. Rochelle wanted it known that respectable people
could dissent in public without being like loud protesters on the "fringe"
of civility. Few if any in ACES wanted to subvert the privatized local
lifestyle completely.

ACES members in fact identified with their locale, even though they
wanted to reform its civic culture. ACES members constructed Airdale
as a community with a common interest in enviromental health. Sam and
Laura had both declared at public hearings that ACES believed a
"community" had the right to take part in any decisions about the local
environment that could affect it. ACES members did not often speak of
Airdale as a source of positive cultural or political attachments. But this
does not mean that the activists dissociated themselves from their residence there. Rather, it was an implicit part of their social identities, one
that did not often need elaboration except in relation to outside activists
who came to Airdale. Everyone could share the joke, for instance, when
Laura reported the comments of one activist from a metropolitan center
who had come to Airdale for a state-sponsored hearing:

Laura: "He had never been to Airdale before. And it was a cultural experience
for him to hear an articulate member of the community. He told me he was

especially impressed with your statement" (pointing to Rochelle).
Jack (lightly sarcastic): "We didn't bring any cows."

Laura also explained how even though ACES shared with its more flamboyant Greenpeace allies a "broader view" of the causes of environmental destruction, "we are taking it down to the community." "Down" did not imply a condescending attitude. Sam and Liz, for instance, sounded like concerned, involved residents more than distant moralizers or political sophisticates when they said they hoped more local residents would attend hearings and events. Liz spoke of her door-to-door petitioning as an opportunity to educate "members of the community" so they would be aware of the risks, regardless of whether they signed her petition or not. Laura, who had by far the most experience representing ACES in metropolitan and regional coalitions, went so far as to reject the label "activist" itself. "Ten years ago I used to respect activists but think 'they're not like regular people'." Contrasting herself and her locally active friends from activists in the metropolitan center, she observed: "We don't go to Sunshine to buy our groceries here, we go to the grocery store."[5] And when they went to public hearings, they would "deliberately disperse themselves around the room ... we want to put across that we are members of the community."

It was a challenge for ACES to situate itself as both "in" and "of" the "community," since many aspects of that community militated against discussing environmental or moral controversies in public. On the one hand, ACES members did not build their entire lives around culturally alternative, politicized identities the way some of its metropolitan allies did. They lived everyday lives within Airdale's placid, culturally mainstream milieu. They did not "go to Sunshine," they did play on local intramural sports teams, and one member had kids in the local 4-H club. They were "of the community" in cultural terms. On the other hand, they also wanted to challenge the privatized atmosphere in Airdale enough to create an ongoing public debate about Microtech. Local civic culture gave them few shared traditions or institutions for doing so.

ACTIVISM AND PRIVATISM IN SUBURBIA

Speaking out in a "company town"

It is safe to say most Airdale citizens lived in a different cultural atmosphere than Ridgevillers.[6] The Ridge Greens had never assumed that general opinion in Ridgeville would be hostile to their efforts. The mayor of Ridgeville was even a speaker in one of the numerous lecture series the

Greens put on. The mayor's local political organization invited the Greens to nominate a member to its steering committee. ACES members on the other hand mused continually about the difficulties of getting an "alternative" view of the military contractor across in Airdale.

This is not to deny that the local social environment shaped activism in Ridgeville and Seaview. The point is that ACES members considered their locality highly problematic. Greens did not – even when they pursued a relatively contentious local issue like a state-sponsored freeway expansion project.[7] Locality mattered in two, interrelated ways for the culture of ACES. First, members spoke of Airdale as a "company town." They developed a repertoire of anecdotes to demonstrate how the contractor tried to control public opinion in Airdale, and how the contractor's looming presence itself put a damper on criticism. Second, members of ACES thought that Airdale residents discouraged critical public discussion of either the contractor or other potentially contentious public issues. Negotiating the privatized local milieu was a central task for would-be activists.

ACES members' complaints about Airdale's "company town" atmosphere might suggest an overwhelming economic dependence on Microtech. Some of our images of "company towns" come from powerful literary accounts of nineteenth-century villages peopled with the likes of Emile Zola's ragged coal miners in *Germinal*, workers and their families who lived out miserable lives in the shadow of the same industrial firm. More recently, Gaventa's (1980) widely read treatment of politics in a company town made a strong case that the company chilled opposition among its mostly poor surrounding residents in subtle and not-so-subtle ways. Airdale needs to be understood in different terms. Its median income ranked sixth out of sixteen cities in its county (US Bureau of the Census 1983). And while Microtech was Airdale's largest employer, employing roughly one in five adult workers residing there,[8] Airdale has increasingly been settled by commuters in search of cheaper housing.[9] In the most extreme imaginable scenario, were the contractor simply to depart from Airdale altogether – a fate that ACES did not advocate – the effect on Airdale would be profound. Yet a substantial number of residents would have other reasons for residing and working in the area. We cannot fully ascribe widespread detachment from public debate about the contractor to local residents' economic self-interest.[10] Still, images of Airdale as a kind of "company town" were an important part of the ACES members' background knowledge.

The ACES image of the contractor's local influence matters because it affected the ways members understood the meaning of activism in

Airdale. Members discovered in the course of their activism that they had been carrying assumptions about Microtech's influence, and their activism sometimes reinforced those assumptions. For instance, Sam said in an interview that when he first saw his name amongst the plaintiffs in a lawsuit over a contractor environmental impact report, he thought to himself, "what if they (the contractor) try to take my house away?" Liz discovered during petitioning that "in this town, in terms of organizations, everything seems so tied up with Microtech." Group lore included numerous examples of Microtech management trying to bolster its power and legitimacy in Airdale by controlling public opinion.

An important way that Microtech sought continuing public trust was by holding close the mantle of technological expertise in public hearings and meetings. Studies of toxic contamination in communities find similar uses of technological expertise to maintain control in public forums (for instance, Edelstein 1988: 126; Kaminstein 1988). One extended example from a state-sponsored public meeting on groundwater contamination will suffice. ACES members joked that attendance at a series of such meetings had declined because the meetings were boring and offered little room for serious discussion. Determined to change the climate for participation, Barb gave her own presentation on alternative clean-up technologies:

Barb introduced herself and her credentials – a science baccalaureate and some other technical training. She had prepared a packet describing the alternative technologies, and maintained a non-dismissive tone towards each: "Each treatment has its pros and cons and we should know the pros and cons." Her comments emphasized the citizen role in the choice of treatment technologies. At the end of the presentation she instructed, "We have a responsibility to provide input ... to request information when we don't know it. We're all [human] – it doesn't take superhuman ability to go to the library and call people up."

During Barb's presentation, the only comments from the audience were made by a man from ML's own Safety Department (SD). He spoke up three times to correct her. Laura tried to deflate his expertise a bit by translating his short excursus on the "carbon absorption" filter treatment into simpler English: "Yeah, the grungier it gets, the less efficient it is." Barb mentioned the "biological degradation" method of groundwater clean-up had the drawback of a possible odor problem, to which the SD man added a snappy "as in a sewage treatment plant." He then brought up another type of biological degradation process than that which Barb had discussed. SD personnel wanted to put an authoritative cap on a non-expert's presentation.

During her talk Barb showed the intimidation that Laura has said many feel (including she herself) when speaking on technical issues in front of contractor personnel. Barb apologized several times that she was "not a scientist." "If you have any questions, I'll try to answer them – I'm not a scientist, well, a little bit of science background ... " Though having emphasized to the audience that they could learn some of these details for themselves, she conceded that "the public library doesn't have the good science magazines. (In a tone of resignation) Maybe the best is to go to the EPA." The EPA man in the audience grinned broadly. If the authoritative texts are at the EPA, a community resident might conclude that one should simply trust the experts on technical matters. Why bother getting involved?

Following Barb's presentation, Clement volunteered to present "a more efficient biodegradation process," involving electric currents.

ML scientist (perplexed): "I've done work in geophysics for years ... and putting electric current in the ground does not make water flow."
Clement: "Yes it does ... it's been known for 150 years."
From the audience: "Do you have a reference?"
Clement: "Sure, any high school physical chemistry text, or college text."

Contractor personnel tried to control the terms of technological debate and keep ACES speakers on the defensive.

ACES members also believed that the contractor had the power to constrain critical discussion in other ways. An employee's wife who had gone to several ACES meetings spoke against the incinerator proposed by Microtech. She was wary of the contractor's power to retaliate: "If it gets down to threats on First Amendment rights, we may have to leave," which she said would be too bad because "we like this place." At another hearing, ACES members suggested that the press keep track of a Microtech employee who had spoken out against the incinerator. ACES also mused on how the contractor sometimes "forgot" to send notices of upcoming state or federal hearings to interested parties. In all, ACES saw itself as running up against systematic barriers to disseminating critical views on contractor policies.

Although the "company town" image mattered for the group's self-understanding, no amount of direct or indirect manipulation by Microtech would determine exactly how local residents accommodated the presence of ACES. Even residents fearing for their spouses', friends', or their own jobs at Microtech would have various ways of reacting to the petitioners and the talk about toxics in their town. To understand residents' chilly reactions to ACES, which left such an imprint on ACES' collective identity, we need to know more about the pre-existing culture of civic life in Airdale. Baumgartner's (1988) field study of a suburb describes the kind of culture which shaped Airdale residents' reactions to ACES.[11]

"Suburban" culture in Airdale

Baumgartner characterized suburban culture in terms of a "moral minimalism" that keeps suburbanites out of each other's way and focused on their private affairs. The "weak" suburban moral order relies on few overt sanctions, and yet produces the much-criticized "controlled" feeling of suburban life that Baumgartner found in her own field site. ACES members saw themselves as having to deal with a lot of privatism and conflict avoidance in the course of publicizing environmental issues in Airdale. The relative lack of public, political engagement in Airdale, as much as the contractor's influence, shaped the way residents became activists in ACES. ACES members and supporters criticized the privatism in Airdale, but lived within it all the same.

It is important to establish first that ACES members did speak of Airdale as a kind of "suburb" rather than either an independent urban area or a self-sufficient community. On the first day that I volunteered for petitioning, I drove with Liz from one shopping mall to another to find shoppers that had not already been "saturated" by earlier petitioning efforts. Liz joked that I was getting a "tour of suburbia." "We don't have any fancy houses so we'll show you our shopping centers." John remarked that ACES had to "go to the people" in Airdale, which he and Liz both explained meant going to suburban-style shopping centers with large outdoor parking lots.[12] Laura joked about a benefit concert for activist groups in metropolitan Ridgeville as "a chance to get out of Airdale for a night."

Both the politically radical and the more conservative members of ACES feared the consequences of being seen as bearers of public controversy. Every member I met imagined Airdalers would tag them with a wide variety of derogatory labels. Fending off expected derision was a regular part of being involved in ACES. One member, Rochelle, suggested that ACES not endorse a county nuclear-free zone initiative because she did not want them to look like "anti-nuke, peace kind of people." On another occasion she took pains to distance herself from Microtech's description of its opposition as a "nut fringe" based outside of Airdale. Jennie, another member who had become active in the incinerator campaign, told me "we are perceived as being these radical anarchists, but we are all concerned about our families." She insisted at a public hearing: "We're not flaky; we're people raising families and trying to live responsible lives." Liz argued the benefits of carefully crafted flyers for ACES: "We should hand out flyers that would really tell about what ACES is ... more people would join our group if they don't think it's some radical-leftist organization." And Laura once said that flyer distributing was a good exercise because then Airdalers would see real people and not think ACES members were "monsters with two heads."

The activists did not seem worried that Airdalers attributed to them specific "anti-nuke" or "anarchist" or "radical-leftist" ideologies. Rather, these tags functioned to stigmatize people who, like monsters with two heads, disrupt routine public order with irrational controversy. In a "company town" situation like Gaventa's Appalachian valley, the stigmatizing tag "communist" might actually reflect, in however distorted a fashion, a threat to a company's specific economic interests. In Airdale, the tags "radical" or "leftist" or "communist" signified threats not just to economic or political interests but to a local civic milieu that prizes polite, circumspect comportment. "Making a scene" would challenge local morality almost as much as questioning the employer that helped to underwrite economic security in Airdale. This is the best way to understand Jennie's ambiguous couplet "radical anarchists"/"concerned about our families." Jennie wanted to put across that it was possible to oppose the contractor without opposing "family values," the private bedrock of collective life in Airdale. Liz and Jack's frequent jokes and comments about "radical leftists" make sense in this light too.

"Radical" did not simply denote an ideology on the left–right political scale. Liz and Jack joked that Laura was "a member of those radical-leftist groups" and raised the theme of "radicalism" several times during an interview. It was by no means clear what "radical" meant, and I asked twice for them to explain it. After my second query, they implied a "radical" was someone who simply "hates" the contractor and thinks "all weapons" and all things military for that matter are "bad." By this definition, someone who favored total conversion of ML's projects to non-weapons related work could be a "radical." Yet, Liz and Jack did not flatly oppose this kind of conversion, and ended their above explication of "radical" by observing that it would neither "be the ruin of Airdale" nor "end" the community even if the contractor departed altogether. And Laura had made it quite clear at meetings that she favored ending weapons development at Microtech and elsewhere in the region. Liz and Jack had been impressed with Laura and Barb's presentations at a meeting Jack attended because "they weren't just radical about it and weren't jumping up and down on the table. They were very calm and deliberate ..." Once again, "radical" signified someone who broke civility norms, not just someone espousing a particular point of view.

Though all members demonstrated some cognizance of suburban civility norms, members devoted varying amounts of allegiance to them.

As is clear above, Liz accepted them to a large extent. She called the scientist costume she wore in the annual town parade a "mask" that would conceal her identity in public. She told me she had been "incensed" by what she learned about Microtech's handling of volatile materials and wastes, and had begun to wonder if a son's health problems may have been related to airborne releases from the site. Yet while petitioning she told me she "doesn't want to be confrontational; the contractor hasn't been confrontational." It would be inaccurate and unfair to call her politics inconsistent. As a "peace advocate," she preferred that her own son go to jail over either going to war, or else fleeing "to Canada." But she herself did not "feel comfortable" crossing the bounds of civility because that would be "inflammatory." She told the group on several occasions, "I'm not ready to get arrested."

Local civility norms had less bearing on Laura's activism. She appreciated the local teenagers' satire on ordinances against skateboarding and "cruising" in placid, family-oriented Airdale: "there's nothing else to do but sex and drugs." But even Laura, a college student in her 40s with management experience, spoke of her own uneasiness in public arenas, and I sensed it did not simply derive from shyness about public speaking. Comparing herself to an outspoken and sometimes outrageous Greenpeace activist, she declared "my mother taught *me* to be polite!" John felt least constrained by the suburban anti-conflict milieu. He both amused and disquieted other members with his boldness in telling state health officials that Microtech was a "greedy capitalist" institution.

No doubt the apprehensions in ACES did reflect real contacts between ACES and Airdale residents. But in a different "company town," resident activists might have found the strength to buck common opinion through a communal institution like a church, or a shared local culture that could inspire dissent.[13] But in suburban Airdale, what residents shared most was privatism and an avoidance of public controversy. Of course suburbanites in Baumgartner's study or in Airdale might attend various churches or volunteer in service groups. But there are relatively few *publicly shared* cultural affiliations in a private-oriented suburban locale. Whether or not ACES activists personally upheld suburban civility norms, they lived in a situation with few widely shared bodies of folk wisdom or cultural authority that they could bring to ACES. Members found diverse sources for their activist identity. And as Laura summed up about the whole group:

ACES is made up of what we have in common ... Carrie is the society and religion coordinator at her church but doesn't come on with Christianity [at meetings], and I have certain spiritual commitments to peace, justice and the environment, but I don't come on strong with them at meetings. Sam has other things going on – everyone has other things going on too.

Without common, institutionalized cultural authorities to draw upon, ACES needed another basis of togetherness for individuals who all had "other things going on." So ACES drew on personalized notions of commitment that encouraged community members to speak out as empowered individuals.

PERSONALISM AND LEADERSHIP AMONG SUBURBAN ACTIVISTS

Personal expression as an option, not a mandate

The ACES group culture combined an openness to personalized expression with a shared rootedness in Airdale. As the leading influence on the group, Laura structured ACES as a Green-style democracy of equal selves. For their part, other members considered ACES a group in which they could try out risky opinions in a safe atmosphere. But they did not assume the way Greens did that each individual carries an elaborately developed, individual political will. They "did their bit" for ACES and for Airdale with the good of the local community as their arbiter of worthwhile activism. Commitments made *as Airdale residents* did not require the special activist identity and lifestyle that Greens created in the absence of a shared sense of communal belonging. Personalism in ACES did not result in expectations about individual political virtuosity. Instead it created acceptance for different levels of individual engagement, including Laura's highly personalized – and time-consuming – engagement. ACES members were willing to let each other define different limits for involvement, and they were happy to let Laura lead them.

A shared respect for personal opinions enabled members to sustain disagreements. More than once, Laura interceded in a disagreement with an appeal to the equal validity of any sincerely held viewpoints. At one meeting, for instance, Margo and John sparred over how confrontational a stance the group should take towards the contractor:

John insisted that ACES was not growing because members were so used to technical talk that "we don't talk about people." He concluded that it would be best if ACES was blunt and said that people working at the contractor were, in effect, "killers." Margo objected.
Margo: "Well I do think ... that you can polarize people, and the words you use are very important."

John: "You hate the place!"

Margo: "Well, I can say that here – I would never say that in public … I think there are many ways to approach this and they all need to be looked at."

Laura (broadening on Margo's statement): "All the voices need to be heard, everything needs to be said … It's a tapestry – you're not wrong and your way isn't the only right way. There is no one right way."

Margo conceded that John "always brings up the moral issue" and "the moral issue is the basic issue."

No one offered a different moral argument than John's on how to frame the environmental hazards of work at Microtech. Laura's resolution was, in effect, definitive. Her resolution appealed to the intrinsic worth of all contributions and all contributors, rejecting a standard for judging between them.

A "tapestry" of self-expression was a suitable metaphor for external as well as internal relations. When the ACES agreed to help a metropolitan peace group plan a Peace Day rally for the Airdale area, Laura told ACES how different groups attending might engage in different activities. There were, for example, the "anarcho-punks" who might want to do civil disobedience and get arrested. "I want to validate that that's OK … (because) that's what they do." Laura wanted to "validate" different people's conceptions of political action as intrinsically worthy – coming from within the person. There could be different activities, so that people whose idea of participation in the rally was "sitting" (she gestured a stiff pose with hands folded) could go to the event and so could people who intended to risk arrest for direct action.

Laura wanted to do more than create liberal tolerance for individual preferences in ACES. She assumed that group participation ought to include a lot of personalized expression. It surprised her, for instance, that I had characterized ACES after one of the general meetings as a "friendly" group:

Laura: "I think we're not friendly enough. We should have more time for process."

PL: "What should people talk about?"

Laura: "We should talk about *ourselves* … how we feel about things." She gave an example of a man new to ACES who had previously worked in the weapons industry, saying that he must have feelings about the work but that there's so much business to get through, there is not enough time to talk about his feelings. "We mean to support him – we really are a supportive group – but there isn't enough time."

Like that of the Greens, Laura's everyday definition of participation included both political and personal expression without a strong division between the two. I commented once that I was struck at how a short, spontaneous exchange about American democracy and the cold war had erupted amid one of the general meetings. The meeting had included a lot of technical information about work at the contractor. Laura said "that kind of thing" needed to happen more often, because "that's what ACES exists for – to empower people." She continued, wondering whether meetings sometimes suffered from "fact overload" and suggested that meetings might strike a different balance between "facts" (technical presentations) and "emotional support." Talk about American democracy and emotional support were interchangeable in this definition of participation and "empowerment."

Personalist language certainly was not foreign to other members. Stacy, a newer member, conceived her own participation in ACES-related activity in terms of an inner, intuitive self. Carrie entered peace and environmental activism from experience in a church-based social action group that encouraged a very personalized way of adopting issues: her commitment to a "peaceable world" included family relations maintained through "conflict resolution" and "affirmation techniques" at home. Even John, steeped in both Catholic and union organizing traditions, was able to trade on notions from popular psychology – the idea of being "centered" as a person, for instance. He taught his catechism students that making the sign of the cross was also a symbolic way of "centering" oneself. Showing me how he crossed himself, he named the different hand positions: "Here, left, right – you're centered. See, Jesus was a Zen Buddhist." He said the kids really got it.

But not all members defined their participation in terms of personalized expression. Liz, for instance, cast herself as a good citizen taking advantage of her right to speak out in a democracy. When I asked her whether she saw ACES meetings as an opportunity to express her personal feelings about criticizing contractor policies, she said she preferred to keep those feelings to herself. Clement cast himself as a rationalist who could speak out because he saw through what he considered the cult-like "dogma" of technological advancement at the contractor. Members all said they appreciated the opportunity they had in ACES to participate. But they did not all emphasize the openness to talking about their own feelings that Laura had made available in ACES meetings. These different orientations to expressing themselves came out at a fundraising workshop, when the trainer began by asking the group, "Why have organizations?":

Jack: "Clout."
Barb: "To get things done."
Laura: "Sharing with like-minded individuals ... the community of it."

Even if other members did not talk about activism the way Laura did, they understood her assumptions about groups and commitment well enough so that participation in ACES could start feeling comfortable to them, not awkward.

The meaning of "consensus"

Discussion and decision-making formats in ACES were, in theory, similar to those of Greens. And similar to Greens, the ACES wanted to equalize leadership and responsibility. But in practice, the ACES group culture gave these structures and goals different meanings. While the Greens fought over what they perceived as imbalances in power and participation, the ACES quite gladly ceded to Laura *de facto* responsibility for developing group projects and maintaining contacts with other activist groups. The ACES did not share the Green-style norm of intensive individual initiative and participation. So while Greens had defined consensus as the optimal format for enunciating individual political wills, ACES considered consensus a loose and practical way to decide things quickly in a small group. They used "consensus" somewhat interchangeably with "loose" – an adjective few Greens would append to their version of the process. In tones reminiscent of the Greens, the original ACES mission statement had emphasized consensus as central to a "democratic environment wherein each person's opinions and concerns are valued." But Laura had explained the form of decision-making in ACES as a matter of convenience as much as group identity. And she used the word "consensus" to describe the loose ACES organizational format in general:

The group had discovered their mailing list was not a hot list for fundraising. I wondered whether people would feel more inclined to give money if they thought the organization was "theirs."

PL: "Did you ever try having people sign a sheet and become a member?"

Laura: "No. We thought about it ... but consensus has worked so far – you know what I mean? We have not had to [distinguish between] 'you're a member, who can vote,' and 'you're not' (pointing to hypothetical members at a meeting). We haven't had a problem so we didn't want to make a problem."

Here, Laura equates "consensus" with an informal meeting style in general, even though the term usually denotes a specific decision-making procedure that can be as elaborate as Robert's rules of order. For Greens as well as the other activists in Chapter 2, consensus was itself a hotly debated procedure. In ACES, consensus meant that all participants had space to voice their opinions. But it also signified that no one expected contentiousness between individuals.

In fact, members' understanding of "consensus" shows that they were not particularly concerned with enhancing their own opportunities to participate intensively. I asked Barb during an interview if she thought that consensus was an important aspect of ACES as a group.

I think this is the first group I've been in that's used consensus officially – with no hierarchy or chairperson ... It was a different thing for me to move from meetings where they have votes and "I move that ... ", to go from that to this. I mean when the decision is whether our banner is going to be red or green you don't need the official kind of voting and I personally don't want ACES to become such an important thing in my life that these decisions that we make are so important. So I'm willing to go along with whatever – I trust Laura's judgment but I don't want to become a leader of the group ... We all feel comfortable expressing opinions on whatever issue it is we're deciding to do. She takes our input and she respects our input.

Barb associated "consensus" with lack of formality, the opportunity to express her views, and the *de facto* position of Laura as leader of a group with "no hierarchy or chairperson." Liz as well took "consensus," informality, and Laura's considerate leadership, as being all of a piece. She contrasted ACES meetings with less "loose," more formal ones. Sam, too, said that he thought consensus worked out "because Laura is the leader."

Unlike the Greens, members of ACES saw no contradiction between consensus decision-making and the longterm leadership of one person. The reason is that no one depended on the consensus procedure as a means to enhance individual members' political efficacy. While certainly committed to the group, members of ACES did not carry highly individualized political commitments requiring a forum for expression. They wanted to situate ACES within the mainstream of their suburban community while at the same time coaxing that community into more public debate. Personalist language could help everyone feel welcome in the sometimes risky public forum ACES was constructing.

Room for leadership

Laura most closely approximated the highly individualized commitments of Greens. Far from making her more private, personalism enabled her to go public by defining an "authentic" self liberated from suburban conventions. She described to me once how classes in psychology and Eastern religion had taught her that there was "no one way" to see the world. This perspective sustained her efforts to break the spell of legitimacy that company science and suburban privatism created for Microtech. Since she had situated her personalized commitments squarely in Airdale, she carried those commitments less as an individual agent, and more as someone morally interdependent with others.

Both core members and new volunteers in ACES assumed that newer participants could learn about speaking out at public hearings from more experienced core members. Newsletters would remind members of technical points they could raise about alternative types of waste containment, about the thoroughness of feasibility studies, about emergency preparedness. One member gave impromptu talks at some monthly meetings about the chemistry of burning hazardous wastes. Laura, and especially Sandy, the woman from metropolitan anti-military circles, encouraged members to challenge received terms of debate by questioning state and federal policy on hazardous waste removal. While the Greens saw themselves melding roughly equal, individualized commitments into a group in which all members were "leaders," ACES maintained informal tutelage relationships.

Members often deferred to Laura before deciding on a new project. During my field work, most proposals for ACES to co-sponsor an event, to plan a community meeting, or to develop a new strategy were either Laura's initiative or the product of conversation between Laura and another member. Other members contributed indispensable volunteer time and technical skills to ACES, and were attentive participants in decision-making. Once having decided upon a project, members took up essential places in an informal division of labor. After the anti-incinerator petition drive had been initiated, for instance, one member made herself responsible for door-to-door petitioning in neighborhoods, while another put himself in charge of calling volunteers to petition at shopping malls, and a third offered to write model letters to state representatives that other members could copy and send. Laura affirmed that she could not possibly have played her own active role without the contributions of other group members. Still, she was indisputably the leader. The tutelage relationship became especially clear at the one meeting I attended which Laura missed except for the last half-hour:

Barb raised the next agenda item, on the question of whether and how to join other activist organizations in campaigning for a proposed comprehensive nuclear weapons test ban treaty. Jill said tentatively, "It's something we want to show we're concerned about." No one said they were convinced about this. Jane offered up in a sprightly way that she would get involved and even make an educational mission to Airdale groups. She wasn't sure whether to go alone or with other members. No one else definitely volunteered to go with her. She asked, too, whether the idea was for activist groups to make statements in concert, or whether ACES should make its statement alone as a local group. Jill: "Let's wait until Laura comes and see what she intended." Later, Laura explained her "intentions" and quickly offered to write a one-page statement on why the test ban was a good idea. Members at the meeting agreed the campaign was worth their involvement.

Like Jane at this meeting, ACES members were neither passive volunteers nor unconcerned spectators. They became involved not as individual agents of social change but as concerned local residents contributing their time and gladly accepting direction from a more experienced activist.

Laura surmised that other members would take on more individual initiative by practicing with slow "baby steps" – taking on small specific tasks. At one meeting, for instance, she insisted that someone other than herself be the facilitator. Liz volunteered, but also made clear she still considered Laura the arbiter of a well-run meeting. As in Green meetings, the facilitator began by assigning amounts of time for discussion to each agenda item. Looking directly at Laura, Liz asked, "You want to determine the time for each?" Laura replied that Liz ought to read off each item so the *group* could determine how much time each deserved. Liz read each one, looking directly to Laura after each, expecting Laura to advise her on the amounts of time. Laura supplied them.

By accepting tutelage within the group, ACES meetings were a different kind of educational forum from Green meetings. While Green initiates were open to learning more about particular environmental issues, Green organization-building stressed the importance of room for individual creativity and initiative – hence the proliferation of "working groups" in the Ridge and Seaview Greens. In ACES, it was much more common for new or non-core participants to excuse themselves from getting more involved in group work because they were "still getting educated" as several new members put it. Greens more often excused themselves from further involvements on account of over-commitment to the various projects they were already juggling.

At the same time, members of ACES exhibited less willingness than Greens to involve themselves in directing the group. Nearly every core member expressed the desire at one time or other for the group to grow. But only Laura and John, a former union organizer, ever brought up the group itself as an object of discussion at meetings. John complained at one meeting that the group was not growing, that the mailing list needed to be thinned of inactive people, and that the group needed to discuss its overall direction *vis-à-vis* Airdale. His comments were bitter, and other members sat stoically, waiting for the verbal storm to pass. At another meeting Laura asked how people thought the group was working, and what they thought would get them more involved. Feedback was slow in coming. One member suggested that "not everyone is willing to sit through a meeting" and that "maybe it's best to call people and give them something to do."

In sum, the informal tutelage in ACES gave members options for participation. They could become fully enfranchised decision-makers, or they could confine their participation to "worker bee" status as Laura once called it. ACES members were in the cause together, with a leader in front. Being a good activist meant contributing to a good community group more than practicing individual political virtue. Combining personalist norms of participation with an often unspoken commitment to a locale, the core members of ACES sustained a group that lasted even as its specific issues changed. Still, John's comments struck at a truth about ACES: it could only do so much public educating with a core membership of seven.

PERSONALISM AND MOBILIZATION: "EMPOWERMENT"

In evolving from a small affinity group to community organization, ACES increasingly theorized about what made people able to publicly question formerly unquestioned work at the weapons contractor. Their different theories are congruent with the different ways they understood their own entry into activism. The theory heard most often, and given the most credence in ACES, was Laura's theory of "empowerment." Empowerment happened to separate individuals as a matter of personal development. The personal self was "empowered" if it became politically aware of or critical of issues once taken for granted. Empowerment was a personal process that did not depend on an institutionalized setting.

The empowerment theory got ACES into a bind: on the one hand, notions of personalized empowerment served important functions in a suburban milieu that gave little support for critical thinking about Microtech. On the other hand, these notions did not foster strong recruitment practices in ACES. While the ACES mailing list nearly doubled from approximately 200 to 400 names during my field work, the number of highly active core members – those who both attended general meetings regularly and performed the bulk of group maintenance tasks – increased by only two from the original five in 1983.

Interestingly, several theories of activation and quiescence were current in ACES during my field work. These theories tended to match the way ACES activists themselves broke though the suburban chill. Several regular members brought out their theories at a general meeting held shortly after the contractor had rescinded its request that the EPA approve its plans for operating an old waste incinerator. Despite the policy turnaround, some managing officials at Microtech, including members of its Safety Department, had gone to a public hearing to speak for the soundness of the incinerator plan. Later at a meeting, the activists mulled over how company scientists could have made statements about safety that ACES, federal EPA regulators, and even some Microtech employees considered wide of the mark. Members' own theories of activation and quiescence shaped their explanations of how the employees could think and speak as they did:

Rochelle declared, "They have their technology-god." She said when her husband found out what Microtech was doing with its wastes, he got very upset because "he believes in science."

Liz said that when she had been a secretary at Microtech (25 years earlier) "we didn't get told anything we weren't supposed to know," and that if she had "understood some of the things I typed I might not have taken a job there."

Laura now commented, "I have a number of friends who are therapists, and they say that it [insisting on the safety of Microtech's waste treatment] is like a form of 'denial.' It's like when an alcoholic at first denies he has a problem. So they must be in denial."

Clement spoke for a long while about how he was beginning to think it was just a different "mindset" at Microtech. Employees there weren't just "stupid," but there was a "science dogma" that was like religion for them.

Jack added, "It's like an experiment I learned about in a sociology class." He went on to describe the Zimbardo prison experiment. He concluded, "if there's a function to be performed, people will fall into it and act that way."

There is striking diversity in these theories. Liz associated the contractor officials' statements with a lack of information. If only good citizens were properly informed, they might think differently. Rochelle and Clement imagined some Microtech workers to be under the sway of an irrational technological mindset. Laura had a similar theory but elaborated it in psychotherapeutic terms. And Jack figured that an organization would produce appropriate behavior and thought in its workers – though it is not clear whether he considered the contractor literally analogous to a prison. On other occasions, Rochelle, Clement,

Laura, and Liz had all used their own theories to understand general opinion in Airdale about the contractor, and general reactions to ACES.

Even with the diversity of understandings about "the other side," Laura's had the strongest influence on the group's community relations. She believed that the overriding goal of ACES was to "empower" the Airdale area. Wondering how "empowerment" would work, I asked Laura and Jennie, a peripheral ACES member, about a man I met while distributing leaflets for ACES during Airdale's annual parade. He had told me with boozy exuberance that "I put all sorts of toxics in my body" and told me that the mercury in his tooth fillings were toxic too. How would ACES "empower" someone with this line of reasoning on toxic hazards? Laura said someone like him "isn't ready." She would give him a leaflet and just say he could read it when he gets a chance, but wouldn't push the issue. Jennie concurred, saying that it would be like trying to toilet train a six-month-old baby.

PL: "So who are the people you can empower – people who are already questioning?"

Laura: "Yes, there are two types of people you can empower. People who are already questioning and 'ready'" – and then she explained you can also let (other) people know that "there IS an alternative."

PL: "So the float[14] is good to do because it lets people know there's an alternative ..."

Laura: "It plants a seed in people's minds – "

Jennie: "Yes, it plants a seed – "

Laura: "So when they're ready sometime later they'll have in the back of their minds the idea of an alternative ..."

"Denial," "not ready," "planting a seed": the vocabulary of empowerment in ACES drew on developmental metaphors. People would naturally arrive at a critical stance on Microtech if given the chance to express their true, developed selves, free of psychological impediments. When people were "ready," they would stop taking the contractor's pronouncements uncritically. And then, Laura explained to me, they might want to join ACES so they would have "a place to go" where like-minded others would validate "alternative" ways of thinking. They might need support for expressing unpopular opinions in Airdale.

While Laura articulated her approach to recruitment in more psychological terms than some other members, no one contested the empowerment theory. In part, ACES members had enough confidence in Laura's leadership and experience that they were not likely to put forth different ideas about recruitment. In a forum in which "all voices need to be heard" as Laura said, but in which no one felt compelled to push an individual opinion, members were willing either to listen politely to other points of view or else to try translating between them. For instance, Laura once described how an upcoming "town meeting" on the environmental risks of Microtech's research and development work would include a talk on the psychological state of "denial" that enabled people to put the risks out of their minds. Clement addressed her: "I don't use your vocabulary, but what you're against isn't science anymore – for some of them it's mythology, religion, dogma."

Ideas about psychological suppression and empowerment also carried the prestige of association with current thinking in peace and environmental movement circles across the country. The audience at the above-mentioned "town meeting" heard a talk on the "cultural implications" of weapons work by Joanna Macy, a noted peace activist and lecturer who devised "empowerment" workshops in a book entitled *Despair and Personal Power in the Nuclear Age* (1983). Macy took "cultural" implications as synonomous with implications for psyches. After the talk, Sandy, the longtime activist-lawyer associated with ACES, began talking in terms of "denial." And Clement was ready to substitute the psychological language of empowerment and quiescence in place of the religious conversion metaphors he used earlier:

Clement: "When I talk to them about how ridiculous it is to do open-air tests – it's as if I've questioned their manhood ... "
PL: "But what about the people in the middle, people who live in Airdale who don't work at Microtech – do you think it's a mindset with them, or –?"
Clement: "Sure it is – I think that woman (pointing at Joanna Macy) put her finger on it."
PL: "What would get people out of this mindset?"
Clement (shrugging his shoulders): "You think I know where a social conscience comes from?"

The notion that activism hinges on the state of the inner self carries implications for recruitment. If people can only become activists according to a schedule of personal development, then there will not be much point to aggressive community organizing drives. The best recruitment strategy will be one that "plants a seed," that makes a clear statement but does not try to coax or convince. ACES continued to work on the assumption that Airdalers would join their cause on the basis of a slow awakening of consciousness. It may be true that some Airdale residents understood themselves and their potential public involvements in terms of personal development; the dominant theory of recruitment in ACES may have corresponded to everyday understandings in Airdale.[15] We cannot know this without a separate community study. ACES as a group worked on the assumption that Airdalers would become radicalized public actors the way Laura and a couple of other original ACES members had gone public – as empowered selves. With the support of outside "expert" thinking on empowerment, ACES continued to favor a personalist approach to organization-building. Members like Liz, Barb, or Sam who did not articulate their commitments in terms of empowered personhood would most likely let the dominant approach to organization-building stand, and let other members take care of recruiting.

EMPOWERMENT AS A CULTURAL DILEMMA

ACES faced a predicament in trying to mobilize Airdale residents without simply scaring them off. Their predicament resulted not from a failure of commitment on their own part, then, but from a lack of shared bases for public-spirited, critical citizenship in their suburban culture. Members of ACES, like many residents of US suburbs perhaps, could not invoke publicly shared religious or communal sources of authority for undertaking collective action. In this milieu, personalist notions of community involvement sustained ACES in a number of ways. They enabled suburban activists to take risks in a group that was loose and welcoming enough of diverse individuals to make risk-taking more comfortable. One did not need to sever ties with the prevailing culture of privatism to join ACES. Prospective members would be welcomed into ACES on the basis of whatever (privately held) commitments had motivated them.

It would have been difficult at best for ACES members to recruit more aggressively than the personal "empowerment" theory would suggest. Aggressive mobilization for any controversial issue would have run the risk of seeming irrational to people whose shared culture consisted foremost in a dedication to private life. Appeals to economic self-interest or family health would not goad many local residents out of their privatism if these appeals could not be accompanied by well-publicized accounts of some toxic disaster already having taken a toll on local residents. ACES and other activists knew of "accidents" at Microtech over the years, but the effects of these accidents on residents' health could not be easily substantiated. On what basis, then, could an ACES neighborhood canvasser convince the person at the door to become involved in ACES?

"Empowerment" gave activists a way to talk about breaking suburban civility norms. Contesting suburban civility would mean awakening politically quiescent selves to a better, or more real, practice of selfhood. It meant contesting one kind of (privatized) individualism with another kind of individualism that actually enabled suburban residents to go public, each on an individual schedule, one by one. This kind of individualism empowered but also limited activism in Airdale: for people who believed that Airdalers suffered from individual, disempowered "mindsets," a well-established organization with strong recruiting practices would not be part of the solution. For example, Laura once explained to me the ambivalence in ACES about getting an office front. On the one hand, the office would lend the group a "veneer of credibility." On the other hand, maintaining an office front would send the message that "ACES can do things" and detract from the goal of getting Airdalers to feel empowered, to "feel *they* can do things." She compared her preferred image of ACES with the Sierra Club's image, which to her said that "Sierra Club can do it." Attributing efficacy and responsibility to the organization would, in this view, only perpetuate the individual powerlessness and quiescence that ACES saw itself as challenging. So the empowerment theory directed attention toward awakening individual consciousness rather than expanding an organization.

Communitarian theorists might argue that ACES ought to have nurtured a political culture of "citizenship," avoiding notions of personal "empowerment" that limited the group's own growth and public visibility. For if everyone agreed on the goodness of good citizenship, then no one would fault ACES for aggressive recruiting and organization-building. The problem is that going public in ACES implied dissent from taken-for-granted notions of good citizenship in Airdale. "Good" local residents were "concerned about our families" as Jennie put it, and did not get involved in "flaky" or "radical" causes. The usual categories for talking about responsible citizenship in Airdale did not make much room for activists publicizing controversial issues in even the sincerest public interest. ACES could not simply neutralize skepticism about its efforts by claiming a moral high ground of citizenship. This is all the more the case when Microtech could already claim unimpeachable good citizenship by contributing to the national defense with its military contracts. ACES would, at least, need to make clear it was advocating a *different* or more "real" practice of good citizenship. This is in fact the route ACES took, legitimating itself by appealing to the "reality" of personal empowerment that breaks through constraining social conventions.

Further, the "good citizenship" of Liz, Rochelle, and Mrs. Starkey motivated them to get involved as helpful volunteers, but not as leaders in formulating strategy, confronting Microtech's management, or building ties to other activist groups. The empowerment theory limited the ACES' recruitment and its breadth of appeal, but it also gave Laura the means for making lasting, risky commitments that challenged local conceptions of (quiescent) good citizenship. Laura could sustain her leadership of ACES partly because she identified her commitments more strongly with a specific locale than did most Greens, but also because she had made her politics an ongoing part of her whole identity the way Greens did.

Communitarians held that personalism was inimical to pursuit of a common, public good. Yet, personalism allowed Laura and some other ACES members the freedom to contest privatism, in the public interest. In Airdale, personalist notions of empowerment and commitment gave at least some members of ACES the means to advocate for a new communal good – safety from military-related toxic wastes – a good that ACES claimed should concern everyone in Airdale, regardless of their employment. Rather than privatizing public issues, personalist culture gave activists a basis for working together and for trying to reach other Airdalers within local cultural constraints.

ACES was a successful activist group by a number of standards, including its own. Its petition drive had collected 10,000 signatures against the proposed hazardous waste incinerator. Both ACES and its metropolitan allies credited the petition drive with forcing the contractor to abandon its incinerator plan. A local newspaper editorialized that ACES was one of the "highlights of 1989," providing one of "the examples that energize a democratic society." Still, nearly every member of ACES puzzled over why more people did not join the group as regular participants. After the first of ACES' "town meetings" Laura conceded that nearly all of the relatively few local residents who had addressed the audience during the open microphone period were members of ACES. The other residents were afraid to speak. "We still have a lot of empowering to do," she concluded.

There are a number of reasons why more Airdalers would not participate in ACES. The two most salient for this study were the everyday political stratagems in a "company town" and the privatized culture of suburban life. Other possible reasons – economic interests, for instance – might become clearer in a comprehensive community study of Airdale. In this study of political commitment, what matters most is not "why people joined (or did not join) ACES" but *how* people joined. What cultural means did they have for making themselves activists in a civic milieu that suppressed conflict and lacked publicly shared cultural authority? Activism based on personal "empowerment" and rooted in a specific locale sustained ACES as a vital, though small, group.

It is debatable whether or not a different culture of commitment might have produced a larger group in Airdale. But it is clear that ACES would not be able to find this out as long as it understood recruitment in terms of empowerment. ACES would not be able to develop a larger core group, nor "empower" a larger number of residents to speak out, without a theory of activation and a form of group solidarity that enabled them to recruit residents more aggressively. ACES would need to appeal to some shared communal or political identity that could make sustained organizing drives seem reasonable rather than simply invasive to Airdale residents. That identity was not readily available in Airdale.

4

Imagining community, organizing community

Activists who went door-knocking[1] for Hillviewers Against Toxics (HAT) felt little of the apprehension that hung over the ACES petitioners in their grocery store parking lots and suburban neighborhoods. HAT fought some of the same kinds of hazards that bedeviled Airdale – toxic air releases from industry, the threat of catastrophic explosions. HAT's community, like ACES', was enmeshed in a web of ties to one industry. But being a part of the "community" meant something different in Hillview than in Airdale; it meant among other things that no one would slam the door shut at the sight of an activist canvassing a neighborhood. HAT's construction of its community gave it a far wider mandate to do organizing work in Hillview than ACES allowed itself in Airdale. Activism in Hillview felt less risky for HAT members than it did for ACES activists in Airdale.

During my brief training as a "door-knocker" for HAT, I accompanied my "trainer," Mrs. Davis, to a house. Her appeal to the elderly African American man living there included the word "community" at least six times. "HAT is community people who are getting the community involved," she explained. "The organization *needs* you," she affirmed, associating HAT's needs with those of the (black) community as a whole. Mrs. Davis easily launched into an impromptu pitch that an ACES member like Liz would probably never have thought of trying in her own door-knocking campaign. Mrs. Davis' seemingly unremarkable appeals to "community" took on fresh meaning after I had heard Liz carefully word her way through a rationale for why it was all right for her to be petitioning at all. And HAT's equation of its needs with those of Hillview sounded very bold in comparison with ACES, whose members downplayed their group affiliation at public hearings because, as Laura had explained, they did not want to look like pretentious cadres giving off to other Airdale residents that "we're from ACES and you need to agree with us." With the support of a communal civic culture lacking in Airdale, HAT did not need to be bashful about community leadership.

HAT illustrates a local level of the community-belongingness envisioned by communitarians. HAT defined its constituency as a community in which residents shared a sense of interdependence rooted in a common history, a common peoplehood.[2] This community made communal belongingness an ongoing condition of local life rather than a goal of individualized questing as in the Green groups. HAT was a predominantly African American, grassroots environmentalist group, a cultural descendant of civil rights struggles of the 1950s and 1960s. A group such as HAT could claim to represent the broader community it invoked – even if some members of the community disagreed with some of its claims – as long as it upheld shared communal standards and reference points: the church, the struggle for racial justice.

This chapter explores HAT's practice of community, and contrasts it with more personalized versions of community. Personalized and communitarian types of community both have strengths and limits in the way they sustain political commitment. While the communitarian theorists devalued the contribution of personalism to public commitment, this chapter shows that they have tended to overvalue the communitarian alternative.

COMMUNITARIAN-STYLE COMMITMENT IN HAT

Unlike the Greens, HAT did not self-consciously articulate a new set of values or organization-building practices. HAT's by-laws made no special mention of egalitarian decision-making routines; they sounded no appeals to a broader "consciousness" of environmental decay, or economic or gender inequalities. HAT members committed themselves to a kind of "community" obligation that differed from that practiced by ACES, or the Greens. HAT members' sense of peoplehood and their ties to authoritative community institutions – the black church in particular – have no direct parallel in the cultural sites that have given rise to the other groups in this study.

Though members referred to HAT's constituency in a taken-for-granted way as "the community," we should not fall into the trap of taking this community as self-evident or "natural." The "pre-givenness" that HAT imparted to its surrounding community was itself a construction, not an immediate reflection of primordial ties.[3] This does not mean

Hillview residents lacked a sense of common identity until HAT articulated it for them. When HAT's staffperson thundered about corporate injustices done to "the community," when door-knockers appealed to residents' sense of responsibility to "the community," they were not just making up an entity from scratch and imposing it on Hillview residents for the sake of gaining support. HAT's construction of "community" in Hillview, based on a sense of economic and racial injustice and a shared Christian faith, resonated as common sense with many in the African American neighborhoods to which HAT sent its door-knockers. But it is important to remember that HAT itself was not just a natural outgrowth of local ties and local standards. Occasional conflicts between HAT and some of its would-be constituents show that HAT had to imagine its community, as did the other activists in this study, and HAT's imagination was not always identical to that of Hillview residents.

The ways that HAT members constructed a community for HAT raise some questions both for HAT's style of commitment and for the communitarian theorizing that would uphold HAT as a model. HAT's culture of commitment both enabled and limited its ability to politicize its members. On the one hand, the community with which HAT identified itself offered publicly shared sources of strength for collective actions that most ACES members would have considered too risky or uncivil. And HAT could certainly take for granted a shared sense of local rootedness, a communal identity, that played little part in the Greens' search for common ground. On the other hand, HAT's imagery of a strong and united community gave it a relatively weak basis for accommodating divergent interests in Hillview, or divergent opinions in HAT. HAT's appeal to communal standards gave HAT a kind of togetherness that sometimes excluded some residents of the locale it embraced as its "community." Within HAT, individual members had a hard time acquiring a sense of ownership of their organization, partly because their image of community emphasized unity without providing a clear picture of how individuals might contribute to it.

HAT and the Greens stood opposite each other on a spectrum of challenges. The Greens' challenge was to maintain space for highly individualized political participation in their organizations without endangering collective stability. HAT's challenge was to keep its organization running while ceding more efficacy and explicit responsibility to individual members. The kinds of community imagined by personalist and communitarian activists certainly differed, but both led to movement-building practices that were in some ways parochial in relation to a wider context of social movements and public debate.

For many Americans, communitarian images of political commitment are common-sense enough to make the complaint that began this book a familiar one. Yet, relatively few studies have examined how a strongly communitarian form of commitment would work in grassroots movements. This case study of HAT is one of the first in-depth analyses of everyday routines in a communitarian, environmental organization.[4] And it is one of few detailed looks at everyday practice in a group that descends from the Saul Alinksy community organizing tradition; recent studies of similar groups, though not environmental ones (Delgado 1986; Lancourt 1979), have not paid close attention to questions about culture and commitment. Table 4.1 compares the "communitarian activist" with the typology developed in Chapter 2 for "personalized politics." The ACES fall between the two ideal types here, since they shared some characteristics of both types. Like the ACES, HAT was part of a national upsurge in local activism against environmental hazards. Local anti-toxics activism has drawn in part on the community organizing methods that Saul Alinsky developed in the 1940s and 1950s, continued by youth-led community activism networks in the 1960s, and extended by national community organizing networks in the 1970s and 1980s.[5]

HAT claimed a number of victories since its inception in 1986. It became a participant in local environmental policy-making, and received coverage in the daily newspaper serving Hillview. It won itself a seat on a county environmental regulatory board after mobilizing Hillviewers to complain about the way the fire department and corporate officials managed an industrial fire that was allowed to burn for a week. It influenced the terms of a new county hazardous materials treatment plan. Its pressure helped lead to the beginnings of an early warning system designed to notify Hillview residents in the event of a toxic fire, large industrial accident, or other emergency. And it won a 50 percent reduction in the amount of hazardous waste that the state health agency would allow Petrox, a large chemical company in Hillview, to burn in its incinerator. From its beginnings, HAT sought to engage Petrox in broad negotiations aimed at reducing Petrox's varied toxic emissions. After earlier talks were suspended, HAT succeeded in 1990 in bringing Petrox back for what appeared to be drawn-out negotiations with very uncertain prospects.

Though it has a largely minority constituency, HAT had whites on its board, and was officially a "multiracial" group attempting to attract representatives of other local groups as well as individual Hillview residents into a coalition. Whites usually joined as experts and organizational allies, not as "community members."[7] During my study the board

Table 4.1 *Personalized and communitarian cultures of commitment*

	Personalized politics	Communitarian activism
commitment duration	long-term, continuous, indefinite	short- or long-term
ideal model of interaction	individuated, egalitarian, collective action	collective action under one or more leaders
main goal of commitment	innovation in political culture/ expansion of political debate; secondarily policy change	attain policy change through local participation
typical forms of organization	"affinity groups," rotating leadership councils, discussion groups	committees, executive boards, general membership meetings
constructed constituency	politicized individuals	a geographical region
case example	Ridge and Seaview Greens	Hillviewers Against Toxics
provisional examples	anti-nuclear and peace activists of 1970s–early 1980s; 1970s grassroots feminists, cultural feminists; Earth First!, animal rights activists of 1980s, some anti-war activists	ACORN, "Citizen Action" groups in 1970s and 1980s; *some* anti-toxics local groups ("Grassroots Movement for Environmental Justice")[6]

representative from Environmental Advocates helped HAT negotiate waste management practices with various Hillview industries, and he aided HAT's organizing strategies with technical information about local industrial hazards. White experts have deferred to the black chair's and executive director's definitions of the community on whose behalf they are working. So the great majority of this chapter focuses on the black local residents who were leaders or members of HAT, rather than on the technical experts.

HAT's experiences have implications for the prospects of cross-class and multicultural activist politics in the US. They illustrate the possibilities and predicaments for lower-income blacks who enter an historically white, middle-class movement arena. African American communities have become increasingly active as environmentalist constituencies (Bullard 1993, 1990, 1989; Bullard and Wright 1987). Major African American leaders have entered the environmental fray; Jesse Jackson delivered an Earth Day sermon at a church in a HAT neighborhood stronghold. Multiracial, grassroots environmental alliances were just beginning during this study. This chapter suggests that different cultures of commitment have important consequences for multicultural alliance-building.

ANTI-TOXICS ACTIVISM IN HILLVIEW

Double jeopardy in a company town

Hillview is a multiracial, relatively poor, industrial city of a little less than 100,000. Its mean family income in 1980 was 31 percent below that for its county as a whole. At that time, blacks constituted 48 percent of its residents, while whites and people federally designated as "Hispanic" made up 40 percent and about 10 percent, respectively. While relatively low income levels characterized both non-white and white residents, black Hillview families earned around $3,500 less than the average. The 1980 census recognized twenty-eight "neighborhoods" in Hillview, some of which overlap closely with locally understood neighborhood boundaries. HAT concentrated a lot of its organizing, and drew some of its leading members, from two largely black (average 88 percent) Hillview neighborhoods abutting the large Petrox chemical plant. In those neighborhoods, roughly 25 percent of families lived below the federal poverty line, and the median value of owner-occupied houses was roughly one-third that of the county. In those two neighborhoods, 35 percent of adults (over 25) had eight or fewer years of formal schooling, and 41 percent had graduated from high school – about half the proportion for the county as a whole.[8]

In a pattern similar to that of industrialized locales around the nation (Bullard 1990, 1989; Commission on Racial Justice 1987), all of the Hillview neighborhoods bordering major industrial generators of toxic waste had low income levels (20 percent or more families under poverty line). And all but one had a high proportion of black residents (70 percent or more) as compared with all Hillview neighborhoods. The one neighborhood with relatively fewer blacks had one of the highest concentrations of Hispanic residents out of all Hillview neighborhoods. All of the largely minority neighborhoods in Hillview bordered one of three major industrial zones. HAT has counted the predominantly black, often low-income residents of those neighborhoods as its primary constituency.

These residents live in double jeopardy, being both socioeconomically disadvantaged and more likely than other Hillviewers to suffer the consequences of exposure to toxic hazards. For this reason, HAT leaders have

taken up the struggle against "environmental racism," a term popularized during the time I was doing field work in HAT (Bullard 1990;
Russell 1989; Commission on Racial Justice 1987). HAT leaders, like
minority anti-toxics activists in other locales, have seen race as an important factor in industry decisions to site waste incinerators, storage facilities, and production plants that generate large amounts of toxins. During
this study, Cornerton, one of HAT's two neighborhood strongholds,
hosted several chemical manufacturing facilities, hazardous waste trans-
porters, and a landfill. HAT was pressuring county agencies not to locate
an additional, proposed hazardous waste treatment and transfer facility
in the neighborhood.

Cornerton sits next to a miles-long sprawl of chemical plants owned
by Petrox, which produces more hazardous waste than any other of the
numerous manufacturers in Hillview. Petrox cast a large shadow on local
politics as well as the local environment. In fiscal year 1987–88, the city
received roughly 28 percent of its total revenues from taxes and services
fees paid by Petrox. Petrox also made contributions to civic organizations in Hillview, including $400,000 to rebuild the Hillview Boys Club,
$7,000 for the Cornerton community center, and funds for a school
program that gears job skills to the needs of business. Even $7,000 is a
large sum for a low-income locale, and HAT considered some civic
leaders in Hillview and some city council members to have been "bought
off" over the years by Petrox. HAT leaders complained about the reluc-
tance of some local pastors and neighborhood leaders to join its anti-
toxics struggle. It assumed donations like those from Petrox were part of
the problem (figures from local news article, author's file).

Petrox's influence in Hillview has led some HAT members to talk
about Hillview the way ACES members described Airdale – as a
"company town." Since there are no figures available on the proportion
of Hillview residents employed by Petrox's Hillview plant, it is difficult
to assess the degree of Hillview residents' immediate dependence on
Petrox. With their low income levels and chronically high unemployment
rates, it was unlikely that black Hillview neighborhoods provided a large
proportion of the unionized blue-collar employees at Petrox. It was less
clear how many black Hillviewers may have worked non-contract jobs
there. Certainly the great majority of Petrox's office labor force did not
live in neighborhoods like Cornerton. In any event, HAT's claim is cred-
ible that Petrox's financial contribution to Hillview posed a challenge to
a citizen group trying to make local industry and government take toxics-
related issues seriously.

HAT as a community organization: history and structure

HAT evolved out of a twenty-year history of community organizing in Hillview. Three of HAT's core members originally met during a five-year campaign in the 1970s to win compensation for Hillview residents displaced by a freeway expansion. With the help of the Citizens Action League (CAL), a California-based analogue to the national ACORN network, residents won "a house for a house," a victory often recalled with pride. The CAL core activists next tackled utility companies on rate policies, and then moved on to confront toxics in Hillview. "People were dying like flies" recalled HAT's chairperson. The links that early anti-toxics activists in Hillview perceived between illness and toxic pollution got supported by an EPA study that found the lung cancer rate in the industrial belt spanning Hillview and adjacent cities was 40–50 percent higher than in the rest of the county. A state-sponsored study later in the 1970s produced similar findings for all forms of cancer.

In all, three citizen organizing networks assisted local Hillview activists in their bid to limit toxic emissions from local industries. Originally members of CAL in the 1970s, Chairperson Ben Norton, Mrs. Sherman, and Mr. Hamilton worked with the newly merged CAL-ACORN in the early 1980s after the old CAL had "flitted out" in Norton's words. But the infusion of resources and advice from the multi-state ACORN network was not always dependable. By 1985, the above-named activists and others in an informal Hillview anti-toxics group decided to accept an offer of financial sponsorship from American Communities Fighting Toxics (pseudonym), another multi-state organizing and technical assistance network. In 1986, HAT formally organized itself under ACFT's sponsorship as a community coalition with an executive board that would be made up of members of different local organizations and neighborhood associations. During this study, the ACFT was the major financial and organizational sponsor for HAT. Board members continued to identify themselves with their local volunteer organizations, and several named their primary affiliation as CAL-ACORN.

Each of the networks assisting HAT had framed (Snow *et al.* 1986; Hunt, Benford, and Snow 1994) Hillviewers' grievances in terms that counterpose local, low-to-moderate income residents to the state and corporations. Each sought, with varying degrees of success, to mobilize Hillviewers in neighborhood divisions that would unite to pursue city-wide toxics (or other) issues while continuing work on issues specific to particular neighborhoods. And each observed a division of leadership peculiar to the community organizing tradition by separating the role of "organizer" from that of "grassroots leader."

The "grassroots leader" in HAT, as in other community organizations (Delgado 1986), is a local resident with ties to a particular neighborhood or pre-existing organizations. The leader is someone who can enunciate local grievances, backed up by some clout in the local social order. While connected within local networks, such leaders are not necessarily accomplished activists or local "movers and shakers." Neither would a community organization like HAT expect a prospective leader to enter with an extensive knowledge of particular issues – toxics in this case. Rather, the organization would expect to groom such leaders from among local members. During my participation in HAT, a chairperson informally identified several members for prospective leadership on account of their effective speaking at public hearings, their specialized writing or technical skill, or their initiative at suggesting new projects. While the unit of "grassroots" efficacy in the Green movement was the single "empowered" member, in community organizations like HAT that unit is the local leader, and by implication, the leader's local constituency as a whole. Both leaders and other members of HAT did voice concern that individual members be able to speak their minds. But unlike Green groups and similar movement groups noted in Chapter 2, HAT did not choose its organizational structure to accentuate individual participation.

In the community organizing tradition, the "grassroots leader" role has been a device for ensuring that local organization members could develop a political will within the local culture, without undue influence from expert advisors' possibly differing priorities. By developing these leaders out of the membership, a group like HAT would "own" its expertise and use it to further the members' aims. "Empowerment," then, implied a collective project shared by an organization as a whole, rather than a quality that an activist could carry individually. It relied on an unambiguous division of labor between leaders and new members whose learning would further "empower" the organization as a whole, as well as themselves. This is not the kind of empowerment that ACES or Green activists practiced. Chafing against the personalistic tone to much talk about empowerment, a black pastor speaking at a national conference about his anti-toxics experience in Alabama declared, "You don't 'empower' poor folk! ... Leadership arises out of the community."

HAT's structure would require a pre-existing local culture that could perceive "grassroots leaders" and collective empowerment as legitimate expressions of communal opinion, not infringements on personal choice. In Airdale with its lack of publicly shared cultural authority, ACES needed to create solidarity among members with disparate, privately held commitments. ACES did not have the cultural basis for sending community organizers out to Airdale neighborhoods with realistic hopes that many residents would take them seriously. In Hillview, publicly shared authority and a community organizing tradition reinforced one another, and supported a communitarian-style solidarity.

COMMUNITARIAN COMMITMENT IN HAT

As with the other groups in this study, I sought out HAT members' own understandings of public commitment. And just as in the other case chapters, I discerned what being an activist meant to HAT members by listening for how they placed themselves within some larger context of political institutions and cultural authorities, and by noting how they talked about their own membership in HAT. These "social identities" shape the kind of togetherness the group can construct as a whole. And as we will see later, they may also influence the kind of larger, nation-wide "movement" in which a local activist group participates. Most HAT members grounded their social identities either in other specific local organizations, or in institutions of "the black community" in general. Members anchored themselves in a local milieu, then, in contrast to the Greens who carried their commitments more as individual agents of social change than as members of organizations or of a specific locale.

Chart 4.1 lists the core participants in HAT, along with examples of typical ways they talked about themselves and their membership in HAT. All of the core members below are African Americans, with the exception of technical advisor Bill Reagle, Co-Chair Dee Trapper, and new member Rona. Staff person Lester, Chairperson Norton, Mrs. Davis, James, and Rona were in their 40s. Other members were in their middle 50s or older. Members all lived in Hillview with the exception of the technical advisor and the Co-Chair. Particularly pertinent information is italicized.

Chart 4.1 Creating activist identities in HAT

Lester Burrell, HAT's single paid staff person and officially executive director, regularly enunciated his role as *fighting for "the community."* He said people like him were *doing work in the community that the churches should have been doing.*

Ben Norton, the Chairperson of HAT's board, mentioned more often than anyone else on the board the *importance of having a minority presence* in the environmental movement. He emphasized his role in a campaign to get more minorities onto large environmental organization governing boards. At an Earth Day program featuring Jesse Jackson at a local church, Norton reminded the audience, "*we may be poor, we may be black, but we're somebody.*" He spoke on several occasions of the *church as a source of strength for blacks.* While fighting for greater minority influence in general, he drew his own legitimacy from being a "grassroots leader," in contrast to organizational big-wigs who "wrote books." He had a long, local organizational history with the Citizens Action League.

Dee Trapper, the Co-Chair, was fondly *called the "mother of toxics"* by longtime local anti-toxics activists. A *former mayor and a city councilwoman* in a neighboring city, Dee was involved in a number of volunteer organizations.

Mrs. Sherman was secretary and a founding member of HAT. "*A woman's place is where she's needed*" she quipped once, and referred on several occasions to her *organizational history with CAL,* and with *welfare rights campaigns.* Mrs. Sherman *regularly gave the opening prayer* at board meetings. She belonged to the local *Gray Panthers* chapter, a group for retired volunteers who serve lunches at community centers, a *legal assistance organization,* and the local Rainbow Coalition.

Mrs. Davis *volunteered in 5 community organizations,* including the *National Association for Negro Women, and the NAACP,* and (late in this study) announced that "*as a black woman I'm running for city council.*" She spoke often about *working for the betterment of "the community,"* which included anti-drug as well as anti-toxics work. HAT members respected her for having been a teacher, and holding B.A. and M.A. degrees. They acknowledged her as HAT's most active recruiter of new members.

James Shaver joined HAT with a *college background in natural science.* He spoke of his *desire to see more diverse racial and class backgrounds in the environmental movement.* While he considered his own politics further to the left than those of HAT as a whole, he soon became one of HAT's speakers at public hearings. Though ambivalent about the black church as a main cultural authority in Hillview, James declared he joined HAT so that he could "*contribute to the community.*"

Mrs. Louis was a founding member of HAT. She spoke very little at meetings and said she had been a nurse, for which she won an award.

Mrs. Irwin spoke rarely at the meetings I attended. Her relatively few comments often included *allusions to biblical wisdom.*

Mr. Hamilton was a founding member of HAT and during introductions
at board meetings always identified his *affiliation with CAL*. He was
an usher at his Baptist church as well. He did not often speak at
meetings, but occasionally asked questions to clarify a policy matter.

Rona was introduced to HAT by Dee Trapper and soon was elected to
the board. She *joined as someone with experience working at Exco*, a
target of HAT campaigns. While highly supportive of HAT's efforts,
Rona *disagreed with HAT's custom of opening prayers*, saying that
there was *no place for religion of any denomination in a "government-
based" group* like HAT.

Bill Reagle was a *technical advisor who represented Environmental
Advocates* on the HAT board. He updated board members with
information on hazardous waste production which they used to
determine targets and goals for organizing drives.

Unlike for most Greens, membership in HAT signified a cultural continuity, either with prior community organizations, shared religious traditions, shared African-American peoplehood, or all of these. And unlike
Greens, none said that these identities made them feel "different" from
their surrounding culture. Rather, they grounded their commitments in
shared cultural and organizational authority, or else in a shared difference from a larger, predominantly white society. As with the ACES, it
did not matter that some members – even core members – did not participate often as individual contributors. In HAT, participation got defined
in terms of a collective product much more than as a matter of individual
contributions.

As with ACES, we should ask whether "commitment" for HAT simply
meant the collective pursuit of private interest. With obvious pollution
rising up from industrial smokestacks and dump sites blighting the local
landscape, it could be that HAT members went public to fight for their
own health and safety more than for a public good in general. We might
expect them to appeal to similarly endangered, uninvolved residents in
terms of their self-interest too. The grassroots organizing manuals
distributed by the major US citizen anti-toxics resource center instructed
leaders to select and organize those neighborhoods most affected by toxic
contamination, and to "close in on the sale" to residents by phrasing
involvement in terms of some form of self-interest – an interest in safe-
guarding family health, or else an interest in *feeling* like one is doing the
right thing.[9] But HAT defined "getting involved" as rising above self-
interest. The definition drew on communal themes familiar to other
African Americans in Hillview, even if these local residents did not

always live up to their own standards. HAT activists and some Hillview residents viewed self-interest largely in critical, sometimes satirical, terms.

Self-interest versus the "community"

Of the five most active, most influential individuals in HAT (apart from technical advisors), only two claimed to have suffered a physical malady directly related to toxic exposure. One of these members had incurred the illness as an industrial employee, years before joining HAT. I never heard him mention his health condition when explaining his involvement to others in public settings. This is not to suggest that HAT members have overstated their claims of toxic imperilment in Hillview. There are no systematic, current, local health surveys for Hillview as of this writing. But clearly, many black Hillview residents thought local toxic hazards endangered their health. At three community forums I attended during this study, residents attested to unusual breathing conditions, chronic and acute skin conditions, sudden hair loss, high blood pressure, and other conditions that they traced either to one of the catastrophic industrial fires in the area or to prolonged exposure to air pollution from Petrox. Those who had sufficient time and strength to attend meetings and become active HAT members were not necessarily those with the most serious health conditions.

Whether healthy or ill, HAT members seemed never far from environmental health dangers. During this study, one woman who attended two board meetings did speak regularly at rallies about the effects on herself and her son of toxic fallout from an explosion at Petrox. Several board members mentioned relatives or local friends that became unusually ill from what they presumed was toxic exposure. And Mrs. Sherman, a loyal attendee, developed numbness and high blood pressure after trucks mysteriously dumped hills of dirt near her apartment. A neighbor discovered from a letter accidently sent to his house that the dirt contained high levels of mercury.

But active HAT members *spoke* of self-interest as a motivation of last resort, or else as a legitimate basis for private law suits, but not as an entrée to local public life, or to HAT. Staffperson Lester groused to me during one very slow door-knocking campaign, "People aren't thinking in terms of toxics ... they think once they get compensation, that's the end of it." Co-Chair Dee Trapper expressed her amused frustration at having to indulge local residents to get them to attend air quality control board hearings. Reflecting on the participation at one "community forum" on pollution from a local chemical firm, she drew a distinction between reacting to immediate toxic threats and longer-term involvement in HAT:

PL: "I'm glad people in the end started speaking up."
DT: "I'm glad they *showed up*." But she said that getting them interested in "our work" is something else again.
PL: "Isn't this (the forum) 'your work'?"
DT: "But will they come to a meeting? They come when it affects them, their neighborhood. But when it doesn't ... (sighs) People don't join things anymore – they watch TV."
She then told me how when she was doing anti-toxics organizing "all by myself before this group existed" she used to "drive people (to hearings), offer them free lunch, and drive them home – *then* they'd come."

A black Hillview resident with a history of community activism related a similar story to other residents gathered together for a house meeting with a HAT organizer. The house meeting was part of a campaign to turn residents out for a community forum that HAT organized to criticize the way city and county officials handled an industrial fire. The fire had burned uncontrolled for a week.

Mrs. M had been involved in welfare rights organizing some twenty years ago. During a house meeting in advance of the forum she told of how her welfare rights group had tried to involve local residents. She explained that her organization announced to one targeted neighborhood that the government was threatening to cut off their checks altogether. Residents jammed the meeting hall and it was "standing room only" she recalled, cracking up with laughter. The whole living-room audience roared.

The "house meeting" is from the standard community organizing repertoire, and this one further illustrates the relation between self-interest and "community" feeling in Hillview's civic culture. At house meetings, neighbors meet with an organizer who encourages them to articulate their grievances, and to discover a common plight and a common, usually corporate, foe. This time, six or so residents described the ash that had been deposited on their cars, and the numbness and dizziness they had experienced since the fire. The organizer I had accompanied prodded more discussion, accentuating the conflict: she called the $200 offered to some residents "hush money" – "They will try to buy you off." Residents were certainly interested in a fair monetary compensation. Some had gotten lawyers to pursue claims. But compensation alone was a secondary point that neither the organizer nor residents dwelt upon for very long. Residents found more compelling the injustice of the fire and the seemingly obvious racial contours of the response to it:

Mr. M.: "They just don't care."

Organizer: "That's right. They don't care about the community."

Mrs. M.: "They – (glancing directly at me) – and excuse me for saying this – warned people up in Crestville about what to do. But they didn't evacuate the people right nearby ... I was in the beauty shop on Seventy-Fourth Street and it was full of stuff."

"Getting involved" meant acting more as a *member* of a wronged "community" than as an individual with an individual cost-benefit ledger.[10] The staff organizer in particular referred to struggling on behalf of "the community" numerous times at each board meeting. In fact, HAT leaders and other members always referred to the constituency that HAT constructed for itself simply as "the community." Unlike ACES, HAT could draw from its community shared sources of cultural authority and identity.

Shared standards: "They don't have enough God in them"

At least one very clear arbiter of the black Hillview "community" was the church, a local authority acknowledged by both HAT's elder faithful and its less traditional, liberally educated, black staff organizer. Following a tradition of religiously supported, African-American political struggle (Morris 1984; Lincoln and Mamiya 1990; Henry 1990), HAT expected local churches to allot time occasionally for a member to present HAT's case to congregants. HAT monthly board meetings themselves each began with a Christian prayer. The prayer itself may have been perfunctory but the symbolism of giving it was potent: when a new member once objected that religion had no place in a "government-based" organization, the chairperson instructed, as he had done elsewhere, that in "slavery days" the church was "all black people had." Neither the other local residents nor the white technical advisor on the board argued here for a separation of church and state. ACES members, in contrast, had rooted their commitments in varying faiths and philosophies. And as Laura the leader had explained to me, they maintained the tacit understanding that no one would "come on" too strong with their particular beliefs at meetings.

While the ACES group culture treated unpoliticized Airdale residents and ML employees as personal selves in need of development, Christianity was a shared yardstick against which HAT members measured the virtue of local leaders, civil and religious. Frustrated with the intransigence of some local churches on toxics issues, one member exclaimed, "They don't have enough God in them!" Even the more skeptically minded staff organizer held that HAT was in fact doing the work that local churches "should have been doing." When one of HAT's new grassroots leaders decided to run for city council, several of her endorsement speakers – including her pastor and a member of an association of religious broadcasters – spoke at length on the candidate's virtues as a Christian woman. The implicit contrast with incumbent council members – widely perceived to have been "bought off" by Petrox – was hard to miss.

The construction of a Hillview "community" got a further assist from populist rhetoric HAT shared with other local anti-toxics groups in the "Grassroots Movement for Environmental Justice."[11] The staff organizer sometimes described the Hillview anti-toxics struggle as one of "community control." He announced during one particularly fiery speech at a rally that the "bottom line" is a "question of power":

It's a question of who's going to rule in our community. Is Petrox going to rule, are these other toxic polluters going to rule in our community, or are the people, the residents that live in our community going to rule? HAT says that the people are going to rule.

ACES needed to break through the civic privatism of Airdale, and drew on a personalist morality in order to do so. But populist political reasoning, together with a publicly shared, Christian-influenced morality, gave HAT a basis for upholding the common good of local people against threats to their well-being perceived as coming from outside.

The "community" HAT members have referred to should be easy enough to identify, especially since it is largely black and divided into recognized neighborhoods within Hillview.[12] And yet, when probing the meaning of these frequent references to community with two active members of HAT, I had some difficulty getting an unambiguous definition. The trouble was that while HAT officially pursued a multiracial politics, demanding health safeguards from industry and government for *local* residents, HAT based its solidarity and identity largely on local forms of *African American* community life. The next sections show that this culture of "community" life has strengthened HAT members' solidary resolve but has also limited HAT's ability to groom active members, and to deal with conflicting interests in the larger locale.

THE MEANING OF PARTICIPATION IN HAT

Members participated in HAT in order to advance HAT as an organization, and Hillview as its constituency – not to give voice to individual political will as an end in itself. Individual participation was less of a goal in itself for HAT than for the other groups in this study.[13] While some HAT board members passed several meetings with no turns whatsoever, Green members would have considered such lack of participation troublesome, a sign of disinterest or of discrimination against the member. HAT's decisions about organizational structure offer another good case in point. In place of the Greens' "facilitators" and "vibes-watchers" and the ACES' loose form of "consensus," HAT adopted a standard organizational structure for non-profit organizations. With none of the Greens' queasiness about formal, standardized position titles, HAT maintained a Chair, Co-Chair, Executive Director, and Board of Directors. What's more, HAT ratified a provisional draft of its by-laws in roughly ten minutes. At one meeting board members decided upon and voted approval for two candidates for the board in five minutes. The Ridge Greens, in contrast, ran for months on various by-law drafts because the working group devoted to drafting them endured the same individual challenges and centrifugal tendencies as Green groups generally. And Ridge Greens had argued at least once about rights to *attendance* at Ridge coordinating council meetings, apart from council membership. While Ridge Greens quite often stymied routine decision-making by appeals to contrary versions of by-laws, only twice during my two years with HAT did a board member appeal to by-laws in order to question an action of the board.

The definition of "community" and community welfare underlying HAT's efforts gave leading members and advisors the legitimacy to orchestrate participation by other members at public forums. During the organizing campaign in the wake of the above-mentioned fire, for instance, the HAT leadership coached HAT members on questions they could put to county health officials who would be attending. Ben Norton and other HAT leaders emphasized on several occasions the need for HAT to "speak with one voice" at public hearings on toxic waste policy in Hillview. Commenting on potential HAT speakers at a hearing on emergency early warning arrangements, Norton warned that "we need to make sure someone doesn't get up there who doesn't know what they're talking about."

ACES members had similarly trusted their leader, Laura, to plan most of their strategy and tactics at public hearings. But Laura showed a greater ambivalence about orchestrated participation, an ambivalence tinged with a more "anti-authoritarian" and personalist stance on participation. While she wanted to make sure that either she or some other ACES member would raise the major technical issues at a hearing, she also emphasized that the hearings were "not a set-up." She wanted to make clear that "we don't plan exactly how they will come out." Before each hearing she would encourage other members to bring up literally any concern that they may have because individual participation would be good in itself.

HAT's construction of "community" gave it a far wider mandate to organize Hillview than the one ACES allowed itself. Outreach workers like the organizer quoted from the house meeting gave themselves the role of community advocate as a matter of course, whether or not they actually lived in the targeted neighborhood: the latina organizer reminded the black residents at the meeting: "They [the adjacent industry] don't care about the community" – placing herself firmly on the side of the "community" that both HAT and black Hillviewers constructed. This appeal to communal belonging contrasts clearly with ACES' plant-a-seed theory of activation. Without a single, widely accepted construction of "community" in Airdale, ACES was unwilling to project a lot of authoritativeness in Airdale civic life. ACES preferred to let Airdalers discover its virtues by individually cultivating a sense of dissent, by finding strength "from within" to challenge local quiescence regarding Microtech. For the most part, ACES did not make aggressive use of the community organizing recruitment repertoire, though it had access to that repertoire as an affiliate of the CCHW network.[14] ACES did not follow up its principal outreach campaign – the incinerator petition drive – with organization-building events that might have increased the number of regular participants in ACES.

Where are the members? Accountability and centripetal tendencies

HAT tried to structure members' participation with unambiguous definitions of roles and responsibilities. HAT had clearer norms of accountability than the Greens, for instance, whose group culture frowned on traditional "leadership" and sought a harmonious mesh of individual initiatives with relatively little administrative oversight. For the Greens, questing after an egalitarian, but not simply anarchic, organizational model meant living with a good deal of uncertainty regarding authority and the limits of personal initiative. HAT's contrasting schema of co-chairs, executive director/staff organizer, and board members provided lines of accountability that members could follow in order to assess the organization and their place in it. On the one hand, this assured HAT leaders an ongoing legitimacy that often eluded those Greens whose extra efforts earned them the informal and often unenviable position of leader. On the other hand, the same culture that sustained the authority implied in the standard, non-profit organization flowchart also provided only sketchy roles for participants to assume as critically engaged members.

HAT's ongoing struggle to define executive leadership demonstrates the strengths and weaknesses of communitarian commitments in practice. At several points during my involvement with HAT, members debated the division of responsibilities in the organization. HAT's national sponsoring organization, ACFT, delivered a fairly critical evaluation of the executive director's performance. The evaluation stated that the director did too little to develop more "grassroots leaders" and to involve board members in community organizing drives. Pressured by an ACFT officer to dismiss the director a few months after his evaluation, the board instead gave the director a unanimous "vote of confidence." And yet, some fourteen months later, several board members gathered for a special review meeting during which they enunciated criticisms of HAT and its director that paralleled some of those contained in the staff evaluation of the year before.

HAT board members wanted an organization in which members could in fact become grassroots leaders, or at least make contributions integral to HAT's day-to-day operations. They sought this kind of participation as community advocates working in unison, not as Green-style, individually empowered selves. Mrs. Davis, for instance, wanted to get more involved in HAT educational campaigns and give HAT greater public visibility, but thought the director gave her too few openings for involvement. At the review meeting, Mrs. De Rose, who like the rest of the members clearly supported the director, made a striking statement that combined the idiom of communal authority with an appeal for greater individual efficacy under the "community" aegis:

The statement affirmed that "we are all in this together," "as a community," and that "every link in the chain has to be strong." She said she wanted to "put her 100 percent" into the organization but found it difficult to do so. She concluded that HAT needs "leadership," a leadership "that encourages each and every one."

While calling for greater individual efficacy, Mrs. De Rose's statement contrasts with ones Greens made at their own organizational review meetings: De Rose's statement was unambiguous about the need for leadership. The "community" she placed herself in clearly differed as well; she defined it by a unity of purpose more than by a Green-style weaving together of individual initiative. Another board member appealed for more "community education" and included herself among the needy. This member found herself uninformed when at a toxics reduction meeting, Petrox spokespeople wielded "all sorts of charts and things." In all, board members at the special meeting seemingly saw no conflict between allegiance to communal purpose and a wider distribution of responsibilities and knowledge in HAT.

Yet, HAT board members had spurned the earlier, negative staff evaluation without carefully measuring its merits and deficiencies. They had continued to let the director develop door-knocking drive plans and determine organizational priorities primarily in consultation with the chair, co-chair, and technical advisor. They had continued to let him do most of the group's public relations work. As we have seen, most of the board members already had experience in other civic organizations; they were not simply new to active volunteering.[15] I argue that HAT's communitarian culture of commitment brought the strengths of unity in tandem with challenges for participation. HAT members had a basis for appreciating accountable leaders, but fewer well-established understandings about accountability *among themselves* as the guarantors of a democratic group. HAT did not always meet the challenge of communitarian democracy.

HAT members focused their varied dissatisfactions onto the director's wide-ranging leadership. While the dissatisfactions that actually sparked the special review meeting involved matters of member participation, during the meeting these dissatisfactions either dropped out of the review process or else got distilled into recommendations for actions that *the director* could take. HAT members were far from questioning their director's legitimacy in the name of members' personal expression, as Ridge Greens had done with George during their "group process" sessions. Board members just wanted Lester to continue exercising authority in a more "accountable" way. But the calls by the above members for more involvement opportunities, for a "groupier" group, did not get translated into recommendations for action board members themselves could take. Both Lester and the board were caught up in an organizational culture that made it difficult to articulate an image of responsible, involved membership in tandem with accountable leadership.

Accountability meant needing to "play by the rules" as Ben said. For Ben, this translated into the need for the director to keep better account of HAT's income and expenses. For both Ben and other members, accountability was mainly a quality of leaders but not so much other members. Ben had first alerted the board to his displeasure with Lester's accounting practices months before. Now with Ben's concerns particularly in mind, board members agreed that Lester should be asked for regular monthly reports on routine office activities and on HAT finances. Members agreed as well that Lester had been saddled by a position that really demanded two full sets of duties – those of community organizer and those of manager – either of which would have been enough for one person. Clearly, the board would need to become accountable for some of Lester's task burden.

But while there were familiar "rules" for good management, there were fewer rules, or familiar practices, for acting as an accountable, empowered member of a community organization. Implying that the board already had what it needed to jump in and help Lester, Ben reminded the board that it had received valuable training from an experienced community organizer. In fact, the training had presented budgeting, fundraising, planning long-term priorities, and conducting a participatory meeting. In the ten months since the training, Mrs. Davis had initiated several fundraising projects – including a bus trip, a candy sale, and an awards dinner. Most of the other activities presented at the training went unpracticed. As a result, HAT board members "owned" their group less than Greens, who tended toward the other extreme, sometimes endangering their groups by bestowing group "ownership" – and nearly the right to a foreclosure sale – on each active member.

In a group "fighting for the community," people joined as community advocates and supported other members who demonstrated themselves as sincere advocates for the community. The executive director, for instance, earned a good part of his legitimacy from his willingness to work hard for HAT and its constiuency. One older board member who spoke on his behalf immediately following the staff evaluation placed both herself and Lester in the context of a local struggle for the black common good:

Mrs. Irwin started her endorsement by saying "I've been black three times – as a baby, a girl, and now as a woman." She made a brief reference to "we-people" and went on to say that working with HAT wasn't something "you do for money." Rather, "they're doing it for the environment," and she named a number of local and regional toxic threats to underscore the urgency of the cause. She had seen Lester work hard, she testified, and "when you do the best you can do there's nothing else you can do." She had "no disappointments in him."

Mrs. Irwin's comments implied that Lester ought to be judged on the basis of his commitments at least as much as on instrumental criteria.

Ben Norton's evaluative stance differed somewhat from those of other members. Upholding the organization's overall mission, he stated his own endorsement with an assurance that he was not supporting Lester "just because he's black." As HAT chairperson and member of several multi-state environmental organization boards, Ben was more recently experienced than other members in standing up for organizational needs that might clash with communal solidarities. Still, the community organizing language of "grassroots leaders," backed by assumptions about the unity of communal interest, gave Norton – like Mrs. Irwin – a thinner basis for articulating the everyday responsibilities and practices of non-leading HAT members. Norton did mention "ownership" as a positive quality to cultivate in HAT members. But HAT's everyday practice of "community" gave members relatively few opportunities for more ownership as individuals.

If leaders would not make discussion of "ownership" in HAT into a priority at meetings, it is unlikely that non-leading members would push the topic onto meeting agendas. Norton referred several times to the board's training sessions, assuming that the board would leave the sessions as activated participants who could then start doing things differently. If they did not become more activated, Norton would take this as a sign of difficulties with the director, a difficulty that better funding would solve perhaps, but meanwhile members themselves would not learn how to practice accountability. A self-perpetuating cycle ensued, different from the centrifugal cycle that turned Green members against their overworked, *de facto* leaders. In HAT a centripetal cycle drew all energy and legitimacy toward leaders, making other members too indistinguishable as separate actors, rather than too differentiated.

I do not claim that engaged, critical participation is impossible in a communitarian group. Egalitarianism and communitarianism are not mutually exclusive. Neither must a communitarian organization necessarily develop traditional male leadership styles that Lester and Ben Norton both practiced. Communitarian commitments in Hillview provided ready support for leadership, a support lacking in the more "portable" commitments of Greens and other activists in this study. But the communitarian language of commitment in HAT emphasized leadership and common will more than it provided moral or political substance for individual members' roles. So members like Mrs. De Rose did not have a clearly legitimate, widely acknowledged basis for demanding more participation the way women like Lucy and Heidi in the Greens did through personalist culture.[16] HAT members constructed the "common good" in black Hillview as a set of priorities that *all* good members of the community agreed on, almost as common sense. The cultural challenge for HAT would be to find a stronger language of participation commensurate with the well-established civic culture that sustained it.

THE AMBIGUITY OF LOCAL BELONGING: HAT IN ITS COMMUNITY

HAT's everyday practice constructed its Hillview constituency as an organic black community, bound by shared faith and a shared sense of peoplehood chafing at injustice. Commitment to this version of community enabled HAT to move out into its locale with a tightly unified solidarity, but one marked by considerable blind spots as well. Some of these blind spots emerged as HAT members imagined the significance of acts "for the community."

Communitarian-style commitment in Hillview could encompass a wide range of activities, some that most observers would call "service" or "charity" but not "political" work. For instance, a number of HAT board members were involved in other community-related work that did not entail challenging the agenda-setting power of county government or the policies of large corporations the way working with HAT did. I discovered that the most active HAT board members apart from the director and chairperson did not distinguish their work with HAT from other work done on behalf of the community. All such volunteer, public engagements went under the category of community betterment. And these bonds of community obligation, strong as they may have been, included relatively little sense of obligation to or membership in a larger, extra-local community of activists challenging the powers that be.

Community improvement in a localized moral universe

For non-leading members, getting involved in HAT was an extension of community improvement efforts, often propelled by a biblically informed ethic of service. The boundaries of that "community" were largely common-sense and unarticulated; to assume them was in fact part of being a regular community member. As an original board member of HAT and active member or leader in a number of other local organizations, Mrs. Sherman was firmly ensconsed in that community. With HAT she had gone to rallies, spoken at public hearings, and helped make decisions about the organization's overall direction. In my interview with Mrs. Sherman I tried to become more clear on who exactly she thought benefited from work on behalf of "the community," and what kind of activity would or would not count as community service. I had a difficult time asking the question in a way that would elicit an elaboration on "community" itself.

PL: " ... When you say 'we,' who [do] you feel like that 'we' is? Like who do you belong to?"

S: Well I belong to the Grey Panthers, I belong to my church, I belong to the RSVP advisory board (group for meal-service volunteers), I belong to Legal Aid – I'm vice president – let's see where else do I belong, I belong to the HAT – I'm really secretary but I wish somebody else would take the position ... "

PL: "But you mention all these groups – do you feel like they're all part of the same community, or is this just really different stuff?"

S: "RSVP is made up of retired seniors ... they gave me an award ..."

PL: "So is being in HAT different in some way from those other groups or do you think it's all the same?"

S: "It's different because we [are] working on just toxics, and things that concern people's health. And that's a little different from legal aid – that's people who have legal problems, so HAT is only working on things that affect the health of the community."

PL: "You just said 'the community,' so *who*? You mean blacks in Hillview?"

S: "Blacks and whites and everyone else that live in this area."

For Mrs. Sherman, her various groups differed because their particular issues were different, but they were all part of the same overall project: doing good things for the community. Though involved on the basis of religious commitments, Mrs. Sherman declared that the church was not enough. "You got to get into the community and let people know there's things they can do to improve your community. No it's all about helping people help themselves – improving your community." Interestingly, for Mrs. Sherman "the community" did not have to mean African Americans alone, even though HAT's solidarity depended heavily on black-identified cultural authorities. To Mrs. Sherman, getting involved meant starting where one lives; for her, that was a locale in which she could take for granted black cultural authorities, although the beneficiaries of her efforts did not need to be black.

Greens, in contrast, defined commitment in terms of a politics that transcended "single issues" and single locales, even though they sought out local issues on which to focus. The single issues they did embrace were ones that they defined as "political," such as rainforest advocacy or reproductive rights – issues that addressed corporate or state power. I never heard Greens comparing their activism to locally based, volunteer human service work – feeding the elderly, providing legal counselling for the indigent, assisting a church-sponsored anti-drug outreach program. I was not aware that any Ridge or Seaview Greens had ever been involved in this kind of volunteer work.

Like Mrs. Sherman, Mrs. Davis was involved in a number of local service organizations at the same time as HAT. She had contributed greatly to HAT's recruitment, pulling in a local minister and a number of residents through her own networking. She oversaw several fundraising events as well. Like Mrs. Sherman, she got involved as a concerned "member of a community" – not as a toxics victim – who ultimately grounded her commitments in religious faith. Mrs. Davis was writing a book on some of the Hillview issues she had involved herself with, focusing particularly on a local religious couple's drug rehabilitation ministry. As a general theme for her book, she chose the word "growth": "These people are all growing." I asked if this book could include some writing she had been doing about Hillviewers dealing with toxic-related illnesses. She said it could.

PL: "I hadn't thought of toxics in the 'growth' category."
D: "Oh, toxics could be put in every category!" (laughing) "... It's something happening in – our lives. People are dealing with it in every state; each community is concerned. I don't know if it's the same in every community but I think it is."

For Mrs. Davis, toxics issues went in the same category as getting people off drug addictions. It was all part of community improvement.

Just as for Mrs. Sherman, the "community" referred to was at once a strong anchor for a sense of local belonging and an ambiguous identification on a broader map of social movement groups, governmental and corporate power. For instance, I asked if a (largely white) anti-toxics group in another part of the county was part of the "community" Mrs. Davis invoked. "Oh yeah, they're community, everyone's community." Here, community carried a populist inflection, referring to relatively powerless local residents in general who seek justice from corporations or slow bureaucracies (Kazin 1995). Inside her own locale, activism for the community did not require distinguishing between actions that constitute charity, or "single-issue" advocacy, and efforts like those of HAT that have larger "systemic" implications because they challenge structures of governmental or corporate decision-making. Mrs. Davis did see her efforts in Hillview as potentially relevant beyond her own locale; she was not simply isolated from the world of grassroots anti-toxics action. Though other communities may have had parallel problems, Mrs. Davis got involved by starting with the problems she learned about in her own neighborhood. And she grounded her actions in the moral universe of Hillview – one in which black Christianity and black identity are everyday guideposts – and not in an abstract world of cultural struggle between industrial or post-industrial "values." Given this implicit moral universe, Mrs. Davis could even use the therapeutic-sounding language of personal "growth" without diminishing her sense that there were communal attachments that united black Hillviewers.

James Shaver articulated his involvements in different terms than other active HAT members like the above two. But like them, he located the morality and legitimacy of his actions in a local black community and identity. James Shaver worked with technical advisor Bill Reagle, preparing reports on liquid waste storage at Petrox for HAT. He initiated HAT's first newsletter as well, formatting it on his home computer. Similar to Greens, Shaver carried a strong dose of cultural dissent into his activism. "Sometimes I wonder if Christianity isn't our worst enemy," he mused. Shaver preferred to put his trust in the "Creator" rather than Jesus. He saw his involvement in HAT in terms of a larger project to assist the African people in the US. The wall facing his computer at home celebrated his sense of peoplehood; it was covered with newspaper accounts and photos of African-American public figures, from Martin Luther King to Louis Farrakhan. With this broader perspective, he nevertheless drew his immediate worth as an activist from his local black community. "Think globally, act locally," he averred.

Unlike most Greens, Shaver had a specific, highly elaborated definition of local community in which he could firmly locate himself. And even though he chafed at some of its specific modes of traditional, cultural authority, he affirmed the communal authority of black Hillview for himself.[17] Acting locally meant tuning in to the particular qualities of black Hillview, the "black community" which he contrasted with another geographic (and cultural) region of Hillview whose affluent residents "don't give a damn about the community in East Park (a predominantly black HAT stronghold)." Shaver intentionally sought to settle in a black neighborhood of Hillview. More than for other residents, choosing a residence was tied up with pursuing a voluntary, political-cultural life project, and not just a means for surviving as comfortably as possible. He sought out public involvement that would enable him to pursue health-related environmental activism for blacks. In this way, he came to HAT on a different basis than members like Mrs. Sherman or Mr. Hamilton, who were continuing their own histories of local citizen advocacy, or those like Mrs. Davis, who added anti-toxics advocacy to a prior history of charitable civic work. Shaver intentionally chose and articulated his sense of community more than other members who were already "of" the community. But Shaver, Davis, and Sherman all shared the basic similarity of working on behalf of a locally situated community which, though possibly akin to other black communities, provided relatively self-contained authority and identity from which to forge public commitments.

The weakness of strong ties

HAT's practice of community obligation afforded it staying power and a willingness to trust powerful leaders, on the one hand. On the other hand, HAT had some difficulties integrating people with differing interests into its tight bonds of communal obligation.

A religiously inspired communitarianism gave HAT members the strength to undertake "risky" political acts. For instance, I told Mrs. Sherman some people might consider her a "rabble-rouser" for being in a group that protests the largest tax-paying company in the city:

> Mrs. Sherman: "No I ain't. You know what, I got the nerve to fight because I started for welfare rights. We set into welfare office for hours, nobody arrested us ... I think being in action, and action the right way, don't hurt nothing. Because you don't hurt nobody, you don't touch nobody, you just do what you're supposed to do."
>
> PL: "How do you know it's the right thing to do?"
>
> S: "Well, I be led by the Holy Spirit. That's how I know. See I'm a Christian woman, when you have love in your heart for other people, you ain't going to do anything to hurt them. You going to do something to help other people ... I ain't no time gone to jail, because we had it organized, we had it planned out ... and you can't be embarrassed if you know what you're doing."

A sense of organizational discipline undergirded by religious faith enabled Mrs. Sherman to participate in seven sit-ins during her welfare rights activism twenty years ago. The same self-definition as a righteous and well-meaning political actor has given her the basis for contesting large, if local, villains by way of HAT activism. In contrast, Liz of ACES had human welfare at heart too,[18] but conceived her activism in relation to her oft-repeated self-perception that "I'm not ready to get arrested yet." Suburban privatism left her sharply sensitive to the opinions of an imagined, generalized suburban "other," and she had little of black Hillview's strong civic culture to guide her past its withering gaze.

But HAT's way of "fighting for the community" sometimes hindered members from drawing conclusions about differences of political interest amongst black Hillviewers. One of HAT's community organizing campaigns provides a case in point. HAT conducted a door-knocking and community education campaign in conjunction with the state health department's (DHS) proposal to revoke a hazardous waste storage permit from Stor-tox Inc. HAT strongly supported the DHS move, and encouraged local residents to turn out for the hearing and speak in favor of the proposal. DHS inspections had found Stor-tox violated state and federal laws by storing incompatible waste products together, mislabeling wastes, and storing more wastes than permitted. A couple of months before the hearing, a steel drum at the Stor-tox site sustained a toxic "release," and in deadpan DHS prose, "was propelled off the property"; a drum full of rocket fuel had exploded. At a board meeting HAT members condemned Stor-tox as a perpetrator of environmental racism. Chairperson Ben Norton maintained that "they've got people working there who hardly speak English," and angrily pointed out that it was another case of "minorities" having to work with toxic substances. "It's like murder!" Another member interjected, "It's genocide."

After the public hearing, HAT members expressed dismay that some local African-Americans had spoken in favor of Stor-tox. In keeping with the local civic culture, they explained them in terms of either self-interest or failed communal solidarity, or else were left without much of a rationale. Mrs. Davis said she was "shocked" that the local president of the NAACP had spoken against the permit revocation. She was surprised, too, that a locally involved woman from one of HAT's neighborhood strongholds had also opposed the revocation. The woman had told the audience she was

"opposed from the first to this plant. But the community got into a relation with the plant. They helped our children find jobs – men find jobs." She made an appeal for "fairness," noting that smoke from an explosion at another local industry still very much in business had wrecked her carpets and drapes.

In HAT parlance, the woman had been bought off. This is the explanation a HAT leader used in telling the audience that some of "our leaders (have) apparently sold out – it's no secret that people have been paid." Later he told a board meeting that some of "our people" were "on the wrong side," expressing his incredulity that a *black man* (emphasis his) from Stor-tox told him "It's ok now, we've got a new staff."

HAT's communitarianism kept members from dealing with the fact that some members of "our people" may have had different, legitimate interests, or that individual residents' interests may have been conflicted. It is entirely possible that some local residents were "paid off" or promised favors in return for support for Stor-tox. But writing off these residents as victims of community-threatening self-interest does not solve the dilemma of residents who need their health *and* jobs for their children. These needs were not likely to disappear by the time HAT door-knockers returned to the neighborhoods for another organizing drive. Rather than dismissing arguments they pronounced as "self-interested," HAT needed a way to integrate knowledge of these interests into a more differentiated image of their community. The language of "community" struggle in the name of a single communal, black identity was a vernacular that limited HAT members' purchase on the conflicting issues in their locale.

The point is not that HAT, in many ways a successful organization, needed to drop one of its major cultural sources of strength. But HAT would meet its own goals more effectively if it could depend on individual members skilled in talking about their own interests and about potentially conflicting interests within their community. To expand its members' political imagination and their bonds of communal solidarity, HAT would need to alter some of the leadership and communication patterns that accompanied its version of communitarian commitment. Since HAT gave its leaders a wide leeway to represent their interests, and trusted the leaders to represent them knowledgeably, members sometimes learned relevant political realities by happenstance instead of through deliberate instruction. Political socialization of individual HAT members was not an organizational strength.

For instance, a relatively new member, a minister, wondered why his associates told him not to list his HAT affiliation when filling out an application for a city council committee. His associates told him HAT was a "controversial organization." "I don't want to get involved in any controversy," the minister chuckled. "I was surprised – I thought they (city council) would appreciate what you're doing. I don't want to get involved in any controversy, I work with them." The executive director replied knowingly that HAT was just doing what the city government was supposed to be doing, and so the organization was only controversial to government people because Petrox was the "big money" in town. Here the minister was "let in on" a bit of Hillview politics, but not given any overview of relations between city government, big industry, and environmental advocacy in Hillview.

In a similar way, Marie, a new member, was let in on some of the local politics surrounding the Stor-tox issue. Director Lester told her about the relative lack of support from county politicians for HAT. Marie's eyes widened as Lester explained how one presumably supportive local politician had suggested that HAT "cut a deal" with Stor-tox. Marie thought he was "so community-oriented." With some trepidation in her voice, Marie asked whether anyone on the city council supported HAT. To Lester's inconclusive answer and wry grin she responded,

M: "You mean to tell me there's not one elected official with environmental consciousness in the whole city of Hillview?"
L: "Oh, there are politicians who will say they are ..."

He went on to conclude that politicians pursue their self-interests.
M: "So they don't care about the consequences of toxics in the community?"
L: "Not unless someone makes them."

The lesson that members like Marie and the minister were let in on is that one has to stick with the common good of the "community" as constructed by HAT leaders because the alternative is to become seduced by self-interested actors. But members did not get a broader political socialization that could make them less parochial actors in Hillview and give them a more nuanced sense of local political dynamics. They could not bring much local knowledge about politics and money in Hillview to the executive board's strategizing sessions. And so they could not participate in or listen to executive board deliberations as fully enfranchised members of what was supposed to be a member-controlled organization.

HAT certainly had some of the cultural resources for accomplishing a broader political socialization. One of HAT's strengths was that members accepted tutelage less ambivalently than activists in the other groups, especially the Greens. Political tutelage would of course take time and money that are especially precious for a sometimes thinly spread organization fighting serious local health hazards. And there was plenty to support HAT's cynicism about local government and self-interest in Hillview. Still, HAT might have become a valuable forum for a very practical kind of "civics" education with life-and-death consequences for residents who were dealing with exploding drums in their neighborhoods and indifference at city hall.

This expanded political socialization might give self-interest a context rendering it more explicable, less intractable to a strongly communitarian imagination. HAT might have planned organizing drives and organizational networking to take advantage of this local knowledge. But HAT would have had to institute a greater emphasis on individual participation in order for this kind of education to make sense in the organization. If HAT continued to pose itself simply as the communal "David" to the corporate "Goliath" as Lester once put it, members would have little reason to expect that their own knowledge or efficacy would matter in a company town. Solidarity under a common communal standard would continue to matter more than a broader division of labor and knowledge in HAT. And HAT's construction of communal ties would continue to make commitment in HAT a somewhat insulating practice, closing off HAT to potential allies, such as the woman who spoke out in favor of Stor-tox.

HAT's communitarianism both enabled and limited politicization in Hillview. The combination of religious faith and a singular "community" identity launched some Hillviewers into unquestionably political actions that demanded environmental "rights" from health authorities and influence over corporate behavior. On the other hand, HAT's solidarity put limits on individuals' participation as actors engaged in building a political will. It limited the degree to which HAT members could evaluate the ramifications of their various community involvements for social movements, governmental or corporate power outside of Hillview.

Ironically, HAT's communitarianism both enabled and frustrated HAT in some of the same ways that personalism both enabled and frustrated the Greens. Greens could not simply leap out of their everyday cultural context and set aside individual differences to work for a common good as "citizens" or as mainstream, local community members. Going public for them *meant* being individual political agents who oppose mainstream (non-Green) "values" and lifestyles. Their activist culture was not simply a style they could drop; it gave them their often taken-for-granted notions of what one does in public as a politically committed person. We could no more expect members of HAT to simply drop their locally based social identities and their religiously inspired sense of communal membership upon entering public life. Going public for HAT members meant enacting that particular civic culture. Neither the Greens nor HAT members had at the ready an activist style that could easily sustain a group that would be both highly participatory and responsible to a clearly defined constituency.

Compared with the Greens, HAT had a more concrete constituency. HAT also had a record of policy-influencing accomplishments in Hillview. But HAT's assumptions about that constituency hindered it at points and gave it a somewhat parochial outlook on economic interests and communal identity in Hillview. As we will see below, the Greens' own "community-building" made its very universalist-sounding ideas about coalition politics highly parochial in practice.

TWO CULTURES OF POLITICAL COMMUNITY

Local communitarian community

Activists in HAT and in Green groups both talked a great deal about "community." But clearly, they were referring to very different kinds of social networks and different experiences of togetherness. These different ways of piecing political community together produce nationwide movements with different kinds of togetherness – different bonds. And these differences, I will suggest, can result in difficulties when activists try to produce alliances between movements.

Local communitarian groups like HAT create a kind of togetherness that emphasizes a presumably shared common will over the voices of individual participants. These activists fashion bonds of interdependence that are relatively tight at the local level and do not often stretch beyond local participants. In black Hillview neighborhoods, with their history of local organizing campaigns and their access to the collective identity and authority of "the black community," it is a straightforward, if challenging, task to create these bonds. Mrs. Davis and Mrs. Sherman, for instance, found the source of their commitment to activism in the specific but taken-for-granted locale of Hillview. Sherman and Davis did not regularly bump up against their community's borders on their socio-political "map" of public commitment – hence their relative ambiguity about who exactly the community included.

Other members of HAT with a broader orienting map for their activism also shared a primary allegiance to their locale and its strong bonds. Shaver clearly drew larger implications for African American well-being from his efforts in Hillview. But for him, "think globally, act locally" in practice meant tuning in to the particular qualities of black Hillview, since "each community is different." While he could enjoy the culturally mixed, middle-class milieu in Ridgeville – the kind of milieu he had been educated and employed in – he intentionally settled in Hillview. "I like going to Ridgeville sometimes, (but) I just feel more comfortable here." Shaver took "the community" less for granted than the above two women. Unlike them, he spoke directly about the need to maintain a community identity, to "watch how we use language" when referring to it in public statements. He was thus very conscious of constructing a "black community" in the course of working with HAT, one in which he found his own source for public commitment.

Ben Norton was more involved than other HAT members in national-level environmental activism by way of his participation on the ACFT board and in other multi-state networks. But he too highlighted his commitments to a concrete, local community. Dedicated to publicizing and strategizing against environmental racism, Norton did imbue his local efforts with general significance for African Americans and other minority populations.[19] At the same time, Norton situated himself as a mediator of sorts between a national organization (ACFT) that gave HAT more clout and more resources, and HAT itself, from whence he drew his own legitimacy and moral worth as an activist. Norton spoke warily about ACFT's enthusiasm for "experts" and well-known figures with fundraising appeal. He contrasted them with local grassroots leaders (like himself) on whose behalf he sought more positions of power in the national organization. He contended once that grassroots leaders could perform at least as many valuable tasks for the national organization as people who had "written books." Grassroots activists bred in locally situated struggles were for him the most legitimate leaders of a movement at the local or the national level.

Populist communitarianism in the anti-toxics movement's own literature complemented the culture of community movement groups and the predilections of activists like Ben Norton. Spokespersons for the environmental justice cause extolled the virtues of a decentralized movement based in separate communities and united mainly by "mutual aid" – sharing of expertise and experiences between local groups. Gibbs (1989), for instance, set up a stark contrast between a movement with a "central office" that "tells the Movement what to do" and a movement made up of "people from all walks of life" who "act locally." "Because they are united on basic principles, their local actions add up to cause major change throughout society." Gibbs reasons further:

When you block an unsafe facility, shut down or clean up a polluter and win the clean-up of contaminated sites, you add to the nation-wide movement for environmental justice, even if you never leave your own backyard or do another thing! (1989: 1)

What remains unclear is how these local actions would "add up" to a sum that would be greater than the parts – a movement that could sustain an organized, collective will over the long haul. The priority and the self-identified strength of a community movement like the Grassroots Movement for Environmental Justice (GMEJ) in the early 1990s was locally based action.

In fact, CCHW (Citizen's Clearinghouse for Hazardous Wastes) writers and editorialists advocated that the best and least manipulative bonds of obligation would be those that tied activists together mainly at the local level. In contrast, a "national" movement meant one in which "people come from all over to one central location and march together" (Gibbs 1989) or else sit-in at a national corporate headquarters (Newman 1991). National movements, in this view, are dictatorial. A description of CCHW's first nationwide "Day of Action" invokes the national spectacle/local autonomy dichotomy to emphasize CCHW's commitment to separate, local organizations as sole sources of movement legitimacy:

Our first impulse was to make it a tightly coordinated and orchestrated affair where we called the shots ... Quickly we realized how wrong-headed this was: what makes the Movement strong was the integrity, strength and independence of local groups, not the amount of control exercised by CCHW as coordinator or "instigator." When we saw ourselves headed down the path of becoming a Washington-centered, bureaucratized institution with delusions of grandeur, we pulled back. (CCHW 1986: 24)

ACES and HAT achieved some of their goals in the face of remarkable obstacles. But the movement literature cited above and the case of HAT point to a crucial weakness: the logic of local communitarian activism has little place for actions that would, in a participatory, democratic fashion, unite communities into a collective identity that could survive beyond an occasional spectacular demonstration or campaign.

Personalized communities

Some US activists have defined community in terms of individualized commitments to principles which they do not immediately identify with any geographical locale or any specific social group. Personalized political communities treat individual members as each carrying a great deal of responsibility and efficacy for realizing principles in practice. Their groups share a kind of togetherness in which individual voices resonate loudly within a collective project. Personalized political communities have become widespread in the US in the past twenty years. Members of these political communities could find themselves at home in similar enclaves throughout the US (Flacks 1988) in which participants have shared the assumption that politics is a highly personalized project, that general principles of feminism, ecological awareness, or anti-militarism should resonate thoughout one's individual life.

The personalized form of community has been described elsewhere (Buechler 1990; Breines 1982) as "community" in general. One important account characterized the alternative bookstores, crisis centers, and discussion groups of the contemporary grassroots women's movement as a "social movement community" – defined as a loose network of "politicized individuals with fluid boundaries, flexible leadership structures, and malleable divisons of labor" (Buechler 1990: 42). But it is important to distinguish between the different kinds of bonds that can tie political communities together, rather than taking a personalized form for granted as "community" itself. Only certain kinds of people want to and are able to construct personalized communities as defined here, and they are the "politicized individuals" who personalize their politics.

As with local communitarians, the boundaries of "community" for these activists can be ambiguous. The Ridge and Seaview Greens, for instance, constituted Green movement communities, and also considered themselves a small part of the very loosely defined, regional "peace, ecology and social justice community." The loose regional community shared general principles similar to those of the Greens, many of which were in fact codified in the Greens' "Ten Key Values" listed in Chapter 2. Greens collaborated on a monthly calendar of events relevant to the regional community. Events on the calendar ran the gamut from pro-choice and anti-intervention protest marches to speaker series, to spiritual awareness workshops. Members of groups like the Ridge or Seaview Greens might join in a massive march against a Supreme Court ruling on abortion, or attend a conference on redesigning cities. One was a member of this loose regional community by personal volition.

Ambiguity works differently, however, for personalized communities than for groups like HAT: the bonds tying together personalized political communities are more flexible than those of local communitarian groups, and might potentially unite more widely dispersed activists. While both Greens and anti-toxics activists *practiced* and validated their commitments mainly at the local level, Greens could imagine themselves obligated to a national "Green" community, or even a worldwide Green movement. They could articulate their own work as one small contribution to a much broader project. They could feel like participants in a national movement charged with slowly building a national Green political will. Ridge and Seaview Greens, along with grassroots Green groups across the US, spent considerable time drafting statements for a national Green platform. It was of course a very open question whether nationally dispersed Greens in personalized communities could mount the sustained, concerted campaigns necessary to make the Green movement, or a Green party, a highly visible presence in national political arenas. The point is that the form of togetherness behind the "Green" identity might sustain a national political community more easily than a kind of togetherness based very largely on relationships in a local moral universe, and secondarily on a relatively ad hoc "mutual aid" principle. "Green" principles and "enviromental justice" principles were certainly both national in scope, and made possible nationwide collective identities, but the forms of togetherness underlying them differed significantly.

Numerous activists besides Greens have practiced a personalized form of community. They have defined themselves as individual, politicized bearers of commitment rather than as members of a collectivity who – like HAT members – drew on one specific tradition or locale to create bonds of togetherness. Accounts of contemporary grassroots or radical feminist groups suggest this personalized version of community (Buechler 1990; Echols 1989; Freeman 1975). Anti-nuclear activists in the Clamshell and Abalone Alliances, and the west coast Livermore Action Group

(LAG) put a similar stress on personalized community-building (Epstein 1991). As one LAG member explained, for instance, the goal of community-building was to "create a version of participation that was as complete as people could imagine ... " For LAG, communal feeling eased the decision activists made *as individuals* to get arrested:

> Each person was confronted with a decision: whether to step over the line and get arrested or not ... When people made the decision to step over the line and get arrested, they found that they also made the decision to step into a community that felt fulfilling and liberating (quoted in Epstein 1991: 8).

Compare Mrs. Sherman's perspective on sitting-in at welfare offices: with the same credo of "non-violence," Sherman based her actions on a sense of cultural authority that made individual acts meaningful through pre-existing membership in a collective identity.

Individuals in personalized communities cannot simply will themselves into the kind of community that sustained Mrs. Sherman. But politicized individuals like Greens have sometimes assumed their own practice of community is universally valid, that it satisfies universal desires. The LAG activist quoted above, for instance, stated that "*people* crave a certain kind of community" (emphasis mine). When movements practicing personalized politics use their assumptions about community-building to appeal to non-middle class and minority audiences, we can see the very particular, social parameters of their universalism.

Ridge and Seaview Greens, for instance, participated in "multicultural organizing" workshops designed to strengthen their ability to attract a non-white constituency. A workshop revealed this kind of universalism could be quite bounded culturally. But it also revealed why Greens would not be able to construct for themselves the more traditional community bonds that sustained HAT.

Multicultural ideology, culture-specific practice

The workshop on "racism and power" wove together themes of institutional power and personal change. It treated racism as an institutionalized form of cultural oppression.[20] The workshop facilitators expounded on the white "monoculture" to which most of the workshop attendees implicitly belonged. Equating "Western culture" with consumer capitalism, they described the "Wonder-breading process," through which majority (white) culture in the US obscures or weakens minority cultures. Along with this account of intergroup relations, the workshop taught the twenty Greens in attendance that making the Green "community" more culturally diverse meant being an individual culture-bridging agent. Multicultural alliance-building would mean making friends with people of color. Workshop facilitators wanted the workshop to integrate individual exploration with discussion of broad movement recruitment priorities. They asked participants to break down into small groups and discuss "what's my worst fear of dealing with racism?" and "what could the Greens gain from dealing multi-culturally?" We concluded by pondering both "what is the next step for me personally?" and "what is the next step for the Greens?" With a format that highlighted individual agency, the workshop assumed not only that activists would create a broader movement *as* individual political agents but that targeted groups would accept and appreciate the efforts of activists as individual culture-bridgers.

The activists understood their own cultural heritages through personal biography much more than through shared traditions or communal belonging. For nearly all of them, cultural background produced a very nuanced and conflicted sense of "I" much more than a membership in a "we." For example, one of the workshop exercises called for each attendee to briefly describe both "something positive" and "something negative" that they "got from their heritage." To my surprise, each of the roughly twenty activists created a well-crafted, seemingly spontaneous, long (3–8 minutes) narrative, far longer than necessary for what was supposed to have been a thirty-minute period of personal introductions. All but one of the attendees were white; a clear majority claimed a middle-class background. The stories bore little immediate resemblance to each other. Most activists specified particular ethnicities in their backgrounds, some expounded upon their religious upbringing. What the stories shared was that most described their narrator as "moving away from their heritages," as one activist put it. One said he didn't like the notion of "heritage" much at all, because heritage usually implied sexism and racism. This exercise itself assumed that people could take individualized, critical stances on their backgrounds as a matter of course.

Some people spoke with passion about their cultural backgrounds, while others struggled to find something noble in theirs; many recounted episodes of racism they now acknowledged in their own lives. The activists wanted to jettison the aspects of their white "heritage" that they claimed had blinded them to minority cultures. One of the exercises, in fact, involved "visualizing" being a member of a cultural minority group and seeing one's homeland destroyed by the products of Western culture. By owning up to racisms they had taken too much for granted in their own society and their own lives, these activists thought they would slowly free themselves of the noxious aspects of their own heritage as whites. The process would clear the way for multicultural contacts. But this self-critical approach to intercultural relations still built on the assumptions of a very specific culture – the culture of personalized politics. In trying to exorcise their cultural biases, the Greens did not see that the individualizing stance toward cultural heritage was itself just as culturally specific and limiting – even "monocultural" – as any of the arguably "racist" values they had learned from their heritages. Greens assumed that individualized expression was naturally good, and that it belonged in any good political relationship.[21]

The workshop gave Greens practice with a cultural form that might limit communication with other groups despite their best intentions. My field observations indicated that personalized community-building did in fact impede the Greens' multicultural initiatives. Greens adopted a strongly multiculturalist ideology, and upheld the environmental justice framework through which activists of color had come to understand toxics and related issues. But Green organizations such as Ridge and Seaview counted on task groups of self-empowered volunteers to carry out the organization's multicultural organizing agenda. Certainly individual Greens did voice strong interest in multicultural alliance-building but they were usually also involved in other projects. Any such project would depend on the willingness of individuals to sustain the project over a long period; the Green culture of personalized commitment made it difficult for the coordinating council to mandate multicultural organizing as an ongoing project and to assign volunteers if none were already available. No one person or group was charged with raising a multicultural organizing priority during discussion of other projects. It was hard for Greens to carry out initiatives that would require a lot of ongoing, centralized direction on behalf of a Green organization as a whole.[22]

Green group practices could produce other dilemmas for multicultural contact too: with a focus on personalized contact, Greens gave less attention to the ways they would represent the Green movement as a single collectivity to outsiders. Members of more tightly-bound activist communities could easily misunderstand the Greens' individualized style and infer that Green organizations must lack a seriousness of purpose or have only weak interest in them. Most Greens would face dilemmas of representing not only a Green collective identity, but a white one too. The Greens would have to appear as *white* activists to potential allies; no amount of contrition or racial self-rejection would neutralize their cultural background in the eyes of others. In their workshop, the Greens learned that they might individually absolve themselves of "whiteness" through critical self-exploration. But they did not develop a *collective* cultural identity *as* whites, though "whites for racial justice" or "cultural democrats" might have served. Activists who define themselves as a culturally united community ("African Americans") and expect that others are doing likewise would not have a ready category for relating to activists who insist that they are not what they appear.[23]

Certainly other aspects of Green activism besides its style of community-building could affect Greens' efforts to build alliances. The point here is that the individualization that Greens and other activists practiced is one of their most important and least discussed cultural characteristics, one with practical implications for building multicultural alliances. Multicultural ideology does not prepare activists for cross-cultural contact if its *practice* in everyday life is individualizing – and therefore limiting for contacts with groups in which individual empowerment matters less. A group like HAT has little basis for understanding or taking seriously an activist who operates as an individual political agent. In practice, the universalism of Green multicultural ideology ended up being parochial in ways Greens did not imagine. But "fighting for the community" the way HAT did limits the horizons of political community, too.

CONCLUSION: SEGMENTED SOLIDARITIES

De Tocqueville (1945) suggested that people who got involved in the life of a local community might learn a kind of civic virtue that could be transferred to broader, perhaps national arenas. In the 1970s and 1980s, the citizen activism of ACORN and the other organizing networks which prefigured HAT regenerated this hope amongst scholars and activists with communitarian sympathies. While Bellah *et al.* (1985: 213) cautioned that this kind of activism focused mostly on local concerns, they held out the hope it could still provide examples of "how a renewal of democratic citizenship at the national level might be achieved." One scholar-activist, who signed onto the first US Green manifesto in hopes of having located a true citizen renewal, has argued that local communitarian-style activism is the seedbed for a reinvigorated national public life (Boyte 1989, 1984). Boyte revisits the argument that local community activism will produce activists who come to develop broader agendas and wider horizons of solidarity:

In *democratic*, populist movements, as people are moved to activism in *defense* of their rights, traditions and institutions, they change. . .They discover in themselves and their traditions new resources and potentials ... They find out new political facts about the world, they build networks and seek contacts with other groups of the powerless to forge a broader group identity (1981: 63–64; emphases his).

In a similar vein, students of anti-toxics activism have wondered aloud whether local anti-toxics groups could become the basis for a social movement with a broader ideological perspective and a broader constituency than toxics victims alone (Edelstein 1988; Freudenberg 1984). From the mid-1980s to the present, anti-toxics activism has continued to spread to locales throughout the US.[24] It is very much an empirical question whether or not this nationwide, community mobilization against toxics will build regional or national institutions that address multiple issues and ally with other movements, or whether it "will remain a broad-based special-interest movement" (Edelstein 1988: 168). One student of anti-toxics activism (Bullard 1990, 1989; Bullard and Wright 1987) has already chronicled a nationwide, black environmental justice movement of activists like HAT members who fight toxic pollution as community-based activists extending a civil rights agenda.

This chapter suggests there are good cultural[25] reasons why local anti-toxics groups and their resource centers may not develop a movement that broadens solidarity beyond separate locales and loose mutual aid. The very meaning of public commitment for community activists such as those in HAT inheres in localized moral universes that in turn sustain limited horizons of solidarity. This is not to claim that the "change" that Boyte writes of glowingly can never happen. But there is no reason to suppose a process intrinsic to local involvement in even the most democratic of civic organizations produces the imagination for a broader political community, instead of a strengthened communitarianism at the local level, and a wary mutual aid perspective at regional or national levels. Anti-toxics leader Lois Gibbs articulated above the overall movement strategy that complements the segmented solidarity in the present anti-toxics movement: "local actions add up to cause major change throughout society."

While anti-toxics alliances and regional networks were still very much in the making during this study, my evidence suggests that Gibbs' strategy has resonated with local anti-toxics activists' notions of how citizen movements do and should work. Both HAT and ACES became members of a new Community Environmental League (CEL) in California, a coalition of local anti-toxics groups. ACES' leader Laura explained that at CEL's second conference, an activist pointed out that decisions about toxics are "centralized" but that the focus of CEL was decentralized and grassroots. Laura resolved, "That's OK, we stop them up," and gestured with her hand as a make-believe "plug" of grassroots groups, stopping up a large corporate "drain." At an earlier conference which formed CEL, group representatives voiced wariness about giving the new coalition the power to make a lot of claims on either their energies or their political allegiances. For instance, the activists preferred that CEL produce a "bulletin" with news updates instead of a "newsletter" with opinion pieces. They opted for CEL to function, in the words of one white activist, as a "resource center" offering information. Concluded a latino man from Los Angeles, "we get together when we need each other; let's fight our own."

Local communitarian activist groups have enunciated populist, localist, or community betterment themes that may resonate with many more Americans than does the individualized cultural revolt in antinuclear, environmental, or feminist personalized communities. Widely shared political themes may draw a more receptive public audience than the abstract, sometimes angry cultural critique of Greens and like-minded groups. But mainstream political ideologies do not necessarily broaden activists' sense of public virtue beyond local horizons. In everyday practice, these widely shared themes have accompanied movements with segmented, local solidarities. A view of political commitment in practice gives reason for some wariness about de Tocqueville's hope, rekindled by contemporary communitarian thinkers, that local community involvements would broaden citizens' horizons of public virtue.

While locally based, communitarian-style activism builds more efficiently organized groups, personalized politics complements a vision of a political community broader than one locale or one people. In everyday practice, both cultures of commitment select for a culturally specific kind of activist. If both cultures lead to different strengths and weaknesses, then why would activists not overcome the parochialisms of each culture, picking and choosing characteristics of each to create the strongest organizations with the broadest scope? Need the cultural differences persist? The concluding chapter suggests how both personalized politics and local community-based activism could in fact overcome some of their limits in a broader political community that would integrate both into a broader division of political labor. But first we must understand why the cultural differences in commitment and community forms have persisted. Chapters 5 and 6 explain these cultural differences, focusing primarily on the factors that sustain personalized politics.

In Chapter 5, we find that activists use the cultural skills that their class backgrounds make available to balance "personal" and "political." They live that balance through their choice of work and private lifestyles as well as their involvements in activist organizations. Embedded in class-shaped preferences that activists often take for granted, styles of political commitment cannot easily be changed.

5

Culture, class, and life-ways of activism

Even though Greens could not rally around communal traditions the way HAT members could, they still wanted to live publicly responsible lives. And they shared assumptions on how to go about it. When Carl and Linda argued about what the Ridge Greens should be doing, neither questioned that good activism meant individualized, self-empowered activism. Why were Greens able to take this assumption for granted? Not all people can or want to make such personalized commitments. The personalized style is a cultural response to a lack of shared, traditional cultural authority of the sort HAT could invoke. But most people do not feel comfortable speaking out as individuals. Most people do not develop their own elaborate, individual political ideologies at length, at least not without explicit guidance from a leader like Ben Norton of HAT or Laura of ACES.[1] Why did Greens assume it possible to build an *organization* out of personalized political wills, instead of just living out their visions, each on her own? And why did they continue carrying individualized commitments even when organizations like the Ridge Greens endured such difficulties?

We can answer these questions by understanding how activists' socioeconomic backgrounds and the broader institutional arenas for activism shape their opportunities for commitment. This chapter and the next treat these two contexts for commitment. This chapter focuses on the class-linked culture that makes personalized politics possible to begin with. Activists' class backgrounds did not *cause* their activism, nor did they cause activists to follow one commitment style rather than another. In the case of personalized politics, the Greens' disparate social identities made personalism a workable basis for togetherness where other

146

bases would not do. Those social identities themselves were precipitates of an institutional context for activism that I treat in Chapter 6. But I argue that cultural skills associated with professional middle-class work and lifestyle make it possible for activists like Greens to share a personalized culture of activism to begin with, in the relative absence of other shared reference points.

This chapter contrasts the lifestyles of anti-toxics activists in this study with those of Greens in order to highlight what is distinctive about the Greens' whole-life commitments. Green and anti-toxics activists' logics of commitment developed within the context of differing educational experiences and career trajectories that became apparent from surveys I carried out with national samples from each movement. For Greens, assumptions about worthwhile work and private life became part of an entire politicized lifestyle that most anti-toxics activists did not share. This chapter illustrates the ways both Greens and anti-toxics activists balanced political involvements with the rest of their lives, but it focuses primarily on the Greens and the commitment logic that they have shared with many other post-1960s activists. Profiles of selected core members from local Green and anti-toxics groups will illustrate the different logics of commitment.

Some accounts explain personalized politics by tracing it to activists' psychological needs (Marx 1979), or to an "extended adolescence" (Habermas 1975) that well-educated activists have the luxury to experience. Accounts of personalized politics amongst college students during the 1960s, for instance, have treated it as part of a psychological adjustment to transitions in the life course (Whalen and Flacks 1989; Flacks 1976; Swanson 1979). In this view, personal expressiveness served to create a comfortable, supportive environment for college-age young people or other socially marginalized people coming to terms with hard decisions about work, family, and personal identity. This account would not answer the question of why these activists would bother to define their collective actions *as* politics. But it might complement the arguments in Chapter 2 about the cultural context of personalized politics: the sense of an individualized break with cultural authorities that Greens articulated might indicate that these activists were struggling with dilemmas of maturation. But evidence from demographic surveys of Greens and anti-toxics activists suggests it will be more useful to link personalized politics with social-structural attributes rather than with developmental needs.

I use data on age, schooling, and occupation to argue that Greens tended to bring different cultural skills to their activism than did anti-toxics activists – skills that are more available to people with a lot of schooling than to others. When widely shared, these skills made it more possible for activists to construct movement organizations with the personalized style. Little systematic demographic data are available on personalized politics in the US. The little published data that exist describe activists that are relatively youthful and highly educated (Scaminaci and Dunlap 1986; Ladd *et al.* 1983; see also Epstein 1991). And few reliable demographic surveys of anti-toxics activists were taken prior to my survey.[2] Grassroots social movement organizations produce a number of extra challenges for survey research. I detail the procedures chosen for surmounting these challenges in Appendix I; here I describe the survey research in brief.

US Greens from twenty states met in Eugene, Oregon in 1989 for a platform-writing conference. The same year, grassroots anti-toxics activists from twenty-seven states met in Arlington, Virginia for a conference organized by the Citizens' Clearinghouse for Hazardous Wastes. I distributed survey questionnaires to participants in one large general assembly at both conferences.[3] At the Green conference, I chose the most important plenary session, the one at which final votes were taken on Green platform planks developed at the conference. At the anti-toxics conference, I chose the address by keynote speakers; other than an awards luncheon, this assembly constituted the largest at the conference. The response rate at the Green assembly was roughly 52 percent; at the anti-toxics assembly it was roughly 50 percent.[4] These response rates compare favorably with those obtained in the very few similar surveys of post-1960s social activists.[5]

Anti-toxics activists and Greens not only tended to come from different parts of the social ladder, but their family lives also differed. It would be misleading, though, to say the activists' social backgrounds predisposed them to one culture of activism or the other in a single, unidirectional relationship. We need to think further about how social background relates to activism. I argue that activists make ongoing, interconnected decisions (or assumptions) about work, personal life, and political activity which are part of different logics of commitment. In everyday experience, work and private life are *part of* decisions about political involvement, rather than purely independent variables that cause or inhibit political commitment.

FORMS OF THE ACTIVIST LIFE

Life-ways

Commitment to activism is part of what I will call a life-way. By life-way I mean an overall pattern of public and private involvements – in work, family, and political life – within one biography.[6] Committing oneself to activism means making ongoing decisions about how much of life and what parts of life one will devote to political activity rather than other aspects of life. Life-ways show through in everyday interaction, but are not necessarily deliberate plans; we can think of them instead as patterns of deciding and improvising one's way through the life course. They are, in other words, kinds of practices. The theory of practice that I applied to the question of commitment in Chapter 1 is again useful here. Recent cultural theory suggested that we think of culture influencing action by offering shared ways of doing things – practices that people take for granted most of the time. Culture provides the life-ways, or patterns of practice, that people enact as they build their own lives. Some theorizing about practice has used the term "strategy" to denote patterns of deciding and acting, not necessarily deliberate, that a sociologist can reconstruct from observing a group or an individual in everyday interaction (Bourdieu 1990, 1984, 1977; Swidler 1986). But the word "strategy" is misleading; it implies thoroughly deliberate, strategic planning, rather than taken-for-granted practices that may or may not be chosen intentionally. I use the term "life-way" to avoid the unwanted connotations of "strategy."

Different life-ways produce different life chances over time. An activist who leaves a graduate school program to become a low-paid, full-time movement organizer both alters his immediate position in employment markets and his long-term market chances. He also makes possible for himself a different kind of commitment than that of an activist who limits her political involvements to ones that fit into time left over after work. That is why I emphasize that relations toward work and personal life are part of one's relationship to political commitment, and not simply prior determinants of it. We can think of occupation, family life, and activist involvements as interactive variables whose form of interaction depends on the life-way of which they are part.

Two life-ways of activism

How do activists decide that they should juggle their careers, families, and activism in one way rather than another? Life-ways do not get individually re-invented from scratch in thousands of activist lives. Different movement cultures presuppose, and encourage, different life-ways in their members, and I will call these life-ways of activism. Many Americans who become political activists have done so in order to make private life more satisfying (Flacks 1988). This temporary trade-off between public, political involvement and private life is the predominant life-way for citizen activists in the contemporary US. Those relatively few Americans that commit themselves to "history-making," to political activism over the long haul, endure tensions between public, political involvement and building a private life.

Many activists in both Green and anti-toxics movement groups experienced a tension between private life and political involvement. I heard complaints about long meetings and a sense of being "over-committed" in ACES, HAT, and the Green movement alike. But while these complaints were both nearly universal and constant in the Green movement, highly involved anti-toxics activists voiced them mainly during large specific projects or organizing drives. Activists defined the tension between private life and activism differently in anti-toxics and Green groups, and they defined "politics" differently too. Greens wanted to change the meaning and practice of both "everyday life" (work and personal lifestyle) and of "politics." Most anti-toxics activists, on the other hand, saw a tension between the two in terms of physical demands, but mostly assumed them to be separate spheres of activity. For the most part they did not try to innovate new definitions of "political." The anti-toxics activists were not for the most part concerned with innovating new kinds of political practice. They did not practice nonconventional lifestyles or nonconventional relations to work as part of a politicized way of life. The two kinds of activist participated in movement cultures that encouraged different life-ways of activism entwined with different socioeconomic opportunities.

PERSONALIZED POLITICS AS A STRATIFIED PRACTICE

The survey results indicated that Green activists averaged roughly the same age as anti-toxics activists, with a roughly parallel age distribution (see Table 5.1). If personalized politics results from developmental dilemmas as some accounts have argued, then we would have to ask why Greens had more developmental dilemmas than anti-toxics activists at the same stage in life. It is entirely possible that the psychological transformations that accompany becoming a Green-style activist are different

Table 5.1 *Age distribution at Green and anti-toxics conferences*

	Greens %	Anti-toxics activists %
AGE		
18–29	7	11
30–34	28	17
35–39	13	20
18–39	48	48
40–44	18	20
45–49	13	9
40–49	31	29
50–54	8	5
55–59	3	5
60 and over	11	14
	n = 72	n = 133

from those that people undergo when they join a local anti-toxics effort. But it is one thing to say that different life-ways produce different kinds or amounts of personal stress in contemporary American culture, and another thing to say that psychological differences or abnormalities cause different life-ways. At the cultural level of analysis, we need to ask what kinds of (culturally transmitted) life-ways underlie Green or anti-toxics activism.

While the age distributions at both conferences were fairly similar, the education, occupation, and family lifestyle typical of attendees at each varied markedly. Greens' schooling levels formed a nearly perfect bell curve centered over "some graduate work," while the clear majority of anti-toxics activists had received a lesser amount of schooling (see Table 5.2).

The figures on anti-toxics activists vary somewhat from what we would expect given the movement identity that anti-toxics leaders have promoted. CCHW leaders have described anti-toxics activists as high-school educated and working class, like anti-toxics pioneer Lois Gibbs. The figures here certainly allow that to be the case for some activists, but it is possible that CCHW's characterization fits its local, non-activist constituencies somewhat better than it describes all *core grassroots members*. Since CCHW literature has emphasized the role of people of color in the anti-toxics movement, a note on race is in order too. The survey indicates that grassroots leadership in local anti-toxics groups

Table 5.2 *Highest amount of schooling obtained by Greens and anti-toxics activists*

Schooling	Greens %	Anti-toxics activists %
Some high school or less	1	2
High school graduate	1	8
Some college	15	47
some technical school or community college	n.a.	9
tech. school/comm. college degree	n.a.	10
some college or university	n.a.	29
College or university graduate	19	14
Some graduate work	26	9
Master's level degree	19	12
Doctorate	17	6
	n=72	n=131

continued to be largely white at the end of the 1980s – 93 percent of my survey respondents.[7] By the start of the 1990s this may have begun to change as minority locales began mobilizing specifically to fight toxic hazards (Bullard 1993, 1990). HAT was one of the very first such groups in the US.[8] Some research finds that minority locales have a greater likelihood of being selected for toxic waste sites, even with income or property values controlled (Bryant and Mohai 1992), leading us to expect greater minority representation among core activists. While research on waste sitings suggests potential minority constituencies for anti-toxics activism, it does not directly inform us about the racial background of leading, local anti-toxics activists at the start of the 1990s.

The above statistics point to a structural basis for the different lifeways of activism described before. A grassroots movement organization mainly comprised of members with a lot of schooling has the resources for a different kind of group togetherness than one in which the average amount of schooling is closer to that of the general adult population – 12¾ years (Bureau of the Census 1980). Higher education at four-year colleges and universities teaches, reinforces, and certifies highly individualized skills, personalized expression, self-direction, and "original" achievements (Bourdieu 1984; Bourdieu and Passeron 1977; Bernstein [1971, 1973] 1975, 1976; see also Bowles and Gintis 1976). So it is likely that people with much college-level schooling will have had more practice with individualized ways of doing things in organized groups. They will have had more reinforcement for individualized skills than people who attain less or no college-level schooling. These practices are not equally accessible across the population of an advanced industrial society, then, and people with higher levels of schooling have greater likelihood of access to them. "Self-actualization" is also an important component of high cultural status in the US (Lamont 1992) – a basis for erecting interactional boundaries against those not judged as self-actualized.

It is useful, then, to think of personalized politics as a stratified practice. The term "stratified practice" reminds us that the taken-for-granted skills upon which personalized politics depends are not equally accessible to all. A group that has the option of practicing this kind of politics needs for most of its members to share cultural skills that are socially stratified. Greens' high average levels of schooling suggest that they could for the most part take for granted and share an individualizing orientation to their politics.

Skill at producing an individualized, articulate style could be considered a form of "cultural capital" because this skill is associated with social advancement or cultural honor (Lamont and Lareau 1988; Bourdieu 1984). Cultural capital is a metaphor for skills that cultural elites – teachers and school counselors, managers, critics – value and can thus lead to social advancement (Bourdieu 1984). In a society whose institutions value individual originality and self-direction, people who act, talk, and judge as separate, even unique, individuals are ones that carry a lot of cultural capital. A person who has grown up in a family with a lot of cultural capital and has a university education, especially if in an elite institution, will "naturally" move through everyday life as a distinctive individual, taking for granted a virtuosity in language and self-development, assuming that personal ideas and opinions *matter*.

While "cultural capital" can be an effective short-hand way to signify valued cultural skills, it introduces troublesome assumptions and connotations that I want to avoid. As Lamont and Lareau have argued (1988), cultural capital has gotten defined in widely varying, inconsistent ways as scholars probe relations between power and culture. I do not want to claim that personalized politics itself is a route to greater social or cultural power for activists, as the term "cultural capital" could imply. The term has been used sometimes with the assumption that people want to display their cultural capital in order to secure prestige. Yet I emphasize that activists' personalized ways of acting or speaking result from taken-for-granted preferences and orientations, not conscious attempts to impress or exclude others. Erroneous but still-common misinterpretations also read the term cultural capital as designating skills that are somehow "better" or more desirable in absolute terms. I use "stratified practices" to describe taken-for-granted skills or ways of doing things that are unequally accessible by a broad population, regardless of their consequences for social or cultural mobility, and regardless of their "intrinsic" worth.[9]

The Greens displayed their taken-for-granted cultural skills in the way they articulated the abstract Ten Key Values and in the way they emphasized talk itself. They took for granted that new recruits had such skills too. Airdale anti-toxics activists, on the other hand, did not put so much emphasis on ideology and abstract values. Recall that being "in the ballpark" ideologically was "close enough." Board members in HAT did not greatly emphasize ideology either; they accepted the staffperson's arguments about the "community" will and about environmental justice without debate. Further, Greens committed themselves to activism as highly empowered individuals who took their own efficacy for granted. Being an activist for them meant developing and expressing articulate, individual viewpoints, being able to talk about how Green values worked in one's own life.[10] Green movement groups prized individual effort and recruited new members on the assumption that they would want their own individual voices to resonate strongly in collective projects. They would want to identify themselves as much as their "community" as a whole with social change. In this vein, it is interesting to hear how a leading US Green theorist (Spretnak 1986) summed up the predicament of Greens who try to become more like communitarian-style activists:

In spite of the genuine enthusiasm I have witnessed in Green audiences when Harry Boyte presents his ideas on community-building, the demographic swell that is the Baby Boom generation is probably the most individualistic in history and does not know how to be otherwise.

Some of the best work on the everyday interaction styles of the educated middle class predates the wide diffusion of cultural stratification research. Like Bourdieu, sociolinguist Basil Bernstein (1971, 1973) associated individualized expression with high social status, and went further than Bourdieu in specifying its qualities in everyday perception and talk. Bernstein found highly educated, middle-class people more readily individuate themselves in speech than do working-class people, using more expressions like "I think." They rely more on patterns of speech that facilitate abstraction and self-expression, and less on common folk phrases or expressions that assume speaker and listener share specific experiences within a specific community. Once again, Green activists with their lengthy debates over platform statements, their consensus decision-making process, and their frequent go-arounds of participation at meetings depended on shared cultural skills more readily available to and comfortable for highly educated middle-class people than other strata.

The contrasting communication styles Bernstein studied produce different modes of valorizing the individual in collective action. The more individuated style constructs a distinctive self of relatively great importance within a group, a self whose private thoughts and acts matter to collective harmony. As a sociologist of education, Bernstein applied his inquiry to pedagogical questions; he wanted to understand the difference between a pedagogy of strict rules and a seemingly looser pedagogy in which formal rules mattered less, but personality and private habits mattered more in assessing educational achievement.[11] The same principles have been applied to studying work cultures[12] and they make sense for comparing social movement cultures too. Greens with their individualized, portable commitments made their own personhood an important site for political action. As we will see, they lived personal lives in line with the abstract categories of their politics, without the support of traditional community institutions. Most communitarian-style activists put less emphasis on the political value of individual efforts and stress collective efforts within the bounds of formally public life. Following Durkheim, Bernstein characterized his two contrasting communication styles as producing different forms of group solidarity. His analysis complements my own comparative study of group togetherness.

Access to relatively rare cultural skills can work like an "entry fee," then, giving activists the resources for participating in a movement group that requires a great deal of self-expression. Activists with these kinds of resources can play the role expected in a movement that stipulates, as we saw earlier, that "all Greens are leaders." Not all activists have the means for this entry fee, and so it constitutes one important basis of social selection for personalized politics.

Of course, access to these cultural skills does not by itself determine that activists will use them to practice personalized politics. At the 1989 conference, for instance, the Left Greens mentioned in Chapter 2 had chafed at the personalized tone of the conference. These activists were not appreciably different in age or background.[13] And despite the "left" name, they did not differ dramatically from other Green activists in their basic Green beliefs: Left Green caucus members had planned a very small caucus gathering and were very surprised when 75 or more Green activists showed up. The Left Greens found out that many other Greens agreed with the critique of capitalism they promoted, though disagreeing with using explicitly "anti-capitalist" language.

The most important difference between Left Greens and the others was a *style* born of a different social identity. Left Greens identified themselves in terms of a tradition, a reference point for their social identities – the "Left." Affiliation with the Left offered a standard for togetherness that made activists more like fellow "comrades" in a cause than like politicized individuals who, lacking a well-established standard for membership, needed a more personalized basis for togetherness. Left Greens were able to participate in the conference's "alternative," personalized organizational formats; they could perform in the individual "go-arounds" in working groups because they had access to the necessary cultural skills. Their social identities as "left" meant that they had more in common than other Greens too, but the other participants at the conference did not share in their "left" reference point. The personalized organizational norms at the conference withstood their criticism.

In contrast with the Greens, anti-toxics activists tended to bring less schooling to their activism than Greens. While they varied in their educational backgrounds, there was not an overwhelming majority that shared the experiences and preferences of college graduates as there was among Greens. Anti-toxics activists on the whole would be less likely to share in the individualizing predisposition of many Greens. They would be less likely to think it natural or appropriate to talk at length about themselves in groups the way Greens did in the multicultural organizing workshop, or to contribute a highly elaborated, individually nuanced opinion the way Greens did in lengthy debates over their platform. The anti-toxics activists as a whole were less likely to have the cultural means, the "entry fee," for participating in highly individualizing groups. Those anti-toxics activists with college educations, like James Shaver of HAT, and the ACES leader, had the cultural skills that would reinforce their own personalized politics as described earlier. But they also shared with the rest of their respective groups a social identity that was rooted in a specific community. They acted in relation to their specific local communities as well as in reference to a more abstract, imagined community of empowered individuals. They upheld the group norms of local community-based activism in their organizations.

The anti-toxics conference did not devote nearly the same amount of energy to general ideologies as the Green conference did. At the Green conference, participants spent much time whittling down a 500-page collection of locally drafted position papers to a roughly 23-page platform. A Green leader talked about breaking down the abstract Ten Key Values in order to make them more accessible to a broader public. At the anti-toxics conference, in contrast, activists went to pre-arranged workshops on organizing, technical issues, using the media, and a single philosophically oriented session entitled "Working for the Long Haul." These activists did not speak of needing to package their ideology for those less skilled at ideological sophistry. While some certainly had the means for engaging comfortably in this kind of discourse, they did not predominate as a majority. And crucially, these activists shared a common rootedness in local community milieux and an interest in applying any general ideological statements to their specific locales. "Good activism" did not mean creating extensively developed ideological positions.

THE MEANING OF "CLASS" FOR LIFE-WAYS OF ACTIVISM

Greens and anti-toxics activists tended to differ in their occupations as well as their schooling. Greens more frequently fit inside the occupational categories of the broad professional middle class. This is not surprising given the figures on schooling and the perception shared by many employers, education professionals, and sociologists that much professional work depends on self-direction and individual articulateness. The data on schooling and livelihoods (see Table 5.3) combine to suggest that it is useful to retain class – in a broad sense – as a term in the discussion about personalized political commitments. The trouble with many arguments about class and recent activism is that they are limited by the assumption that if class relates to activism, the relationship works through a *class interest* in movement *issues*. They assume that class matters only if it turns out that an identifiable class will benefit in economic or status terms from, say, a change in environmental policy. Arguments that reject a determining role for class in recent activism are rejecting the same hypothesized relation between class interests and movement issues (Habermas 1987; Offe 1985; Kitschelt 1985). Whether or not class interest plays a role in an activist's attraction to a specific issue is a different question from that of the relation of class to commitment style. While some would argue that class *interest* shapes the orientation to personalized commitments as well, I argue it is more acccurate to conceive of class *culture* – distinctive cultural skills and preferences – rather than class interest as making personalized commitments appealing.

Table 5.3 *Selected comparisons of Greens and anti-toxics activist livelihoods**

Livelihood	Greens %	Anti-toxics activists %
Managerial	5	8
Technical specialist	8	4
Social/cultural specialist	48	18
(human service)	(15)	(8)
Clerical	9	15
Skilled, semi-skilled, unskilled labor	3	10
Housekeeper	0	14
Retired	9	10
	n=65	n=115

* figures do not add up to 100 percent

If we see how Greens and anti-toxics activists distribute themselves by occupation, we will find that life-way patterns and commitment style illuminate more regarding the role of class than does a class interest interpretation. To explore the thesis on class interest, I distributed Green and anti-toxics activists' occupations in terms of categories derived from Kriesi's (1989) work on class in new social movements, and from US census categories. A substantial number of Greens fit into a part of the professional middle class which Kriesi and others have termed a "new class."[14] Different arguments have given this "new class" different boundaries, and ascribed to it different kinds of opposition to other classes.[15] New class theorists have argued that people with valuable cultural skills have an objective interest in constructing social arrangements that reward cultural virtuosity rather than money or property. They have an interest in valorizing their own cultural skills. In this view, the Greens' "alternative" culture and their personalized commitment style could be a strategy for promoting their class interests by displaying opposition to capitalist materialism and advocating humanistic self-realization instead. New class theorists have included "social" or "cultural" specialists – workers in the arts, media, and pure sciences – within that class because of these workers' educations and because their occupations do not involve managing the interests of capital (Gouldner 1979; Kriesi 1989; Brint 1984; see also Parkin 1968; Ehrenreich and Ehrenreich 1977; Ladd 1978).

Following Kriesi, I limited the new class category to "social/cultural specialists," those professionals and semiprofessionals in teaching, academic research, social work, the arts and journalism, and medical services. I borrowed Kriesi's category "technical specialist" as well, which included natural scientists (but not academic faculty), engineers, computer specialists, and laboratory technicians – all of whom would be highly educated like social/cultural specialists but involved in different, less humanistic uses of their schooling. The managerial category included managers and administrators in small firms as well as large companies.[16] The proportion of social/cultural specialists among Greens was two and one-half times that for anti-toxics activists. And twice as many Greens (61 percent) made livings in an occupation typically dependent on college education and/or highly specialized technical training as did anti-toxics activists (30 percent). These figures by themselves would suggest that new class interest does have a relationship with personalized politics.

The Greens' typically high levels of schooling gave them cultural skills that they could have used either for work in Kriesi's new class occupations, or in relatively lucrative jobs involving technological expertise which Kriesi did not include in the new class. Greens pursued both kinds of occupation, but more did decide to pursue "humanistic" work in social and cultural specialties that would tend to earn less income than their skills might otherwise win them. In fact, 62 percent of Greens in the survey reported household incomes *lower* than $25,000 a year, while only 34 percent of anti-toxics activists drew on household incomes this low. Jobs that "help people" or else don't directly "perpetuate the system" are often ones that involve just the sorts of social work or cultural specialization Kriesi emphasized. These are also jobs that enabled activists like Greens to integrate work into a life-way that makes private life and personal choices directly part of one's politics. Anti-toxics activists, in contrast, did not usually assume that being a good activist meant choosing occupations by explicitly "political" criteria. They were constructing a different kind of life in which livelihood and political commitments are relatively separate.

Some Greens did pursue technical occupations that would also demand high amounts of schooling. It is interesting that while technical specialists made up a small percentage of both samples of activists, the proportion of Green technicians was greater. So we might say those few (five) Greens in that category used their schooling and cultural skills differently than predicted in Kriesi's and some other new class arguments. But we can avoid the limits of class-interest models of political commitment and interpret this finding in terms of cultural skills and commitment. Several variations of the basic Green life-way of activism could accommodate technical employment: being a computer programmer or a lab technician might "pay the rent" as a sort of necessary evil in a life committed overall to Green values. Alternatively, it might involve using those skills to advance "Green values" either through environmental research, or through technical assistance to a non-profit or culturally alternative business. Additional survey information on these five Greens indicates these options account for four of the five. There are certainly technical jobs that could complement Green values, but in the US economy the percentage of these is limited. Schooling and cultural skills provide parameters of opportunity for building a life; information on activists' life-ways clarifies how activists use those opportunities.

The figures on "housekeepers" key us in to the ways cultural skills shape how activists relate to their gender identities, and are worth a comment too. Lois Gibbs and other anti-toxics leaders have characterized grassroots anti-toxics activists as blue-collar workers and housewives. These leaders have drawn a picture of anti-toxics activists as all-American, non-subversive "plain folks." While local constituencies for anti-toxics groups may be strongly blue-collar, the grassroots leadership appeared much less so in this survey, though still more blue-collar than the Greens. Since housekeeping and child care are still largely women's occupations, the differing proportion of housekeepers in each sample might follow from differing gender balances in each: women made up 44 percent of the Green sample and 66 percent of the anti-toxics. But it is striking that not one of the Greens self-identified as keeping house or raising children inside the home. Highly educated, culturally unconventional women activists would probably not consider themselves "housekeepers" even if they had no occupation outside the home. "Housewife" would not be enough of an individually "empowered" position to fit the typical life-way of a Green activist.

Greens and anti-toxics activists would tend to map onto a class grid, then, in different ways. A substantial number of Greens fit into a narrowly defined "new class" category, while some others fit a loosely defined "professional middle class" only. Differences in schooling meant that groups of Greens and anti-toxics activists would likely have different opportunities and preferences for political commitment. Cultural skills learned or reinforced in school structured Greens' opportunities for creating life-ways around personalized politics. These life-ways could include either the more humanistic or the more technological occupations within the broad professional middle class.

The strongest interpretation of the link between Greens' social backgrounds and their personalized commitment styles, then, is one that

Table 5.4 *Family life characteristics of Greens and anti-toxics activists*

	Greens %	Anti-toxics activists %
Partnership status		
Single, never married	44	17
Married	26	71
Partnered	n.a.	8
Divorced or separated (presently)	28	5
Children		
Yes	43	66
No	42	29
No response	11	5

emphasizes the taken-for-granted *culture* of the broad professional middle-class strata, rather than specific new class *interest*. If the Greens' personalized style derived from a class interest in appearing culturally distinctive or anti-materialist, then we would not expect them to worry about their difficulties in maintaining their organizations. Their individual virtuosity would be the end in itself – a display of purity or the ability to thrive in spite of relatively low incomes. Chapter 2 showed that clearly Greens did concern themselves with maintaining their collective efforts. It makes more sense to understand the Green life-ways in terms of everyday cultural skills and preferences, rather than as strategic attempts to gain honor or advantage by displaying cultural sophistication or a fashionable disdain for materialism.[17]

The survey data on occupation abstract one important variable out of an ongoing, practical logic that demographic information alone cannot reconstruct. We can also interpret data on private life in terms of the practical logic of life-ways.

THE PRIVATE SIDE OF PERSONALIZED POLITICS

Being "political" for Greens meant assuming that private as well as public life ought to be lived in light of a Green political imagination. Greens are hardly the first group of cultural dissenters to advocate practicing their beliefs systematically in everyday life. What is interesting is that they do so without the kind of centralized, communal authority that has often supported such efforts.

Anti-toxics and Green activists tended to live different family as well as different career lives (Table 5.4). While 44 percent of the Greens were

Table 5.5 *Television viewing by Greens and anti-toxics activists*

Amount of viewing (hours per week)	Greens %	Anti-toxics activists %
Do not watch TV[18]	(17)	10
3 hours or less	77	33
4–7 hours	13	30
8–14 hours	10	19
15–20 hours	0	5
21–27 hours	0	2
28 hours or more	0	0
	n = 60	n = 126

single and had never been married, only about a sixth of the anti-toxics activists were in this category. Forty-three percent of the Greens had children, compared with 66 percent of the anti-toxics activists. Nearly 30 percent of Greens were presently divorced or separated, in contrast with only 5 percent of anti-toxics activists.

Barring psychological explanations, these figures suggest that Greens brooked more cultural unconventionality in their personal lives. While anti-toxics activists may have had as high a divorce rate as Greens, they remarried more readily. People with a highly individualized sense of political commitment may carry the same commitment style in their private lives. Or, establishing or reestablishing family ties in heterosexual relationships may be a less important part of making a life for Greens than for anti-toxics activists. These figures suggest that Greens were more likely than anti-toxics activists to distance themselves from traditional images of family life, in the same way that they held other, traditional reference points for social identity at an ambivalent distance, as we saw in Chapter 2.

Private consumption habits and over-all lifestyle varied between the two groups as well. Figures on television viewing (Table 5.5) provide a simple proxy for cultural "conventionality" in private life. A number of studies (for instance, Gerbner *et al.* 1982) have argued that TV programming presents a cultural "mainstream" of stereotypical characters and messages, so that viewing over a long period actually "mainstreams" the opinions of viewers on social and political issues. TV viewing is nearly universal, so it can serve as a one-shot measure of participation in the US cultural mainstream.

Individual television viewing averages at least 29 hours a week in the US (Comstock 1978) so both anti-toxics and Green activists are unusual.

Still, the marked difference in viewing between the two groups is interesting because the Greens' particularly low amounts of television viewing
make sense within their typical life-way of activism. In a political
community defined by personalized commitments, private television-
watching had political implications. Since Greens tended to associate TV,
and most mass culture, with manipulative corporate profit-making,
watching any TV at all would represent a lapse of individual political
judgment, and perhaps dull one's politics too. More than one Green told
me that the household TV stayed in a closet, the screen to the wall.
Greens' reception of the survey question itself was very telling. Nearly a
fifth took the time to write in on the survey sheet that they did not watch
television at all. Others wrote notes saying that their viewing needed to
be measured in hours per month or year.

During the two years of field work I learned to read the Greens'
lifestyle choices as politicized choices in a way that those of most anti-
toxics activists in this study were not. I sensitized myself to those choices,
remembering to bring organic or homemade dishes to the Greens'
parties, for instance, while seeking out more conventional, store-bought
party foods for anti-toxics gatherings. While learning the consumption
cultures of the different activist groups, I made some mistakes along the
way; the results could be both embarrassing and enlightening. A pie I had
made from scratch for an ACES party taught me more about gender,
status, and consumption than a whole night's worth of field notes.
Without giving it a lot of thought, I hoped the pie effort might show my
appreciation for ACES at best, or my commitment to helping make their
celebration a success, at least. One of the older men in the group
remarked extensively on the homely creation, and then showed off for
me: standing with me and another member's husband, he engaged the
other man in a long mutual reminiscence, loaded with slang, about the
cars the two of them used to fix up. The wife of another member joked
at some length about how hard the pie crust was, how it would break the
plastic forks we were using to eat it. I gathered that in some circles,
homemade desserts were a little too precious for community group
events, and that at any rate, men as a rule did not make them.

I learned that politics or philosophy made for normal party talk or
phone chat with Greens, while I trod gingerly around these topics at anti-
toxics gatherings as I heard others doing likewise. For the Greens, long
political discussions at parties were simply a taken-for-granted part of
being a "political person," a person who trained a political imagination
on private pursuits as well as public issues. Heather of the Ridge Greens
considered herself a "political person," and articulated for me the logic

of being one. She wanted to redefine the usual meaning of political, attaching it to personal actions usually considered politically irrelevant. Echoing the rallying cry of feminist consciousness-raising, Heather upheld that "the personal is political" and explained during a phone chat how she applied the dictum. "I don't buy toothpaste that's been tested on animals." I wondered how she related individual consumer behavior to other ways of being a "political person."

PL: "So if buying the 'right' things and making personal choices is 'being political', why should someone join a Green Party group?"

Heather: "You can't put your ideals into practice if you have to vote for either a rich corrupt politician or a corrupt politician ... you need to improve your voting choices."

PL: "So are you saying that people should join groups mainly to improve choices that are personal?"

Heather: "We need to create an alternative vision ..."

PL: "So it's not enough to 'be political' in terms of personal choices?"

Heather: "Not if you want 50 percent women in the Senate."

For Heather, buying the right kind of toothpaste was *part* of an overall political commitment that included both private, individual acts and public involvements geared toward creating an "alternative vision." Heather was "being political" by advocating collective action as well as by adding her individual efforts to the construction of a hoped-for polity of consumers who would subject their consumption to a sociological, or ecological, imagination. In such a polity, private, personal choices as well as public roles would be central to good citizenship.

In sum, access to stratified practices enabled Greens to live out political commitments in their individual working and private lives as well as public involvements. Their access to these practices – their ability to relate to their world in such individualized, articulate terms – did not by itself determine the forms their commitment would take. But this access shaped their opportunities for commitment. In the typical Green lifeway, work and private life were meaningful as parts of a politicized life project. Activists who build lives around a personalized politics are not likely to alter one aspect of their commitment style with ease; they have invested themselves in an individualized way of "being political" that is anchored in occupational and family life as well as organized activism. This level of personal investment might make it easier to understand why Ridge Greens struggled with their organizational shortcomings and yet moved on to form a new group with the same difficulties. Their culture of commitment got perpetuated not only by Green organizations but by a whole way of life, such that egalitarian organizations, personalized effort, "socially responsible" work, and unconventional private lives all cohered as a meaningful whole.

Below, some selected biographical sketches flesh out the reconstructions of life-ways from the survey data.

PERSONALIZED POLITICS: LIFE AS A POLITICAL PROJECT

Similar to the Greens at the national conference, core members of the Ridge Green group ranged between their early 20s and early 50s. Half of the Ridge Greens ranged between 30 and 44 years of age, compared with 59 percent of the national sample. The proportion of core Ridge Greens under 30 was 25 percent, however, compared with 7 percent in the national sample. All but two of twelve core Ridge Greens had at least one college degree, and all had at least attended college. Similar to the national sample a little less than two-thirds (64 percent) of the core Ridge members had household incomes of $25,000 or less. During the time of this study, four of the core members were married – two having done so during or just prior to my study. Several others were in long-term relationships though not married; three members had been divorced. Two had their first children during the course of the study. In all, the education, income, and family life characteristics of Ridge Greens approximated those of the national sample, though Ridge Greens were a bit younger on the average, and perhaps correspondingly, had fewer children than we would expect on the basis of the national sample. My participant-observation with the comparison group, the Seaview Greens, made clear that their core members' educational and family backgrounds were similar to those of the other Greens.

Glancing quickly at these activists' work résumés, an observer might conclude that the Ridge Greens experienced a lot of instability. Half of the core members either switched jobs or else went back to school to start a graduate program during the course of the study. A more accurate interpretation of Greens' lifestyles would point out that Greens created lives less in accordance with the measures of a "conventional" life cycle – a steadily building career, a marriage and children in one's 20s – and more according to a yardstick that gauged life decisions by their relevance for a liberal social conscience.

During my participant-observation with the group, nearly every member had commented on the need to have work that either complemented or else did not contradict either political or more broadly cultural priorities.[19] For instance, Donald said that working at Greenpeace was a way to carry out Quaker tenets of social responsibility. Heather clearly prided herself on working for a birth control counseling agency, a job that dovetailed nicely with her feminism. George remained unemployed for several months while he sought out employment that could complement "Green values" and draw on his administrative skills. As the Ridge Green group was folding, he took a managerial job with a non-profit health clinic. He was not entirely happy with it, though: "it's fixing the symptoms, not the problem." Carl had already quit an engineering job on account of his distaste for its bio-genetic applications. Joe held several advanced degrees, and during this study began a job with a small, "clean energy" business. Mike, who had left college during his junior year, held down a job as a clerk at a lumber yard. "I like to rebel against my middle-classness" he told me once, comparing himself to the more affluent and less "radical" people he met in his urban garden collective. After I ended the field research, Mike parlayed his enjoyment of plant and water ecology into a paid, part-time job with the city parks department. Well-educated Green activists sought employment consonant with an individualized sense of social responsibility rather than jobs chosen for building a succesful, financially profitable occupational career as an end in itself.

Greens could apply their computer skills, editorial skills, or well-schooled abilities to well-paying but not altogether satisfying use (George) or else use them to assist lower-paying, perhaps non-profit agencies with a liberal political valence (Heather, Donald). In either case, they saw themselves as needing to resolve a tension between political commitments and the world of work. Greens did not eschew material comfort or highly prize voluntary poverty as did youthful members of the 1960s counterculture. But they wanted more than just their "leisure time" to express their commitments to political and cultural change. The category of "leisure" itself suggests a division between "useful" activity in the public world and "free" time in personal life which obscures the way these activists saw political or social consequences of both public and personal life. The goal was to define both their public and their personal lives into an overall political project.

The economics of this kind of project could be daunting. A politicized life project required the willingness to subordinate comfort to ideals. This was the dilemma Suzanne and Carl explored during a meeting of the newsletter collective:

Carl saw himself as pulled between needing to get on in life, and make some income, and wanting to "build movements for social change."

Carl: "I've got to get a job – I've got to feed my kid. But I'm afraid if I get a job I will drop all this stuff (pointing to calendars and leaflets strewn about the table) and never do anything meaningful."

Suzanne asked if he couldn't get a job with his formidable computer skills.

Carl: "Yeah, I could get a job with what I do – for Lockheed." Merely naming this military contractor dismissed the option. He did recall, with a bit of wistfulness, how much he had made when he worked in bio-engineering.

Suzanne: "I'm afraid to get a job." She feared that if she ended her part-time, freelance editing and artwork, she would not find a full-time job that allowed her to "practice my life commitment and make enough money to live on." She recounted her interests in the environment and in art, and realized "I can't make any money in that." A 20 hour a week job would allow her to do the things that "are really important to me."

George wrestled with a similar dilemma. He preferred to work for a non-profit firm, but also mentioned to me his computer skills could get him a job that would make more money, money that he could even choose to funnel into "Green" activism. Donald, too, needed to juggle his "Green values" with skills that had varied uses and offered varied kinds of returns. He described to me how he "wanted to work for the environment," and also had managerial talent, considering himself good at being "well-organized." He needed to turn managerial talent into employment that could earn him a living without straying too far from his version of Green values.

This difficult calculus of personalized social responsibility shows through in Carl's efforts to find "good work" while holding up his share of family responsibilities and remaining true to his vision of a participatory, democratic movement.

Carl

When I started field work with the Ridge Greens, Carl, in his early 30s, was nearly ready to drop his graduate studies. Texts in genetics shared the floor of his apartment with calendar page items the night we got together to lay out the Ridge monthly newsletter. But as Carl explained, his studies were becoming less and less compelling to him, and time was running out before he would be obliged to leave his graduate program altogether. Having acquired an impressive array of computer skills, he hoped to put them to use in "an activist organization." For the time being, he and his wife managed on her salary as a technician, along with some research funds of his. But it was unclear how long this arrangement would last with a new baby in their household.

The declining fortunes of the Ridge Greens made it more difficult to see activist commitments as worth a precarious financial situation and a life of evenings spent going to meetings and coordinating newsletter and group outreach projects. Carl regularly informed the Ridge group that he was ready to cut back his responsibilities – even if tasks went undone – under pain of severely straining his marriage. Fran, his wife, had been involved in Green activism herself in the Seaview Greens, but had become disillusioned. While committed to the Green philosophy in general, she saw little in the Ridge group to excuse Carl from bearing an equal responsibility for raising their new child. Carl very much agreed on this egalitarian definition of active fatherhood, but would not be able hold up his share of parenting as long as Green activism kept him occupied late into the night, several nights a week. The Ridge Greens' difficulty finding a legitimate sense of authority lay at the bottom of much of Carl's own doubts about the group. Arguments over George's alleged power ploys further soured Carl on the Ridge Greens.

Teetering on the edge of dropping out for several months, Carl finally announced his intentions early in 1990. By then the Ridge group had nearly died and visible Green electoral party activity had yet to emerge. With a limited amount of time left to demonstrate progress in his studies, Carl figured he would give the Ph.D. one last shot. And he would continue his involvement in regional-level, but not local, activities of Greens in California.

No more than four months later, shortly after Greens had won the sole rights to register voters in the new "Green Party" name, Carl was initiating local party organizing. The lure of a completed degree was dimming again. As he explained to me later, he let his degree candidacy lapse: "I was finding every excuse possible for not finishing … I feel better now." To earn both money and political experience, he took a job as a campaign organizer for a county ballot measure. A few months later, Carl took on a half-time job with Green Party organizing in his area. For the time being, it seemed like he had reached his goal of making money working for an activist organization.

Carl's new involvements, even if paid, were making it more difficult to practice an involved, egalitarian role in marriage. Another child had entered the family by then, and Fran was becoming eager to go back to work. But Green activists faced a strict deadline for signing up sufficient Green Party registrants to guarantee the party a place on the ballot. Carl would be needing to spend less, not more, time at home. Carl mused, "someone who doesn't have a life apart from this ought to be doing my job." In an interview nearly two years after the beginning of this study, when the registration drive was entering its final months, Carl confessed,

> She (Fran) needs a father for the kids and I'm not there much. And we need
> money coming in and I'm not providing much of that. Some but it's not what we
> need to really properly raise our kids. But it's mainly the time. I'm just not
> helping much at all with raising the kids.

Carl was not about to suggest that Fran should stay home and raise their
children, and Fran was unlikely to practice a traditional, home-bound
motherhood indefinitely. In fact, Fran had just had an encouraging interview with a biotechnical firm, for a job that would not require her to "do
any experimentation with animals or any of the stuff she really couldn't
stand." Fran was more willing to indulge Carl's political work now than
during his tenure with the old Ridge Green group because at least the
long hours of weekend tabling and weeknight phone-banking were
producing more visible results: the thousands of registrants themselves,
some media coverage, and a still-manageable, still-flattering amount of
"harassment" from the Democratic Party.

Carl was unwilling to drop the committed work that clearly gave him
a personal charge as well as political and moral satisfaction. He would
continue trying to juggle financially destabilizing political commitments
with his feminist-inspired regard for active fathering, while recognizing
his wife's claims on a life outside the house. Two years of life as a political project required that Carl be willing to live with economic uncer-
tainties and a good deal of stress at home.

Why wouldn't Carl have taken a more stable job that drew on his
skills, devoting his leftover time to Green organizing? He assumed that
to be a good activist, and a good person, one needed to make public
involvements and personal life as well reflect a highly individualized sense
of social responsibility. It was not enough to "do your bit" for a larger,
interdependent political community. One ideally lived a socially responsible, "Green" existence all the time, not simply during public, political
activity. Hence Donald's and George's comments to me that it would be
difficult to live a "pure Green" existence, forgoing a car and other
comforts that weighed heavily on the debit side of the social and environmental responsibility scale.

The Greens' personalized politics made it difficult for them to imagine
a political community that would avoid both hierarchical structure *and*
intensive, demanding participation from all members. For instance,
during his time out from Green activism, Carl had asked me rhetorically,
"can working people work in [activist] organizations and not get pushed
around?" He had begun to think a person with the time constraints of a

regular job had to settle for being a "pushed around" volunteer in a group led by a paid staff person, or else endure the "escalation of guilt" he associated with egalitarian, all-volunteer groups like the Ridge Greens. In the Ridge group, tasks seemed to fall to those whose "guilt" made them take responsibility for keeping the group going. He did not imagine participating under the direction of a clearly legitimate, paid leader with the time and resources to keep a group afloat. What cultural allegiances would Carl have shared with other Greens so that they could have invested their group with more authority and responsibility, and divested themselves of some of their heavy individual burdens? This was the cultural dilemma for activists we saw in Chapter 2; the dilemma weighed as heavily on individuals' own lives as it did on their tenuous organizations.

For Carl and other Greens, assumptions about political participation and decisions about work and family life played off one another. Living a politicized life meant sacrificing some of the material comforts his skills could have earned him, while living suspended tenuously between public commitments and his commitment to egalitarian family life. It is no wonder that the figures on divorce in the national Green sample (Table 5.4) were so high.

Other studies

The few other in-depth studies of personalized politics since the 1960s have found what amount to life-ways similar to those of Greens. Epstein's study (1991) is the most detailed. She discovered anti-nuclear activists in the Abalone Alliance and the Livermore Action Group made trade-offs between work and activism as part of an overall, culturally radicalized lifestyle on which activists conferred political value. Epstein also gave some sense as well of the unconventional personal lives anti-nuclear activists constructed: cohabitation was common, and married women rarely took their husbands' names; group living situations were a common way to accommodate both the difficult economics and the collectivist commitments of a culturally radical life. In a similar vein, Whalen and Flacks (1989) noted that radical 1960s youth commonly preferred to avoid jobs heavily implicated in "the system" of bureaucratic capitalism.

"Countercultural" lifestyles are not news.[20] What is interesting is that the logic of commitment activists followed twenty years ago, during a time of economic growth in the US, were similar to those constructed by anti-nuclear activists in the 1970s who saw dim job prospects (Epstein

1991: 84, 109, 145), and again similar to those that activists were re-enacting during the economic decline at the start of the 1990s. It may well be that the group dilemmas of personalized politics have perpetuated, and have been reinforced by, highly individualized life-ways like that of Carl.

Activists like Barb of the ACES and Ben Norton of HAT shared Carl's long hours of low-paid or volunteer activist work. But they mapped out their public and private lives differently. They acted on different expectations about how one becomes a good activist, or a good person.

ANTI-TOXICS ACTIVISM: A BOUNDED SPHERE OF POLITICS

Most of the anti-toxics activists did not relate the whole of their lives to social or cultural transformation. Even the ACES leader Laura, who arranged a Green-style trade-off between activism and relatively low-paying work, insisted on saving some time for living the life of what she considered a "regular person." Laura held a part-time clerical job to leave enough time, and just barely enough money, for her work with ACES. Having earned a bachelor's degree, she toyed with the idea of going to graduate school, but decided, "I'll go back to school when Microtech converts (to exclusively non-military contracts)." In some ways, her life-way paralleled those of the most active Greens. Yet Laura maintained a sphere of life apart from networks of politicized individuals. "When I fall into the stereotype (of what an activist is) and don't have time to go to the movies, play soccer ... I always make sure I do those things." The point is not that activists like Greens never go to movies or enjoy themselves in private. Laura was telling me that she wanted to maintain an image of herself as someone who cared about and was like the other members of her local community.

Most members of ACES and HAT did not need to be as self-conscious as Laura about sustaining "normal" identities in their local communities. And for most of these activists apart from Laura, being involved in a grassroots activist group was not tied up with a movement culture that maintained politicized norms for personal as well as work and movement group life. These activists may have squeezed their pre-existing family life and work routines into schedules crammed with meetings and events. But they did not factor work and family life, or personal consumption habits, into the moral calculus of a politicized life project.

Having characterized the Hillview anti-toxics group, HAT, as communitarian, I want to note that communitarianism has been associated with moral bonds that do indeed connect work, family life, and public involvement (Bellah *et al.* 1985). Communitarian moral exemplars like Mrs. Sherman of HAT define a good life, activist or otherwise, through consistent allegiance to traditions and cultural authorities that weigh on private as well as public life. Mrs. Sherman, for instance, was proud to recycle her household bottles and cans because God's earth needed to be protected.[21] Mrs. Irwin and other participants in HAT had commented similarly that the Lord disapproved of people who pollute the air or land with toxic dump sites. *In the context of a board meeting*, these statements assumed a knowing audience that regularly acknowledged shared moral authorities in public as well as private. They were communitarian – as distinct from "new age" spiritualist, or scientific, or secular "post-materialist" – statements of environmental consciousness.

But while private acts may have carried some moral significance in HAT, they did not carry the political significance they attained within the politicized life projects of Greens. Joining HAT or practicing ecological consciousness in everyday life did not get associated with being a "political person," to use the Greens' language. Some HAT members acknowledged recycling, for instance, as a good thing to do, but never called it a political act. Environmentally significant acts could make one a better person in the same way that charitable acts would make one a better person, one who gives service to a *pre-existing* moral community.[22] Hillview's cultural milieu defined these acts, whether individual or collective, as strengthening a moral community rather than as transforming a political community by politicizing the private.

Activists like Heather, the Green who would not use toothpaste tested on animals, would have difficulties participating on an equal footing in the same political community as most HAT activists. For instance, Carl elaborated on the "balancing act" that the emerging Green Party would need to perform, juggling "Green values" and a commitment to "not be like the other parties" on the one hand and a desire to attract members who weren't all like activists in Seaview and Ridgeville.

Carl: "I think there's something in our platform about minimizing intake of meat. I'm all for that but I also want to reach Hispanic communities for instance, and black communities ... I think we can put out the lifestyle message, and I think a lot of those communities are ready to hear it but not be beaten over the head."

PL: "If there's someone who needs a job and there's a job at an oil refinery, what can you do?"

Carl: "Yeah. Beyond War[23] is an example of an organization that has wimped out as I understand it. They don't give their members a hard time about working at Lockheed and Microtech, and places like that ... On the other hand, we all have to make a living and we can't force our people to go broke over us. I guess I'm kind of torn on that one ... I would like to think we could have some membership that works in those places and start to get them thinking about how they are spending their lives ... and frankly, generate some whistle-blowers."

PL: "So it's an ongoing balance."

Carl: "Yeah, I don't have an answer for that one."

On the one hand, the Green Party wanted to reach out to constituencies not traditionally associated with environmental activism. On the other, it was inviting new party members to experience some of the same dilemmas about personal choice, public responsibility, and the meaning of "political" action that mattered in personalized politics. But anti-toxics activists generally did not politicize personal choices about occupation or about family relationships. I heard only two anti-toxics activists – James Shaver in HAT and Laura of ACES – ever talk about their choice of work as integral to their identities as good activists.

The surveys demonstrated that anti-toxics activists held a range of occupations not as heavily concentrated in the cultural specialist and human service professions as those of Greens. Anti-toxics activists on the whole did not enter activism with the schooling and associated cultural skills of the Greens. Most did not submit themselves to the Greens' dilemmas over relations between political ideals and building a personal life. Most did not talk about redefining "the political" itself, as Greens did who conceived long-term projects like a Green political party and consciously passed up involvements with single-issue groups that might win concrete, relatively quick victories for local constituencies.

HAT and ACES activists did not simply reject broader or more systematic ideologies. Nor did they reject the calls by some environmentalists to change everyday consumption in line with ecological principles. But neither abstract ideologies nor a politics of consumption mattered integrally for their activism the way these did to activists who assume that being politically involved should mean creating an individualized, fully politicized life project. Ben Norton of HAT became vocal in identifying "environmental racism." He called on large environmentalist organizations like Greenpeace and the Sierra Club to develop more racially diverse executive boards. But for him, becoming an activist did not mean being a cultural dissident and creating a new politicized self. His story of involvement shows a political commitment that is both strong and rooted in a sense of public obligation fairly separated from his preferences for working and family life.

Ben Norton

Ben's experiences with toxics predated his work with HAT. Once an operator in a pesticide plant, his daily exposure to chemical by-products made him ill enough to change to cleaner work. Ben's anti-toxics activism developed during the Citizens Action League's (CAL) campaign to wrest equitable compensation from the state department of transportation for Hillviewers displaced by a new freeway. Ben joined up to help his parents, who lived in the freeway corridor. Ben helped start CAL's anti-toxics project in the mid-1970s. He stuck with the project as it evolved into HAT and its sponsorship passed from CAL to ACORN to the ACFT.

During our interview, I could hardly help wonder why Ben had stuck with anti-toxics activism so long. His personal experiences with toxics alone might have prompted many people to retreat to private comforts rather than stick out a twenty-year struggle in the public fray.

Ben: "There's a lot of things that have happened to me, in my life, lots of things you would not believe, and people ask me, 'how come you haven't gone crazy?' ... I try to think of the good things that have happened to me in life. I think of people when I get down and out, people who can't see, deaf people, people that can't walk. And I say you know, 'God is really blessing me', just to have my health and strength ... A person has to really look up and think, 'hey look, I did a lot of things, I helped a lot of people, and in my heart I know that I'm doing the right thing.'"

For Ben, anti-toxics work brought a "feeling of self-satisfaction" from "helping underprivileged people and people that (do not) have the knowledge and the background that I have, or the spunk that I have to keep driving at this thing." Ben wanted to help "people" in general, rather than advancing an agenda of cultural change geared to people of a certain philosophical bent. His comparison of himself with the less fortunate differs from Carl's implicit comparison of himself with the less enlightened.

While Greens wanted to "convert" at least a few people who did not already think and live "Green," Ben's kind of activism calls members of a community to political commitments that get practiced in public roles, though not necessarily in personal or working life. Ben described his long trips to ACFT board meetings, for instance, as activity he fit into a life that included but was not pervaded by a political imagination.

It's more than (having) to be away from your family, in some other state, 3000 miles away, and you're sitting there and you're trying to recall everything people are saying ... I have to take off from my job and be there a day early, Thursday,

Friday, Saturday, Sunday our minds are so blown out, then we have to catch a flight back home and go to work Monday.

Ben put in long, unpaid hours of anti-toxics advocacy with obviously political consequences, without practicing the more or less systematically politicized personhood of Green-style activists. His occasional race jokes would not have sat well with white, well-meaning Greens. (Ben is black.) His unselfconscious enthusiasm for the 1991 Persian Gulf war would have discomforted activists who define their own political worth by how much they question received terms of policy debate in the US.

Norton could carry an ideological agenda without personalizing his politics. He was becoming a vocal opponent of "enviromental racism," an idea that new alliances of black, Spanish-speaking, and Native American local groups were using to contest the disproportionate placement of toxic sites in their locales. Interestingly, other leading members of HAT like Mr. Hamilton and Mrs. Thomas followed a more classically "liberal" position on race, insisting that HAT did good work for "people" in general. They did not consider HAT's politics specifically in terms of African-American advocacy, even though its taken-for-granted form of solidarity grew out of black civic culture in Hillview. Still, Hamilton, Thomas, and Norton all committed themselves to "helping underprivileged people," without needing to politicize their personal lives.

Ben Norton could fight environmental racism under the aegis of publicly acknowledged, shared cultural arbiters that called African Americans to action for the good of the community. Barb of the ACES had to maintain her commitments with neither publicly shared cultural reference points nor a culture of personalized politics to sustain her.

Barb

In her early 30s like Carl, Barb had very marketable skills in accounting and data processing. When I started field work with ACES, Barb was just completing a business M.A. in a part-time graduate studies program while working as a claims adjuster for an insurance company. According to the survey data, she was one of the relatively few anti-toxics activists with an advanced degree, albeit in a managerial field not considered part of Kriesi's politically engaged new class. Barb and her partner shared a household income at least twice that of Carl and Fran. Barb provided invaluable assistance to ACES with her background in administration and biological science. She was a prime support for the organizational "infrastructure" of her group – maintaining its mailing lists and book-keeping. Unlike Carl and more like Ben Norton, Barb kept the main spheres of her public and private life – work, family, and activism – relatively separate.

Barb committed herself to ACES without living a heavily politicized personal life in activist circles. In an interview I asked her why she went to meetings.

> Barb: "We talk about a lot of the meat and potatoes ... I figure once a month for 2 hours, I can commit myself to that. When you take 2 hours out of a month, that amount of time is not that big ... Also I think I feel a sense of responsibility to the organization ... some of the items on the agenda I have to report on."
>
> PL: "So it's not just 'them'; you're really a part of the organization."
>
> Barb: "It's definitely a 'we.'"

Barb took two hours "out of" a month for meetings; ACES was something for which she apportioned time, but it was not integral to the way she built her everyday life the way activism was for Carl. Barb did not see most of the ACES regulars outside of meetings and events, except for Laura. She and Laura played together on town intramural sports teams.

She met her partner of two years in the local baseball league, too. He kept his distance when ACES had task meetings at their house, though he allowed Barb to use some of his leftover office supplies for mailings. Despite her misgivings about the Ridge Greens, Fran, in contrast, shared Carl's "Green" orientation to American society and culture, and had in fact met Carl through Green activism. Their disagreements over Green activism were about methods, not goals; Barb and her partner on the other hand maintained a relationship in spite of different political orientations.

Barb could brook the difference within her relationship because she was not building a life in which both her public and her private life needed to be regular parts of a politicized personhood in a politicized milieu. She could get involved in the team sports program, for instance, and leave her commitments outside the playing field. Airdale's suburban, "company town" milieu might have made it unpleasant to do otherwise.

> Barb: "Our (ACES') positions are so – I don't know – left (long pause) -leaning that you don't tend to bring it up in a cocktail party situation ..."
>
> PL: "You don't see these coming up much on the softball team – ?"
>
> Barb: "Softball practice I tend not to bring up my political beliefs or ACES work."
>
> PL: "What do you think would happen?"
>
> Barb: "I don't know – I guess I'm so accustomed to getting (pause) to getting a

less than warm response that I'd rather be known for my softball abilities than – 'what would happen?' – I don't know. You would probably get a lot of people who might support you. You might get some people who think 'Oh, you're one of those loonies.'"

Even if the Airdale area had been more supportive of activism like hers, Barb did not want to get as intensively involved in activism as had Carl. Barb's activism did not have ramifications for her future money-making opportunities because she did not choose her work in relation to specific political, or culturally alternative principles of social responsibility as had most Greens. She practiced a different sense of public responsibility. She associated her prior work in health services with a "trait of wanting to make things better." She did not, however, wrangle with a dilemma that counterposed career-building to political commitments. Each had its place.

Barb's commitments may *sound* unremarkable, and that is the point. She did not need to personalize her politics in order to "make things better," and she did not need to expound upon alternative values. But this soft-spoken claims adjuster had also taken the remarkable step of speaking out against Microtech's policies in the civic chill of Airdale. For someone who once compared this kind of public speaking with unpleasant gynaecological exams, it is even more remarkable that quietly, conscientiously, she juggled her political commitments in between a busy work schedule and home life.

Barb's life-way did not require that individualized political expression be a central priority. Like other members of ACES she put a lot less investment in the consensus format than most Greens, while liking it all the same:

Barb: "Consensus works out well. Also, if you're not willing to make ACES a full-time commitment you're more willing to let the decision go without your input. I make a conscious effort not to make ACES a full-time endeavor."

Comparing ACES' very loose form of "consensus" with Robert's Rules, Barb observed, "I personally don't want ACES to become such an important thing in my life that these decisions that we make are so important. So I'm willing to go along with whatever. I trust Laura's judgment but I don't want to become leader of the group." While the Green version of consensus had an important place in an overall, individualized moral calculus of public and private life, Barb appreciated the way that decision-making and leadership in ACES enabled her to limit the claims of political commitment on the rest of her life. Maybe only by maintaining a "normal" private life separate from ACES could someone in

Airdale's privatized milieu live with the fact that she was taking risks, boldly contesting the cultural and economic powers that be.

PERSONALISM AND LIFE-WAYS

Chapter 2 argued that personalism made sense as a "common coin," a basis for social bonds between diverse, culturally dissenting activists. Now we can add that this culture is particularly suited to activists who make "being political" into a project for one's entire personhood, public and private. A language of personal development could well fit the needs of someone who makes political commitment into an individual life project. The trouble is that personalized politics aims at political change, but personalist language on its own posits a personal self with no necessary relation to a broader project outside the self. At times, talk about personal change may ease the tensions of "life as a political project." But this talk and the practices that embody it make it too easy to equate changing interpersonal relations with changing political debate and political outcomes.

On the other hand, activists like Greens do bring their whole selves, personal and public, to their movement groups. A culture of commitment that separates public roles from private life will not satisfy their quest for a new kind of group commitment. Personalism offered Greens one way to overcome traditional boundaries between public and private that Greens reject. The self constructed in that language pre-exists "public" and "private" because it is a "natural," essential will. This is not to say personalism is a wholly satisfactory means for creating a political group. But in the context of class-stratified understandings of commitment that stress individual efficacy, it is not surprising that the personal self serves better than the communitarian citizen as a position for Greens to take in relation to the public at large.

Communitarian thinkers associated personalism with the intellectual sectors of the middle class. But they never clarified how relations between class and personalism worked. Rieff, Lasch, and Bell all denounced the culture of the educated middle class – either "intellectual" or "professional" – for being "adversarial," for breaking down moral communities. Personalized commitment develops out of socially structured preferences, and is not simply a morally noxious style that people of good will can drop. It is, in fact, a way of practicing a sense of moral obligation. Heather felt obligated to make her consumer choices consistent with her principles. Carl had difficulties imagining how to convert culturally diverse constituencies to the Green cause because Greens took "lifestyle" issues such as diet as matters of obligation, not just private preference. We discount this personalized kind of morality at the risk of making a partial, moralistic critique stand in for sociological analysis.

THE MISSING LINK IN NSM ARGUMENTS

Arguments about "new social movements" (NSMs) complement some of this chapter's findings regarding the social backgrounds of activists, but the NSM arguments can benefit from a focus on commitment styles. These arguments, introduced in Chapter 2, designated as "new" those movements since the 1960s that have created collective identities outside the well-worn rubric of working-class struggle against capitalists and managers. NSM scholar Alberto Melucci's writing about these movements has emphasized social structural and attendant cultural changes in the genesis of NSMs. These changes include the growth of a professional middle class of cultural specialists. But the scenario of broad-scale change he developed does not successfully explain how or why some NSM activists react to structural change through personalized politics while others do not.

Melucci's work (1989, 1985) has related political style in NSMs to a process of "individualization" and its contradictions in advanced industrial societies.[24] In these societies, both individual and collective action are increasingly the product of rational choice and plan. So they require highly self-directed specialists for social and cultural work, from commercial advertising to social welfare administration. On the one hand, these societies produce at least the appearance that individual needs matter. On the other hand, these societies administer and control the same individuality that they make available for their specialized workers and for the larger population too. In sum, advanced industrial society promises a kind of individual autonomy that it cannot deliver.

Melucci hypothesized that the people who participate in NSMs would be those who are caught between this systemic contradiction. The "contradictions of individualization" hypothesis might explain why highly educated people, often social or cultural specialists, make up large proportions of "new"-style movements, as survey figures illustrated for the US Greens. Their extensive educations and highly independent work could conceivably give them an especially keen sense of individual efficacy and autonomy that they cannot fully exercise. Melucci stated, for instance, that "self-realization" is "encouraged by the production and distribution at the systemic level of such resources as education, technical skills, and universalistic codes" (1989: 209). Scholars outside the NSM theoretical rubric, communitarian theorists, for instance, have also emphasized the growth of self-realization as a cultural trend in advanced industrial society (Bell 1976; Bellah *et al.* 1985; Lasch 1979).

Some of Melucci's empirical work in Milan during the 1970s and 1980s described a very familiar-sounding activist: in these activist circles, just as with the US Greens, personal life became a site for cultural innovation with consequences defined as political. "Alternative" bookstores, music, and cultural services, and alternative personal lifestyles were, according to Melucci (1985), the "latent" dimension of ongoing "collective action" that occasionally surfaces in public political activities such as peace demonstrations. Melucci contrasted this kind of activism with its latent and manifest dimensions with that of working-class politics, in which he said "there tended to be a split between private life and public life" (1989: 206). But *why* do some activists politicize personal life?

The main answer in this line of thinking is that the social contradictions laid out above result in political intrusions on formerly private choices about building a life. These choices are constricted and regulated by bureaucracies trying to hold a complex, self-reflective, individualizing society together. But even if this is the case, it is not simply natural that movement actors would respond by turning personal life into a political demonstration. They might just as logically respond by vigilantly keeping private life private and define political action purely in terms of public struggles against bureaucracies. Or they might retreat into aesthetic contemplation and innovation.[25] A second line of reasoning (Melucci 1991), one less concerned with social structure, suggests that a new sense of global responsiblity influences the new sense of the public–private divide. Greens did emphasize the global dimensions of personal choices as a sort of new morality. But why would activists like Heather or Carl need to demonstrate this morality in their personal, everyday lives, rather than demonstrating it purely through collective public action, such as boycotts of corporate-harvested rainforest products? Why would an environmental moral imagination be articulated by people who act as empowered individuals more than as tight communities of conscience? Ecological thinking by itself need not start with radicalized individuals rather than traditional or long-established communities. In fact, recent work suggests that ecological thinking has been an important part of communal life in non-white ethnic cultures which have not often been associated with high amounts of individualism (Lynch 1993).

The links between wide-ranging sociocultural change and the everyday lives of activists in Milan or Ridgeville need to be filled in. Missing is some analysis of how people translate the (proposed) contradictions of advanced industrial society and the diffuse cultural emphasis on self-realization into personalized politics rather than some other form of commitment in everyday life. Conceptualizing personalized politics as a specific repertoire for activism supplies a missing link in NSM arguments. We can think of personalized politics as a kind of "collective action repertoire" (Tilly 1978; Tarrow 1992a, 1992b), in this case a repertoire of commitment practices. Some activists have more access to this repertoire because of their schooling. And as we will see in the next chapter, some have more need for it because of their position in the institutional arena for grassroots activism. The argument extended in this chapter and the next together offer a level of analysis in between broad theses about advanced industrial society and case studies of movement life.

So far this study has focused mainly on commitment practices, rather than on the political or environmental ideologies that activists articulate. We can now ask how commitment styles relate to the different ideologies in the environmental movement – from "ecofeminism" to "environmental justice." Environmentalist beliefs by themselves do not dictate styles of commitment; this is the misleading assumption that colors some NSM theorizing, as well as common-sense thinking about how beliefs relate to action. But personalized politics and culturally radical ideologies such as the Greens' Ten Key Values can reinforce one another, especially when there are relatively few opportunities to enter those ideologies into institutionalized political arenas.

6

Personalized politics and cultural radicalism since the 1960s

FROM SPONTANEITY TO ROUTINE

In June 1967, "sobersided" older members and ex-members of Students for a Democratic Society (SDS) gathered to mull over the possibilities for a post-student political organization that could flower amid the youthful energy bursting out in counter-cultural color across the US.[1] Bursting into the activists' plenary meeting were three self-appointed emissaries of the counter-culture. Taking center stage, they taunted and intrigued the assembly with news of its impotence before the allure of a free-love, free-wheeling effervescence that was turning on America's youth. The weekend gathering never recovered from its strong hit of shock theater. It never got around to sketching plans for a new organization.

In 1989, at the national Green movement conference in Eugene, Oregon, authorized delegates and other Green activists had gathered to draft a movement platform to take back to their local chapters, and very optimistically, to a wider audience disenchanted with the two US political parties. In the middle of a tedious voting session, the back hallway doors banged several times to successive heave-hos and soon gave way before a missile-shaped cardboard protrusion. Chanting and yelling, a small band of people in torn jeans and sandals hoisted into the auditorium what turned out to be a twenty-foot cardboard reefer. The nominal leader of the Pot People, as they were tagged, insisted his small band would stall the session until the delegates added to their platform a demand for the repeal of marijuana laws.

One of the meeting facilitators talked the hemp spokesman down. She remarked that his group had put a lot of creative effort into their reefer replica, and she offered him a chance to state his case to the assembly before it returned to its business. The facilitator also asked the assembly to give the Pot People a round of applause for their cardboard creation. The pot advocate then took the podium and in preacherly cadences recited the productive and curative uses of "hemp." He received enthusiastic applause. Without deciding a position on hemp, the plenary returned to its business. The Pot People accepted an invitation to the picnic dinner that delegates had prepared for after the session.

The difference between the SDS elders' handling of the hip "Diggers" in 1967 and the Greens' handling of the Pot People in 1989 says much about the evolution in personalized politics since the 1960s. Ex-SDS leader Todd Gitlin writes that what was most remarkable about the encounter in 1967 was that "dozens of experienced organizers, who had set up the conference with a sense of high if vague purpose, permitted three Diggers to derail it." He concludes, "we shared in the antileadership mood – our own countercultural roots again ... we possessed no clear authority principle to mobilize against the Diggers' takeover style" (Gitlin 1987: 229–230). By the late 1980s personalized politics was routine for some activists, not just an intriguing possibility to activists who could be mesmerized by a call to "personal liberation." Personal selfhood had in fact become the "authority principle," the common ground in which they would sow a new politics.

This chapter shows how personalism has provided a principle of membership for a number of post-1960s grassroots movements. Spontaneous protest or youthful angst are what critical commentators have expected from personalism in politics. But for Greens and other activists in a succession of contemporary movements, a shared personalism has focused and routinized rather than diffused political commitment. Activists in anti-nuclear, radical feminist, radical environmentalist, and other movements share not only a personalized commitment style but a culturally radical ideological outlook: they all raise moral and broadly ideological issues outside the usual bounds of political debate in established forums. They not only politicize specific issues but, as Anthony Giddens has said (1991), they question more broadly how we should live our lives. The personalized political style and culturally radical ideologies have mutually reinforced each other – not because ideologies like radical feminism or Green values naturally call forth small, intensive groups and personalized effort, but because ideologies like these lack for institutionalized forums. When we understand the institutional context that culturally radical activists have found themselves in, then we can understand why they have kept gravitating to the personalized style. But first we should very briefly review the development of a personalized political style before and during the 1960s.

The evolution in personalized politics

The modern civil rights movement innovated some idioms of commitment that became routinized as personalized politics by the time of the US Greens. But personalism in politics has a much longer history than that, one long enough to include Thoreau's individualistic stance against the demands of the state. Scenes from that history have been treated elsewhere.[2] It is worth briefly mentioning, though, the intensely personalized commitments among American pacifists of the 1950s who inspired civil rights activists and enriched the personalist legacy for later activists as well. Radical pacifists braved much derision to stand up against nuclear testing and air raid preparedness drills, during a time when such "un-American" activity could seriously be considered a sign of mental illness (Isserman 1987: 145). Four pacifists set sail toward a remote nuclear testing zone in 1958, dramatizing their opposition to nuclear military strategy with a willingness to put their own bodies in the way of dangerous fallout if their mission failed to stop nuclear testing. These dissenters acted from a personalized sense of responsibility, a commitment to act individually on the moral truths one holds (Isserman 1987). They derived this personalist stance from Gandhi more than from a psychotherapeutic imagination. Still, a similar emphasis on individualized responsibility to principle would echo in the more psychologistic talk of anti-nuclear protesters a quarter century later who would put their own bodies on the line to block entrances at nuclear weapons plants.

A subtle but important cultural shift, though, seems to distinguish personalized politics since the 1960s from its forebears. Radical pacifists in the 1940s and 1950s still articulated their commitments in relation to specific reference points of established religion and left politics – the "working class, revolutionary, socialist movement" and the "great religious leaders" for instance (Isserman 1987: 135, 141) – even if they disagreed on strategies and tactics. Early civil rights activism based itself explicitly on church-based credos to which southern black activists could share allegiance. In contrast, anti-nuclear activists of the 1970s and 1980s, even within one regional campaign, would bring with them a variety of Christian, paganist, or other spiritual doctrines, and a variety of relations to the "left" (Epstein 1991). The Green movement similarly took in activists with a wide variety of relations to religious or political institutions, few if any of which provided anchors for a majority of activists. These activists might share personalism without sharing much other inspiration for commitment. As groups, they would practice their commitments at a further distance from any single cultural authority than would activists who acted in relation to the same "divine" or political inspiration even if they disagreed on what exactly that inspiration directed. In other words, I suggest that the post-1960s personalized politics we will examine below got loosened from the institutional constellations that earlier activists could take for granted even as they highlighted personal responsibility. This is not to say recent personalized politics rejects institutions, but that activists who practice it may develop social identities at a further remove from them or with a more deeply ambivalent stance toward them.

The southern civil rights campaigns constituted a crucial node in this development of personalized politics. The Student Nonviolent Coordinating Committee (SNCC), perhaps the most important of the grassroots civil rights movement organizations in the early 1960s, had initially defined its mission in clearly religious terms. SNCC's statement of purpose embodied a liberal Christian morality of mutual love (Carson 1981: 23). But it is interesting that this religiously inspired initiative ended up inspiring white students and some black activists to experiment with new presentations of radicalized selfhood removed from religious grounding (McAdam 1988b; Gitlin 1987). For these activists and the student new left that came directly after them, an imagined, interracial "beloved community" of the righteous became as much a vehicle for redefining personal experience as for forwarding a collective, religiously inspired political will. White volunteers in the SNCC-led Freedom Summer civil rights campaigns came to understand their contribution to social change in terms of their own liberation:

The volunteers came to believe it was just as important to free themselves from the constraints of their racial or class backgrounds as it was to register black voters. They became as much the project as the Freedom Schools they taught in (McAdam 1988b: 139).

A once-religious idiom of commitment had gotten reworked in practice, in communal "freedom houses" and stand-offs against police, shaped into a personalized politics with fewer and more tenuous ties to established institutions. As more traditional reference points for activism – religion or established political institutions – faded for some civil rights activists, personal style and individual acts became sites for political statements. White civil rights protesters borrowed and pieced together a new personal style for a new political stance. From encounters with rural southern blacks, they appropriated fragments of southern black speech and mannerisms, grafting them onto a middle-class politics of cultural dissent (McAdam 1988b; Gitlin 1987). From the 1950s Beats, they borrowed an attitude, a non-conforming personal expressiveness that continued the Beats' critique of the bureaucratically impersonal "man in the gray flannel suit." The humble work shirts and suspenders, and new argot, bespoke a critical stance on old social identities. And they reflected an assumption that political commitment would shape a whole self freed of the conventional, constraining division between public and private. Into the 1970s, some variants of personalized politics evolved toward a radical personalism that opposed established religious or political institutions altogether.[3]

Students of social movements have often identified even the less anti-institutional forms of personalized politics with activists who insist on unbound personal expression anywhere and anytime. It is not surprising that some 1960s activists' flamboyant hair styles and flamboyant rhetoric stand out in the minds of "conventional" observers. But we need to distinguish the enduring features of personalized politics from images of youthful abandon and "spontaneity" that the mass media helped to make synonymous with "activism" in some people's minds. After the 1960s, the Nehru shirts and paisley prints that had become saleable souvenirs of the counter-culture cycled quickly out of popular fashion, and much later reappeared as fashionable, and personalized politics became a routine repertoire rather than an experiment. We need to reconsider the old terms of discussion about personalized politics, so we can recognize the differences between the "individual expressiveness" of nude protesters in a university president's office in 1968, and that of Greens at a Green general meeting in 1990.

Updating the debate about "expressive politics"

Some observers would include personalized politics in the category "expressive politics." Observers and critics from different ends of the political spectrum have counterposed "expressive" to "strategic" or "instrumental" politics. Lost in the dichotomy are important distinctions between actions that express the moral ties of a traditional community, actions that express personalized commitments outside of established communities, and actions that express individual impulses alone; all are "expressive." Accounts of expressive politics have tended to assume that this kind of expression feels good, that it releases individual joy or frustration (Breines 1982, especially the discussion of conservative critics in pp. 1–6; Gitlin 1987; Parkin 1968). For these reasons I have not used the tag "expressive politics", and want to situate "personalized politics" beside it without collapsing the two. Accounts of expressive politics in the 1960s would naturally focus on what seemed new about it – its spontaneity, its emphasis on making politics feel good, its moral rather than material grievances. No doubt for some new left and civil rights activists, activism really was "spontaneous" and really did "feel good." The trouble is that the terms of debate about expressive politics still carry these assumptions, and the assumptions muddy observations of what I have called personalized politics.

For instance, Parkin's familiar account of "expressive politics" in Britain's early 1960s anti-nuclear movement counterposed "moral" grievances to "material" ones. The anti-nuclear CND emphasized moral grievances. This observation would apply just as well to the Greens or other movements described in this chapter. But Parkin overlaid his "expressive-strategic" analytic grid onto CND members' self-understandings without first asking why they defined political activity in moral terms. He assumed that a morally motivated politics was "deviant," not really politics properly understood. These terms do not do justice to a Green "expressive politics" that – whether realistic or not – aims at change in political institutions and electoral politics over a very long haul.

Breines' account of the new left emphasized those activists' insistence on making politics meaningful on a personal level, again a project shared by those who practice personalized politics. In contrast with Parkin, Breines uncritically assimilated her new leftists' categories. She assumed that new leftists' "prefigurative politics" faithfully expressed something intrinsic to individual needs. Avoiding these approaches, I have tried to understand the cultural bases for political commitment without assuming *a priori* that some commitments are not really political, or that other commitments necessarily represent core needs among activists. Parkin's CND and Breines' new left can count as early representatives of personalized politics because their and other accounts suggest that these activists created personalized commitments which they did not strongly anchor in specific institutions or communities. We should be able to talk about a common kind of commitment underlying organized collective action in these movements without taking on board assumptions that the commitment must satisfy basic psychological needs, or that it must fail to qualify as "real" politics by definition.

Accounts of civil rights and new left movements have navigated the question of "political" content in these movements somewhat differently.[4] Some (Gitlin 1987; Whalen and Flacks 1989) have charted separate political and counter-cultural/expressive currents, following both as they intertwine, and sometimes merge, during collective action.[5] In this view, a march for desegregation might embody white activists' desires for

personal absolution and brotherly communion as much as their strategy
for fighting injustice, expressiveness and strategy, both being strands in a
thick weave of activist motives. Other accounts (Breines 1982; McAdam
1988b) perceive more of a single self-expressive/political wave, emphasizing the new combined force of collective action that is self-expressive
and political. They argue that self-development – through Freedom
House living in Mississippi, for instance – really produced a new way of
acting political which involved a whole, personal self.

This latter map of self-expressive and "political" currents fits a little
more closely the terrain I call "personalized politics." But it is a dated
map relative to the political culture of the 1980s and 1990s. Most of
Breines' examples for her argument about a new expressive politics in the
new left are protest events like mass demonstrations and occupations.
These events do not have the same novelty or fresh significance when
they happen in the 1990s. Similarly, McAdam describes a kind of political self-transformation among white Freedom Summer volunteers
comparable to that which still happens in the 1990s, but, given the recent
history of youth radicalization, is no longer an uncharted foray in the
frontiers of the political. McAdam argues that by working and living
closely together as morally motivated comrades, white voter-registration
volunteers in the South became disengaged from the comfortable lives
awaiting their return in the North. They forged new senses of self that
they experienced as more authentic and more significant for political
action. They wanted to sustain these new selves and feelings beyond their
initial contexts. Mass protests and extraordinary resocialization experiences felt good and produced a new sense of self.

In the two decades since the height of the white youth counter-culture,
personalism in politics has evolved beyond temporary protest and exper-
iments in communal living. The post-1960s descendants of earlier personalized politics routinely join and build a movement on the basis of the
personal self. Activists create a personalized form of togetherness despite
the fact that personalized politics in Green and other movements has not
necessarily felt good to activists: the Ridge Greens' "process meetings"
are a case in point. And decision-making by consensus is hardly spontaneous. The Greens' organizational forms, for instance, were stultifying
and frustrating as often as gratifying.

The political community of selves that Greens and other activists have
created contrasts with other, more traditional, bases for political togetherness: universal Christian fellowship, local community membership,
republican citizenship, or internationalist comaraderie. The Green
conference facilitator's implicit appeal to a shared principle of personal

selfhood is what enabled her to finesse the Pot People into the Green conference. To reconstruct the facilitator's logic: "We want to allow you to express your (personal) needs. Our dedication to personalized participation means that we cannot disallow you or anyone else from expressing sincerely felt needs, as long as these are in some way relevant to our (very broad, inclusive) agenda. But you ought not to keep us from expressing our needs either, and we need to get our business done. So we will give you time to express what you want as long as you let us continue doing likewise."

A politics of selves has made sense for many highly schooled activists who lack other shared political traditions and institutionalized identities. Recall how the Ridge Green Party debated an organizational structure, passing up the executive board model, insisting on being politically effective while "doing things differently," and invoking the egalitarian "spokescouncil" model of the anti-nuclear movement. Activists with personalized political wills would not likely choose a model of organization from corporations or bureaucratic public interest groups, much less left-sectarian parties. Having brought diverse social identities to their activism, they needed a shared basis for acting together. They did not share a strong sense of membership in ongoing political or organizational traditions, but for the most part they did share a highly developed sense of personal selfhood. No longer a utopian exercise, or a demonstration of personal emancipation, expression of a politicized self became a routine principle of membership, one that still eluded the SDS elders in 1967. Personalized politics in the 1980s and 1990s has included organizational routines that effectively manage even spontaneous outbursts of "expressive politics" like that of the Pot People.

Attempting to put in practice the lessons they learned from 1960s movements, anti-nuclear activists in the later 1970s and 1980s routinized a form of togetherness that would maximize personal participation and avoid the explosive conflicts within the late 1960s new left. These activists, their feminist and environmentalist contemporaries and successors have continued working from politicized selfhood as the implicit basis for commitment in their movements. These are some of the movements in the "personalized politics" category in Chapter 2. The following brief sketches of just three selected social movements illustrate how personalism has shaped activism since the 1960s.[6]

PERSONALIZED POLITICS IN OTHER MOVEMENTS SINCE THE 1960s

The grassroots anti-nuclear movement: codifying personalized politics

By the time the organized student new left imploded at the end of the 1960s, thousands of young people had been touched by the possibilities of a life-long personalized politics, an ongoing commitment pledged to oneself as much as to any organization or broader polity. They wanted to live "life as a political project," a life that might feel good but one that would also feel *right*. Some took their personalized commitments to semi-rural areas of New England and California, where they might create new communities which would foster individuals' identities as politically committed dissenters from the mainstream culture of careers and nuclear families. When a Massachusetts farmer toppled a tower at the site of a planned nuclear power plant in 1974, there was already a network of politicized cultural radicals in the region who were ready to define this act of civil disobedience as precipitating a new grassroots movement (Barkan 1979; Epstein 1991).

The anti-nuclear Clamshell Alliance that developed thereafter in New England crystallized around a political style that other grassroots anti-nuclear alliances throughout the US would reproduce. One estimate had it that half of the nuclear power plants in the US had been opposed by such groups by the middle of 1978 (Barkan 1979: 24). The political style that Clamshell articulated has been described in terms of its favored tactic – nonviolent civil disobedience – and its organization by affinity groups (Epstein 1991; Vogel 1980). What is striking, and heretofore unremarked, is the likelihood that Clamshell activists and their counterparts in other groups all assumed that movement participants would be able to join as politicized selves.

Clamshell's founding is particularly telling on this point; it gives a glimpse of relations between formal ideologies and the routines that activists take on in everyday practice. Most of the attendees at the initial organizing meetings of Clamshell participated in the alternative cultural networks of Massachusetts or New Hampshire (Epstein 1991). Some were activists, some were communards, some had been involved in 1960s movements, and two were staff members with the AFSC, a Quaker public service organization highly sympathetic to liberal-left citizen politics. As Epstein tells the story (1991: 64) "adherence to nonviolent direct action, semiautonomous local groups, and decision making by consensus emerged more or less spontaneously at [Clamshell's] first meetings." An interview with the man who toppled the nuclear plant tower strongly suggests that Clamshell organizers' everyday understandings of collective action pre-existed and made them receptive to "consensus" as an ideology of democracy:

"As for consensus, it went from 'it's operating this way' to 'there's got to be a word for it,' so Elizabeth [AFSC staff member] said, 'it's consensus.' She laid out how it was used in the AFSC and earlier movements. It was legitimized at our second, large meeting" (Epstein 1991: 64).

"Consensus" articulated what these activists had already taken for granted as part of the post-1960s movement heritage. In terms of a history of ideas, we could say Quakers introduced "consensus" to the Clamshell Alliance – along with the idea of affinity groups. In terms of commitment practices, "consensus" and affinity groups were effective ways to articulate relations between political actors who already related to one another as politicized selves.

Of course without field observation of the founding conference or other Clamshell activities it is hard to be certain about how the activists embodied "consensus" in some concrete form of group commitment. But Vogel's (1980) and Epstein's accounts both suggest that Clamshell activists were unable to institutionalize the leadership and authority in their network that could have broken the deadlocks over disagreements that eventually led to Clamshell's demise. Activists who insisted on living their political principles on the personal level, and preserving individual participation at any cost, could well be activists who, like the Greens later on, tried to create a "new politics" that made personal expression the first authority principle.

The west coast anti-nuclear Abalone Alliance seemed to have intended a similar project. Like Clamshell, it organized mass protest occupations of a nuclear power plant, and in the process built a protest "community," the experience of which came to be an end in itself. Epstein shows that Abalone activists articulated themselves in terms of ideologies that differed somewhat from those in Clamshell, though both networks included large numbers of activists who might have considered themselves "anarchists." The Abalone activists had access to versions of radical feminism and feminist spirituality that played much less of a role in Clamshell activism.

Yet the ostensible difference in ideology did not seem to make so much difference in the collective *form* of activism, the commitment style, that Abalone enacted. Again, personalized expression seems to have been paramount. Epstein quotes (1991: 185) one Abalone activist's statement on the value of a "feminist process" in which "everyone's input was sought and valued":

For me, the most important thing was that in almost every meeting I was in, we went around in a circle and everyone said what they had to say ... we were not forced to vote. That's how I think ideas should develop. That kind of feeling of all of us working together on a problem was real important to me.

Epstein traces this form of group process to the influence of spiritual feminism and paganist teachings about the power and divinity within individuals. But it sounds like the same group style that Clamshell activists articulated in terms of "anarchism" or Quaker ideas about consensus. In everyday practice, diverse political ideologies provide usable languages for the same commitment style.

Epstein's point is well-taken that a major contribution of these anti-nuclear groups has been to disseminate a complex of organizational formats and tactical styles – consensus, affinity groups, nonviolent "direct action." Some of these group practices had already been developed in the more radical wings of the feminist movement (Meyer and Whittier 1994). These cultural tools of movement-building codified and routinized a new personalized politics that has informed environmental activism in the 1980s and 1990s. The personalist cultural current that flowed through the civil rights movement and splashed with announcements of personal liberation in the 1960s became a steadier ongoing stream during and after the 1970s.

We ought to recognize the distance that the personalist tendency traveled from the Christian humanism of SNCC's statement of purpose. Black activists could enact personalized politics within a larger, institutionalized black heritage represented by churches and public service organizations like the NAACP. When some black activists rejected these institutional arbiters of their identity, they substituted alternative notions of peoplehood – the black nation. For white anti-nuclear activists fifteen years later, politicized self-expression had much less of a tangible connection to established collective identities. Activists appropriated old paganist beliefs and "Goddess" spirituality for activism that opposed dominant institutions. Without a single, well-established institutional basis like the black church, or an historical sense of being an oppressed people, anti-nuclear activists like those in the meeting circle pictured above carried their commitments as radicalized selves creating a new community.

The women's peace movement: fighting dichotomies through personal expression

Feeding into the larger anti-nuclear movement in the late 1970s and early 1980s were women's groups scattered across the US which constituted the "women's peace movement." Two activists in women's peace networks (Foglia and Wolffberg 1981) claimed that in 1981 there were twenty-five such organizations in the northeast US alone. These groups and others like them participated in protests at corporate headquarters and in large, women's protest encampments. Their collective actions manifested their insistence on bringing feeling, color, imagination, and other non-"male" qualities into the discussion about nuclear weapons. Assumptions about the whole, individual, pre-social self threaded their way throughout this women's activism. Though these peace activists insistently denounced dualities as instruments of patriarchal thinking, the duality of individual and society informed many of their statements about movement-building.[7] It was a hegemonic residual deeply embedded in their "counter-hegemonic" project.

One of the largest collective political efforts of women activists during the peace movement high tide was the Seneca Women's Peace Camp of 1983 (Brenner 1988; Epstein 1991). Activists conceived the Seneca encampment as a solidary response to the women's protest encampment at the Greenham Common military base in England, the destination of cruise missiles stored at Seneca. The "Women's Encampment Handbook" produced for the Seneca encampment speaks to a woman who appreciates the same notions of self-empowered activism entailed in grassroots anti-nuclear and environmental movements. The Handbook's description of consensus decision-making could have been the model for Green organization-building five years later – and perhaps it was:[8]

The fundamental right of consensus is for all people to be able to express themselves in their own words and of their own will (p. 42).

Familiar appeals to self as the locus of political involvement mark the Handbook's description of affinity groups, the elemental collective unit of women's peace efforts:

Feelings of being isolated or alienated from the movement, the crowd, or the world in general can be alleviated through the love and trust which develops when an affinity group works, plays, relates together over a period of time (p. 40).

The statement makes another familiar assumption – that its reader lives "life as a political project." She merges her "personal" and "political" relationships into a way of life. And similar to the self-expressive universalism of the anti-nuclear activists, the Handbook embellished a brief mention of the history of affinity groups with an appeal to their naturalness as a vehicle for political expression:

[A]ctually affinity groups are probably the oldest and most ubiquitous form of organization by people seeking to make a better world: what makes more sense than small groups of friends who share an "affinity" working together?

Who would argue with the friendly route to social change?

Of course a specifically women's peace activism made a less universal appeal than other developments in personalized politics. But it appealed to the same kind of political actor. Two early observers of feminist anti-nuclearism (Foglia and Wolffberg 1981), activists themselves, imagined feminist activism as conjoining a solitary self with a transhistorical feminine principle:

While each individual [activist] may subscribe to a different relationship with the unifying principle of the universe, the movement as a whole has looked back to the matrifocal spiritual symbols for strength.

Feminist anti-nuclear activists would join a movement on the basis of individualized moralities, ultimately responsible only to the "universe," and united with other activists by reliance on a universal feminine principle. Why would feminists who extol the "feminine" virtues of community and interconnection remain uncritically attached to images of ontologically separate selves? They assumed personal selfhood as the agent of resistance to patriarchy; they naturalized the two terms as opponents, just as Greens sometimes naturalized the opposition of personal expression and bureaucratic politics.

Part of the reason women peace activists created their own networks and sponsored women's protest events was the sexism they experienced in the grassroots anti-nuclear movement. They understood their frustrations with men by conceiving male and female qualities as essentially different and identifying themselves wholly with the female. The way they converted this ideology into practice was by enacting the "female" qualities in terms of personal expression. A women's peace movement would be one in which members are accepted as growing individuals, rather than as competitive political strategists:

The effect we choose to have on others involves concentration on developing personal strength, as opposed to creating fear ... [W]e are able to accept diversity of opinion and approach. The environment is always a supportive one, and it is a pleasure to meet (Foglia and Wolffberg 1981: 451).

This personalized politics, like that of Greens, needed a standpoint outside of mainstream political culture. In this case, they wanted to criticize what they considered the patriarchal practice of separating feeling and intuition from debate about nuclear weapons. They entered peace politics from the standpoint of the personal self.

A "radical" environmental network: tactical variation in personalized politics

The Greens were certainly not the most publicized grassroots environmental movement during this study. The loose network of activists called Earth First![9] received much more attention for its radical tactics and its 1990 "Redwood Summer" campaign. Like the civil rights movement's Freedom Summer twenty-six years earlier, Redwood Summer aimed at harnessing activists' brave indignation in defense of the powerless – in this case, the northern California forests threatened by a stepped-up schedule of clear-cutting.

Interesting in comparison with the Greens, the Earth First! network encompassed activists who favor protest actions over devising platform statements or theorizing the institutional framework for a better society. EF! members (like some Greens) have demonstrated at stock exchanges and business meetings, protesting corporate logging policies. In addition to legal demonstrations, civil disobedience by some EF! members included physically blocking logging trucks, and interrupting logging by "tree-sitting" or "tree-hugging." Rhetoric in the movement spanned both militancy and non-violence. California Earth First! activists with whom I had contact almost universally disparaged the Greens for being "all talk" and ineffectual.[10] In fact, EF! proponents sometimes refer to the EF! penumbra simply as the "radical environmental movement," certifying their own political pedigree while pronouncing other grassroots efforts as either too incremental or beneath notice.

But even though the diffuse Earth First! network has been inspired by ideologists and writers (Manes 1990; Abbey 1975) who favor militant resistance, in many ways it practices the same personalized politics as the Greens. Like the Green movement, EF! has eschewed hierarchical lines of authority and accountability in favor of personal initiative. It has no formal membership at all – hence my elliptical-sounding descriptions of EF! as a penumbra or network. Its participants assume personalized political expression to be a central component of collective action.

An interview with one EF! participant, Randy, made clear how much the network assumed politicized selves as the unit of participation.

Bemused by my organization-oriented questions, he told me "they (EF!) have a meeting when they feel like it." And why do people in such a loosely organized network bother participating?

Some people go because they want to go to a demonstration and they want to see their friends. Some people go because they want to go to a demonstration. Some people go because they want to see their friends.

The idea that loose organization might frustrate commitment clearly came out of a whole perspective on commitment very distant from the life-world of EF! members. Quickly realizing that putting these sociologically motivated questions to Randy was like forcing a conversation between monolinguists of different tongues, I tried to moderate my rhetoric, still hoping to force an encounter between Randy's taken-for-granted world of commitment and the more traditional perspective. I asked how a group could depend on regular press releases and banners to demonstrate with if no one took the lead in organizing regular tasks. Some things, Randy replied, would simply not get done.

PL: "There must be something that makes it worthwhile to be in a group that might not last – something good about organizing it that way."

Randy: "People don't get involved because of the group. They get involved because there are things they want to do – like fighting extinction (of species)."

Randy elaborated that while it might be naive for individuals to think they could be pushing back the frontiers of extinction, "you do it on faith, anything you do, you do partly on faith."

PL: "So people go because they're personally committed on their own?"

Randy did not answer directly, but observed, "You're still pretty wrapped up in these categories." In contrast, EF! members took pride in challenging outsiders' – especially sociologists' – categories for organizational life, categories like "leadership."

Randy was certainly "committed" to EF! causes. He lent his technical expertise to EF! media work. And he did so on his own terms. "I do what I *like* to do" he said defiantly when I asked what sort of work he did with EF! Though he would dislike the term, Randy "organized" his commitment squarely in the terms of personalized politics.

While Randy eschewed the Greens, other EF! participants got involved in Green movement-building activities. One went to several of the early Green Party organizing meetings, displaying varying amounts of impatience at each. Like the Greens themselves, Barth got frustrated at the decision-making impasses that Green groups bumped up against so frequently. At one party organizing session, he compared the dreary work of organizing a party structure and platform – made more tedious by the lengthy verbal machinations that Green groups indulged – with other more appealing images of movement-building.

I went to Redwood Summer and most people said they were registered Green – but didn't expect much would happen ... " Barth then alighted on one Green's fundraising proposal for a large musical event: "So we can have a good platform and committees ... but if we can get 5000 people who think alike to enjoy being together – I want to put my energy into that. We can have a great platform, but if no one *comes* (to join the Green party) ...

At a meeting a month later Barth had become more pessimistic about Green organizing:

We've been talking about the meeting itself – and I know that must be important, but deep in my heart and soul I don't want any part of it ... It is making me consider becoming a Republican.

Barth had broad political concerns, and located their wellsprings deep inside a political self ultimately responsible to no particular organization. "What about education?" he asked at an early Green Party meeting. "There are people in my area who can't read – that's an environmental issue." But when a member of the party coordinating committee asked him if he would bring an issue of concern to him to the next meeting he muttered that he would not be there.

Frustrated with the lack of direction in the Green movement, Barth and other activists like him had available other, more "active," protest-oriented tactics under the same aegis of personalized politics. Earth First!'s demonstrations and "direct actions" – blocking logging trucks or freight trains, disabling sawing motors with sand – combined (temporary) impact on corporate power with a satisfying sense of "doing something." These demonstrators got the opportunity to do what feels right, and perhaps make some converts in the process. They enacted the same notions of self-empowerment politics that Greens did without the endless "talk about talk about talk" as Barth put it at one meeting. Of course, without talk about how self-empowered protesting builds a broader movement, the protest-oriented Earth First! network ended up doing less concrete movement-building work than the Greens, even if their actions received more publicity. Earth First!'s demonstrations and "direct actions" created a wide but temporary spectatorship dependent on further protest episodes in order to remain an alerted – though not necessarily engaged – public. Such relations with potential publics energize new activists by happenstance, not by plan.

Energetic, temporary protest campaigns and abstract cultural criticism are two extreme poles of personalized politics. The Greens have tended toward the latter tendency, although some Greens joined in at Redwood Summer and other protest actions. The two tactical modalities coexisted ambivalently within individuals as well as movements. Carl of the Ridge Greens wanted to develop a new politics around Green values, in tandem with finding self-fulfilling employment. He also felt the urge to carry out a theatrical "hit mission" on irradiated chickens sold in supermarkets,[11] and he privately cheered the eco-tage exploits associated with some Earth First! members. Personalized politics runs the risk of leaving its practitioners a tactics with a weak strategy, or else an abstract strategy of radical cultural change without a clear tactics. Politicized selfhood as a principle of political membership enabled activists in this study to maintain either a broad, elaborate vision or a large quantum of energy for protest episodes, but relatively rarely did the two get articulated together. Most Earth First! members I met spoke for "action." They derided the Greens as "all talk," and put little faith in the party organizing effort. The split between talking and doing was not lost on Greens, including even those most enamored of consensus process and self-discovery.[12] But the options for joining "talk" to "action" that both Greens and Earth First! members saw around them were not appealing.

At one general Green meeting, for instance, a woman asked whether the Greens had tried working with other environmental groups. She had hoped to hear that Greens were working to unite other groups into one large organization. No one was particularly sympathetic to her perspective.

A Ridge Green Party activist: "David Brower says 'don't get so big that you get taken over.'" She said that the Greens were at philosophical loggerheads with the "Big Ten" and "they are not our natural constituency." The Sierra Club supported "politically suspect initiatives." Barth elaborated that the "Big Ten," the "Sierra Club, Greenpeace, or whoever they all are, I don't know all their names" had already made a lot of "compromises." The thinking among groups he was "close to," the "Redwood Summer people and the Earth Action Network," was that "the time is past; it's not that the time is here, it's past. Any compromise is already lost." Barth was sure that entire ecosystems themselves were at stake.

Like Randy, Barth worked on a kind of "faith." He believed that environmental destruction was in too advanced a state to spend the time submitting his beliefs to public debate on whether it really was "too late" or not. Self-empowered representatives of nature's interests, Earth First! members purposely avoided – or never really became familiar with – the established "Big Ten" organizations. They did not try organizing a public so much as jarring one and leaving the organizing to others.[13] Ultimately, they were responsible to their own personal evaluation of environmental degradation, their own faith. They entered the public arena as empowered selves more than as members of public organizations or as new institution-builders.

Activists in each of the three movement networks sketched above committed themselves to intervening in the political arena. None simply wanted to "liberate" themselves or practice dissent for the sake of feeling good. In varying ways, and with varied consequences, each of these movements lodged political responsibility within the self. The world of professionalized movement organizations offered little other basis for culturally radical activism.

THE INSTITUTIONAL CONTEXT FOR PERSONALIZED POLITICS

Political commitment in an anomic arena

Personalized politics complements, and perpetuates, the market-like fray of activist groups in which activists like Barth must define their commitments. Without a single strong organizational aegis or alliance, much less a party-like institution, it makes sense that some broad-minded activists would practice their commitments as mobilized selves, poised for participation in a vaguely defined arena of "social change movements" where activists maintain vaguely defined organizations and fluid memberships. Membership as a personal self implies that one is bound by an individually nurtured sense of commitment more than by allegiance to organizational boundaries and strictures. Politicized selves can travel in an arena of social movement organizations whose main commonality is that they share the expectation of individualized participation, along with an abstract ideology of "progressive" cultural change.

Ex-members of Green organizations have often continued enacting their broad commitments through diverse organizational vehicles. When the fragile Ridge Green organization dissipated, members moved on to other organizations in the same rough "social change" arena – organizations like those I explain below in Table 6.1. Donald went back to working at a Greenpeace office, Carl became a temporary organizer for a garbage disposal initiative on the county ballot, Mike became further involved in environmental restoration and in liberal-left Ridgeville electoral politics while continuing to consider himself an "eco-freak," Larry immersed himself further in spiritual questing, while Joe, George, and Carl rejoined the state's Green movement in its political party-organizing incarnation.

Survey responses from the 1989 Green conference revealed that Greens continue to affiliate with a range of other movement organizations while active as Greens. A strong majority of survey respondents identified affiliations within a spectrum of liberal-left and "alternative" political and community groups.[14] Almost entirely absent from this spectrum were the range of traditional service, leisure, and professional groups that get tallied in standard surveys of "volunteer" group memberships (for instance, Verba and Nie 1972). Lacking standardized categories for tallying affiliations in the "social change movement" arena, I organized the Greens' responses to a question about other political, religious, or community affiliations into the categories listed in Table 6.1. Most Greens had more than one other group affiliation. The numbers represent the number of respondents whose affiliations fit into the category. Some individuals had more than one group affiliation within the same category (Sierra Club *and* Greenpeace, for instance), so the number of specific groups mentioned may exceed the number of respondents who would fit a category of membership.

Despite the variety in organizational affiliations, Greens' commitments observe cultural boundaries. While food cooperatives constituted nearly half of the "community action" category, not one of the respondents named an ACORN-style community organization or citizen rights group. Only one respondent mentioned an anti-toxics affiliation (logged under environmental advocacy). Traditional volunteer service groups (soup kitchen, senior citizen center, Lions Club, for instance) are absent from the list, though some Greens did belong to organizations providing specific environmental or natural resource management services. The communities that Greens build and the constituencies they serve or become part of draw heavily on the alternative cultural products and services that have developed since the 1960s.

Greens do not simply shun more traditional organizations. But the case of religious involvements shows how Greens locate themselves in the more "liberal" niches of these organizations, niches that will host more individual expression. It is striking that nearly 75 per cent of the traditional religious affiliations were with the liberal Quaker or Unitarian denominations. Of the remaining five, three were unspecified, one was Episcopal, and one could be termed New Age-Jewish. In a similar spirit, over half of the electoral political involvements entailed local politics rather than work in a local (or other) branch of the Democratic or Republican parties.

Table 6.1 *Green activists' affiliations with other organizations*

Type of organization	Number of respondents mentioning category
Religious organization	16
Quaker	(6)
Unitarian	(5)
Community action or local advocacy (including consumer co-op, non-elected local task force)	14
Personal or spiritual development group, non-traditional (including co-counselling, "intentional community")	12
Women's, either electoral or cultural radical group	11
Environmental advocacy group (including Sierra Club, Greenpeace, anti-toxics, Earth First!)	10 (7)
Greenpeace	(4)
Peace advocacy group (including regional "peace centers," Nuclear Freeze)	8
Electoral politics*, other than women's (including local, national party, Rainbow Coalition)	8
Rainbow Coalition	(2)
Environmental service or resource management (including recycling association, land ownership trust)	6
Anti-intervention or third world solidarity	5
Environmental hobby (wildflower club, oceanographic club, etc.)	3
Lesbian/Gay/Bisexual	2
Labor	2
Professional	2
Human rights	2
Athletic	2
	n=72

* excluding Green party organizing

None of the above categories of organization covered more than roughly a fourth of the respondents' involvements. The Green movement is an especially important case for examining in the context of the broader social change arena. For in principle at least, Greens wanted to overcome the fragmentation in the "insurgent," left-liberal sectors of the social movement arena. They wanted to unite disparate ideologies in a broad umbrella movement. But the broadly comprehensive ideology that Greens wished to promote through "Green values" runs up against the existing division of political commitments into a myriad of local and regional organizations and national advocacy groups.

It is interesting to note that the resource mobilization approach to social movements (for instance, McCarthy and Zald 1977) takes as given that social movement organizations compete within different movement "industries" for recruiting advantages and other resources. Rather than take for granted the "pluralism" in US public life, we need to understand how the competition, temporary coalition-building, and avoidance between the above organizations shapes the way activists with broad visions define their opportunities for committing themselves. A resource-mobilization perspective does not sensitize us to this question.

Activists who define their commitments in terms of a "long haul" and want to build new grassroots political institutions must ultimately locate the source of their commitments outside the given political arena. That does not mean their commitments to social change are politically irrele-vant. But they are political actors trying to bring new commitments and ideologies into an anomic arena of community action organizations, special interest groups, identity groups, and electoral organizations. The arena is "anomic" because it is not organized for broad-based, sustained public discussion about social and moral priorities. Perhaps for this reason, church groups head the list of Greens' other organizational affil-iations. Lacking a strong institutional niche within the political arena, Greens maintain generalized commitments as organizationally itinerant, politicized selves. Their commitments crystallize into any number of partial expressions.

Within the present-day arena of social change organizations no group can claim a wide legitimacy for constructing a broad alliance of grass-roots environmental or community issue groups. Even were it not for obvious differences in political interests and turfs, no organization would be able to claim a broadly inclusive cultural basis for building citizen political institutions: personalist and communitarian solidarities segment grassroots environmentalism, and similar divisions have cut through the grassroots movement arena more generally (see Table 4.1, Chapter 4). In this segmented arena, it is difficult to construct a *common* basis for membership in a movement. It is difficult for diverse grassroots activists to share the same kind of social identity in relation to the broader array of communal and political institutions. It has been hard enough for local groups with diverse constituencies to maintain togetherness. Recall Laura of the suburban ACES who made sure she would never "come on too strong" at meetings with statements of her own basis for commitment, in an implicit agreement that no one else would either.

Without a thicker basis for institution-building, many grassroots environmental organizations sign onto coalition efforts, with varying degrees of engagement. These coalitions can take several forms, one of which is membership in a nationally organized network. HAT, for instance, worked within ACFT's national network of toxics groups. When the ACFT's administrative priorities clashed with those of HAT, HAT claimed the mantle of political and cultural leadership in Hillview toxics battles. While striving to keep HAT accountable to ACFT, even HAT's official representative on ACFT's national board did his best to uphold local will. HAT leaders treated their contributions to nationwide campaigns organized by ACFT more as fulfilling obligations to an outside entity than as holding down the west coast flank of a national movement organization. The ties of a local political culture took precedence over any broader "movement" solidarity.

Grassroots environmental organizations also join forces with large, well-established, national environmental organizations in regional coalitions formed to tackle specific ongoing issues. Activists sometimes equate these kind of coalition efforts with movement-building. We need to be clear about how this kind of movement organizes commitment and political will. While coalitions of grassroots and large national environmental organizations can certainly produce victories that grassroots groups alone would not, they also tend to perpetuate the "anomic sphere" of fragmented local efforts in an "unregulated market" of movement organizations.

The grassroots and the Big Ten

In this study, both ACES and HAT entered coalitions with "Big Ten" national environmental organizations, including Greenpeace and the Sierra Club. While some members of ACES and HAT articulated a broader sense of mission and scope during their engagements with coalition work, both grassroots groups represented pre-existing, local political wills in these coalitions. Neither had been set up purely as an arm of a national organization.[15] Both maintained their own different movement cultures. The two national organizations they worked with favored different political styles and tactics, but neither actively encouraged in the grassroots groups a broader sense of membership in a political community than already existed. The local groups unquestionably received valuable technical, logistical, and in the case of HAT, monetary support from the national organizations. But relationships with Greenpeace and the Sierra Club did not significantly change everyday patterns of deliberation and self-identification in either ACES or HAT.

Greenpeace and the facilitator style
With more members (2.3 million) than any other national environmental organization, Greenpeace USA has been described as a highly professionalized, compartmentalized outfit, much like a multinational corporation. The infrastructural reality certainly contrasts with the popular image Greenpeace has as a brave band of ocean-going adventurers willing to risk their lives to protect natural habitats from governmental or corporate exploitation. Greenpeace does much to cultivate the image. During a brief stint of field work in 1989 at Greenpeace's west coast regional office, I viewed a new promotional video with office staff. Very short on information about Greenpeace or about the environmental issues it has engaged, the video showed off the deeds of Greenpeace workers: they rendered baby seals safe from hunters by painting their furs with non-toxic dye, they plugged industrial sewer pipes draining into rivers, and they climbed smokestacks to dramatize air pollution. My volunteer shift in the Greenpeace office and my conversations with Greenpeace activists in the field corroborate the recent argument (Eyerman and Jamison 1989) that Greenpeace purposely avoids strident political ideologies. Eschewing ideological debate and talk of new paradigms, it pursues an action-oriented, "non-political" political strategy of pressuring its foes with dramatic, negative media exposure.[16]

In addition to pursuing its own issue agenda, Greenpeace has assisted grassroots anti-toxics groups. During this study, Greenpeace's new anti-toxics campaign linked up with organizations like HAT and ACES across the US. It supplied technical assistance for testimony at public hearings. In addition to its own media-catching exploits, Greenpeace has provided roving, volunteer protesters for local anti-toxics rallies. Along with office work, public demonstrating is one of the few active roles for which a Greenpeace member can volunteer. In the regional office, Greenpeace maintained a list of volunteers willing to attend protest events, and a recognizable bunch kept appearing – in hippie clothes – at the events I attended.[17] Some two dozen Greenpeace workers attended the CCHW-sponsored anti-toxics conference in 1989. In workshops at the conference, at public hearings, and at the founding meetings of the Community Environmental League (CEL) in California, Greenpeace demonstrated a "facilitation" stance toward grassroots groups. It encouraged grassroots activists to become comfortable with a moderate degree of populist militance, while leaving the specifics of ideology and community-building up to the groups themselves.

ACES and HAT had varying reactions to the Greenpeace style, though both groups have gladly received Greenpeace's technical support and have rallied with Greenpeace's enthusiastic protesters at coalition-sponsored events. In Airdale, ACES members appreciated having Greenpeace's help in testifying against various plans to build or rehabilitate incinerators at Microtech. All the same, leading member Laura voiced some ambivalence about Greenpeace tactics, personified in the abrasive style of the local toxics project coordinator. Laura preferred a less combative style and wanted to allow the possibility of slowly raising environmental "consciousness" among health department workers at hearings. The toxics coordinator on the other hand was fond of saying that the EPA was "in bed with the polluters." For public hearings, he favored bringing a large banner announcing that "The People's EPA Says No to Toxic Incinerators." Another Greenpeace staffer bluntly informed California DHS officials at a public hearing that "DHS, EPA [and other agencies] have no credibility with the public whatsoever."

Greenpeace's style proved more jarring to HAT than to ACES. While strategizing for a hearing on a planned incinerator at the Petrox plant, the HAT chair, co-chair, and staffperson considered a Greenpeace staffer's proposal for a "people's takeover" of the hearing. The staffer thought the proceedings should be pre-empted with testimonies from people who had suffered ill health as a result of Petrox. They agreed with the staffperson's judgment that "we are the people who live here – this is our home turf," and so members of the "Hillview community" would have to agree on any strategy. The co-chair added, "If he (Greenpeace staffer) wants to pull some of his antics, fine, but not in the name of HAT." The HAT staffperson instead proposed that HAT demand a seat on the panel that would debate the incinerator at the hearing. Just as the board approved this strategy, a Greenpeace coordinator walked in and began arguing the merits of "creating our own panel," so as not to be co-opted by the EPA.

HAT staffperson: "I don't think any member in the coalition is going to be co-opted by the EPA or by anyone else for that matter."

Co-Chair: "We can't do it as the community because we have too much at stake."
HAT staffperson: "It wouldn't be perceived correctly anyway in the community
    perception –"
Co-Chair (interrupting): "It would scare 'em to death!"

After this meeting, Greenpeace continued participating with the HAT
coalition, but I never saw a Greenpeace staffperson at HAT board
meetings.

For both HAT and ACES, Greenpeace tried to accommodate local
political wills and let local solidarities stand. HAT's claim as the sole
legitimate interpreter of political will on its "home turf" was definitive.
In the case of ACES, Laura conceived the group's role as taking the more
comprehensive, militant environmentalism of organizations like Greenpeace "down to the community level." That meant translating between
political cultures, while preserving ACES' right to define issue priorities
and allocate its energies as it saw fit. Greenpeace brought ACES' and
HAT's campaigns the publicity they might not have received otherwise.
It also did some of the research and outreach necessary to bring HAT
and ACES into a statewide coalition of anti-toxics groups. Greenpeace
facilitated this coalition without re-forging local solidarities into a
broader, integrated, movement collectivity that could act as a statewide
or national force on its own.

Greenpeace moderated its tone for the founding of the statewide
Community Environmental League in 1989. As described in Chapter 4,
local representatives to CEL's founding conference made clear that they
wanted a "network," not a strong new organization with new commitments. The Greenpeace toxics coordinator obliged them. He went no
further than injecting a light populist environmentalism into the proceedings: "Not-In-My-Backyard is fine, but Not-In-Anybody's-Backyard is
better." When a representative from ACES asked why Greenpeace
wouldn't do a newsletter for the new network, the coordinator explained
that it was up to the grassroots to do this kind of organizing. While
providing assistance, "we can't fight your battles for you." He added that
change didn't happen because Greenpeacers got in the news for climbing
an industry smokestack; change happened because lots of communities
organized themselves at the grassroots. The network that Greenpeace
facilitated complemented the "mutual aid" movement-building model of
Lois Gibbs at CCHW: "Local actions add up to cause major change
throughout society."

The Sierra Club and the "influential ally" style

Local chapters of the Sierra Club also maintain toxics projects. Club members provide expertise for testimony at hearings, and they bring the prestige of the Club with its half-million members to anti-toxics battles. With less of an aggressive activist style than Greenpeace, the Sierra Club's relations with ACES and HAT were limited more to providing technical expertise without any implicit tutelage in militancy. Given Club members' more behind-the-scenes role, I observed fewer contacts between them and the grassroots groups. My observations did make clear that the Sierra Club even more than Greenpeace avoided a forthright organizing role and like Greenpeace, did not much influence local movement cultures. In the first four years of HAT, the Club's influence could only have been minimal; its Hillview-area chapter did not join the HAT coalition until late in my study. The HAT co-chair and longtime anti-toxics crusader in the area had approached the Sierra Club nearly twenty years earlier when she began connecting the health problems of some elementary school children with air emissions from the nearby Petrox plant. At the time the Sierra Club had not been interested in the issue.

ACES partook of the Sierra Club's expertise while steering clear of what it perceived as the Club's undesirable organizational style. A Sierra Club representative attended the monthly meetings of a regional coalition[18] begun by ACES and an activist legal agency to broaden the exposure and support for challenging the military contractor. Sierra Club participants took a professional stance, and made clear that they would oppose environmental and health risks from the work at Microtech without debating the politics of military technology or the overall role of regulatory bureaucracies. At an early meeting of the coalition, one of the Sierra Club representatives took umbrage at the anti-nuclear tone of a few other participants and informed the meeting that she could not have been present were it not for nuclear medicine. The Sierra Club's usual toxics representative took a much more measured and less aggressive stance than his Greenpeace counterpart at an important hearing on one of Microtech's incinerator plans. Calling for consideration of alternative technologies and risk assessments, he avoided commenting on the politics of regulation. He closed with a statement of good faith: "We want to work together with the government, the community, and concerned citizens ... " Though valuing the Club's clout and its contribution to the new coalition, ACES self-consciously defined itself apart from the Club. Members did not want to become "like the Sierra Club" by replacing ACES' affinity-group feeling and highly participatory format with a more bureaucratic organization of officers and standing committees. To them, even opening a store-front office posed the unwanted possibility that Airdalers might perceive ACES as a big, self-protecting organization that wanted to enlist citizens, rather than empower them.

Both the Sierra Club and Greenpeace assisted coalition networking amongst grassroots activists. And both won more visibility for environmental issues that originated at the grassroots in Airdale and Hillview – health risks of work at Microtech, and health damage from especially toxic industrial accidents and pollution. The national organizations helped build lines of communication without building new, broader political identities. Entering environmental activism means joining grassroots groups anchored in local political culture or else joining national organizations as a dues-paying member with opportunities to volunteer time in pre-determined campaigns. Neither option has allowed a lot of room for activists to debate broad political or moral priorities in the context of a national public forum.

THINKING BIG IN AN INSTITUTIONAL VACUUM: SELF AS A BASIS FOR CULTURALLY RADICAL POLITICS

The Greens, along with the anti-nuclear, radical environmental and women's peace networks I surveyed above raised broad ideological questions outside the issue-oriented agendas of coalition politics. Only a relatively small percentage of Greens in my survey mentioned Greenpeace or the Sierra Club as affiliations (Table 6.1). Greens and similarly-styled activists "challenge the boundaries of institutional politics" (Offe 1985). They assume members of a society have already won a baseline of rights to political participation and economic opportunity. They pursue instead what has been called a politics of "life chances" (Kitschelt 1985) – a struggle for a better quality of life – or "life politics." In Giddens' words, "life-political issues supply the central agenda for the return of the institutionally repressed" (1991: 224).

The final puzzle for this study is the fact that US activists have tended to raise the broad issues of "life politics" through a personalized style of activism. We should not simply take this combination of ideology and practice for granted. Why wouldn't movements with broad moral and ideological goals be just as likely to favor strong organizational hierarchies, and a firmly established definition of membership in a new moral order? Researchers and activists have posed several reasons for the link between personalized politics and broad ideological goals. None is entirely satisfactory. Each misses the crucial point that a political community of selves is an historical construction, and not a natural accompaniment to particular issues, nor a natural outgrowth of human needs.

Explanation 1: "New social movement" (NSM) identities require personalized politics

Work on NSMs has suggested that personalized politics corresponds to movement goals that differ qualitatively from those of labor and other older movements. Arguing that identity-building is at least as important in recent women's, peace, environmental, and youth movements as is pursuing concrete strategies, scholars such as Cohen (1985), Melucci (1989, 1988, 1985) and others have implied that informal, individual-oriented groups provide the logical forum for experimentation with new political identities. One problem with this reasoning is that it assumes movement participants are readily able to act with a strong sense of individual empowerment. As Chapter 2 argued, this fact of political commitment needs to be explained, not assumed. Second, other recent movements – the US Christian right of the 1980s and 1990s for instance – have spent much of their energies on constructing new collective identities, but have not been characterized by informal, egalitarian, individual-oriented organizational forms. In the US, some grassroots environmentalists have relied on the personalized political style while others have not. The confluence of new styles and new issues in Western Europe did not closely parallel grassroots political culture in the US, where civil rights demonstrators (not practitioners of "life politics") created some of the earliest "new"-style political expression (Carson 1981; Gitlin 1987), and anti-toxics environmentalists self-consciously have constructed local community-centered, not personalized, groups.

It makes sense to look for affinities between identity-focused activism and the personalized style, but NSM theorists have tended to associate the two too unproblematically. It makes more sense to understand personalized politics as a distinct repertoire of collective action, as I suggested in the last chapter, a repertoire that only some of the "new" identity-focused activists enact. When activists such as Greens have "challenged the boundaries" of institutionalized politics as Offe (1985) put it, they have launched their challenges *from* some relation to institutions – from the standpoint of a personalized political self in the case of Greens. They have not simply ridden an ideological vector from out of nowhere into the political fray. In emphasizing the NSM challenge to institutions, NSM research has not attended to the ongoing traditions and repertoires that underlie these radical forays into institutionalized political debates. Personalism is an ongoing culture, and personalized politics has itself become a continuity if not a "tradition" in post-1960s activism.

Explanation 2: Personalized politics "prefigures" a better political community

Accounts of the student new left (Breines 1982) and the anti-nuclear movement (Epstein 1991) have argued that self-development accompanies political relations in the better, future world that activists have tried to model in present-day groups. Taking activists' own terms of discussion at face value, these accounts have assumed that a participatory democracy open to broad ideological debate would also be one with room for personalized expression. But why would a better polity – or one more open to broad questions – necessarily be a more personalized one? Participatory democracy does not have to mean expression of a personal self. HAT members valued participation without assuming that a personal self is what is most salient about a political actor. Personalized politics may prefigure a better polity in the minds of some activists, but it does not naturally guarantee a more ideologically open democracy.

Explanation 3: Personalized politics is purely expressive and anti-institutional

Some critical commentators[19] and some grassroots environmental activists themselves have argued that self-expressive activists simply do not like discipline or are not serious about accomplishing political change. But activists like Greens who practice personalized politics insist on their long-term commitments to social change, even if results have been very slow in coming. Further, it is hard to square the charge of unseriousness with the devotion to a tedious, even rigorous decision-making process in many anti-nuclear, women's, and grassroots environmental groups of the past twenty years. If we uncouple "discipline" from its usual association with vertically organized, tightly controlled organizations, it becomes clear that the organizational ideal in a number of environmental, anti-nuclear, and other movement groups since the 1960s has indeed highlighted discipline. These groups have located discipline more within individual members than within the organization as a whole.

All of the movements of personalized politics surveyed above raise general cultural and moral issues about how people should live their everyday lives. These issues have political import but have lacked strong institutionalized channels through which citizens could discuss them and form identities around them. Local anti-toxics activists can legitimately raise at least some of their claims in the context of state-mandated public hearings, city council meetings, or county waste disposal boards. But no clearly defined political institutions exist in which citizens could debate "radical feminism," or "eco-feminism," "deep ecology," or "post-industrial values."

And who would someone have to be in relation to the rest of society to raise these issues? Other political issues have been associated with longstanding institutional forums and social identities. For instance, Americans have usually debated economic issues as citizens under the aegis of national political parties, or as labor movement members in unions, or else have found small left or far-right parties in which to theorize fundamental economic change. Perhaps for this reason, grassroots activists have occasionally been able to get "military conversion" and the post-cold war "peace dividend" into public forums; the Congress and the political parties are ostensibly the regular forums for discussion of economic priorities. Though the amount of debate on the post-cold war "peace dividend" at the start of the 1990s disappointed many peace and environmental activists, it exceeded that devoted to evaluating the merits of "industrialism" or assessing the relations between women and nature.

Foreign policy likewise corresponds to definite institutions and institutional memberships: citizens can discuss specific policies in their role as members of a military state, even if they disagree with that state's priorities. Proponents and opponents alike usually say "*our* forces won" or "*our* government engages in covert military action." When activists disagree fundamentally with US policy, and stop saying "our," they may take on the identity of "internationalist" or solidary sojourner with an oppressed third world people. The images if not the lived experiences of organized liberation movements in other countries have given some activists an identity to don when they raise radical criticisms of US policy. Whether presenting themselves as the loyal opposition or as radical critics, activists position themselves in relation to political institutions and publics, even when these are the institutions or public of other nations.

But activists who try to publicize comprehensive ideologies of environmental sustainability, world peace, or transformation in gender relations, do not have institutionalized social identities to don. They do not have new forms of political membership to go with their broad new claims. Instead, these activists must cast anchors in the multitude of protest movements, community organizations, networks of "alternative" culture, or an occasional high school or college class that add up to a fragmented, "alternative" sphere of radical political and cultural dissent.

This is the legacy that was left for the Ridge Greens we saw at their potluck party, anchoring their social identities in a scattered array of sites – a "subversive Unitarian church," a course at a women's college, a culturally radical, spiritualist network. Personalized politics is not then a narcissistic search for a politics that is immediately pleasing to individuals. Nor is it a "natural" expression of a deep environmental consciousness. The position of "person" is practically all that is available for activists who raise ideological issues that, in Giddens' words, have been "institutionally repressed."

7

The search for political community

POTENTIALS AND LIMITS IN PERSONALIZED
POLITICS

What are the prospects for personalized politics? What does a focus on
commitment teach us about the conditions for a democratic grassroots
community of different social change movements working together? It is
time to take an accounting of personalized politics, and then to use those
observations to speak back to the radical democratic visions introduced
in Chapter 1.

Personalized politics takes on some challenges more effectively than
others. The activists who practice it have raised broad moral and political questions about ecologically sound lifestyles, basic gender inequalities, and the priorities of industrialism that do not often get raised in
institutionalized forums. These activists maintain a broad vision and are
willing to talk publicly about it, which is no mean feat in a society
increasingly habituated to media cynicism and the constraining
"realism" of interest group politics. And these activists have sometimes
carried out unquestionably "political" action in the most traditional
sense of the term – electoral organizing, for instance – along with
protests and public education campaigns. For all of these reasons,
personalized politics has been an important, even vibrant, part of the
grassroots political landscape since the 1960s.

A strong feature of personalized politics has been its dedication to
inclusive participation. Of course, a community of individually articulate
activists is one fenced in by social parameters of the sort examined in
Chapter 5. Lucille Davis and Mrs. De Rose chafed at HAT's lack of
space for individuals to make a difference in HAT, but it is unlikely they
would have felt comfortable among the self-empowered political

virtuosos at a Green meeting. Some women, however, have found amongst the Greens, anti-nuclear activists, or feminist peace advocates a space for their voices which they had failed to find elsewhere.[1] Women like Linda of the Ridge Greens still felt less powerful than men in some instances, but personalism gave them a basis for contesting gender inequalities within the group in terms that men in the group could not discount. Women had strong grounds for criticizing and even changing group routines in a community of equal selves. This kind of political community has also welcomed those who do share an identification with the well-established cultural authorities or traditions that have anchored other movements – a local civic leadership, a left-sectarian party, a religious tradition, or the tradition of debate about how to create a socialist society, for instance. The Greens and other contemporary movements have accommodated activists whose commitments come from a variety of political or religious identities or else from politicizing experiences that they do not associate with any specific institution or tradition.

Organizational stability appears to be a particularly strong challenge for personalized politics. Clearly, Greens, anti-nuclear activists, radical feminists and others created organizations ridden with conflicts over procedure that could at points threaten the organizations themselves. In the Green movement, we saw activists themselves speaking of their difficulties in finding common ground for working together. In the Ridge group, Mike wanted members to talk about their "common values," and Donald wanted them to recognize a "responsibility" to the group. We saw how much time Seaview and Ridge Greens put into talking about their organizations and their frustrations with them. It is very likely that at least some of this strain on collective effort resulted from a highly personalized commitment style. Cultures of commitment of course do not operate in a social vacuum: we would need a larger comparative study of movement organizations over time to determine how scarce money and time, or an unwelcoming political climate, may interact with the personalized style to compound its challenges.

We can also see some of this apparent weakness as a virtue. While a personalized politics is challenging for organizational stability, this culture sustains commitments for individuals who remain poised for new political involvements even if their extant organizations wither. These activists remain members of an imagined community of committed, politicized individuals open to new opportunities for activism. Greens in fact assumed an already-alert constituency oriented toward cultural and political change when their recruitment meetings invited potential members to talk about the meaning of "left" values. Grassroots movement organizations wither for many reasons aside from those immediately attributable to movement culture, and through personalized politics, culturally radical ideologies such as "Green values" achieve a survival value beyond the durability of specific organizations.

Since the 1960s, people participating in the diffuse, ongoing culture of personalized politics have become core activists or participants in a succession of culturally radical and liberal-left movements.[2] When the 1991 Persian Gulf war erupted, some activists in this study from Seaview City, Ridgeville, and Airdale quickly joined in several weeks of large anti-war demonstrations, along with others whose opposition to the brief war may have come from a more traditionally leftist or "anti-imperialist" stance. Social movement theory has characterized activists like Greens as walking signposts communicating messages of political and cultural dissent even if they do not produce long-lived movements (Melucci 1985). This study adds that these "human signposts" can be very durable ones. When the old Ridge Green group sputtered toward a quiet demise, core members like George, Mike, Carl, and Donald went on to new political involvements or else returned to the Green effort as electoral party activists within the following year. While the pull of family obligations or simple exhaustion limits the staying power of personalized political commitments, we should recognize the dedication these commitments have elicited in activists who define their goals in terms of a long haul.

The US Green movement represents only one version of personalized politics, and given the social movement arena of the 1980s and early 1990s Green activism required an especially strong stress on personalized commitment. During this study, Greens articulated their activism in terms of highly abstract ideologies and they liked to say that "everything is related."[3] In contrast with many other movements, including some with a lot of personalized politics, Greens pursued single issues not as ends in themselves but as sites for articulating Green ideology and putting it into practice. They needed this personalized commitment in order to keep alive broad, multifaceted visions of social change that would not easily fit into the relatively narrow, established institutional channels that separate various issues Greens saw as connected.

The culture of personalized politics has influenced many activists whose commitments are less personalized than those of most Greens and more anchored in specific locales or institutions. In ACES, for instance, Laura articulated herself in terms of both personalized commitment and belongingness to a local community, and her own familiarity with personalized politics helped ACES maintain unity amidst the diverse political stances and cultural identities of its core members. Laura had made a self-conscious decision to settle in Airdale because its semi-rural setting made it a "good place to raise kids." At the same time she identified most strongly with the relatively few others in town who dared to "think differently"; she enjoyed a chance to "get out of Airdale for a night" and go to a political benefit event in Ridgeville, and one day pointed with some pride to a "new age"-oriented shop opening in downtown Airdale. Two other members of ACES told me that they were "really still from Ridgeville down in their bones," having gone to college there long before. These activists did not personalize their commitments in the same way as Greens did, but the diffuse culture of personalized politics influenced them nonetheless.

Many activists pursuing community-centered efforts on environmental, educational, or economic issues have picked up some of this culture – the politicized lifestyle, the organizational practices, for instance – whether or not they feel the ambivalence that ACES members felt about their locale. In the late 1960s and early 1970s, some activists took their personalized projects for social change "back" to local communities, having decided that local politics might be more satisfying than broad national programs of social change in general. These activists did not simply *become* unselfconscious members of locales; they reappropriated local community as a site for carrying out personalized projects for social change. They got on school boards, or started "alternative" schools with egalitarian teacher-student relationships and curricula emphasizing critical thinking and cultural diversity. They organized and staffed low-cost women's health clinics. They created grocery cooperatives. They campaigned for city rent control initiatives. They acted as personal agents of social and cultural change, but within the more manageable bounds of geography or profession than society at large.[4]

Some professional activists in regional coalitions or established, national organizations have carried personalized commitments into their work as well, even if they do not participate in grassroots movement organizations. These activists may have continued living "life as a political project," adding organizational identities to their prior sense of political or radical selfhood.[5] Public service lawyers that advocate for people with low incomes, paid staff in "liberal" organizations such as Common Cause, local organizers for national environmental organizations such as Greenpeace: these are professionals whose work may still satisfy a personalized sense of commitment, albeit a commitment strongly hewn by occupational demands. Of course many of the Greens already treated their jobs as aspects of "being political"; Heather, for instance, spoke this way of her work at an abortion referral center. I am suggesting that some *former* participants in grassroots activist organizations may define their professional work as "being political" too, and may relate to their work as a personal contribution to the public good even if they do not belong to organizations that articulate it this way. The culture of personalized politics may continue to influence their stance toward the meaning of work.

This study has concerned itself mainly with movements advocating the public good for putatively broad constituencies. But identity-based movements with narrower potential constituencies than those of environmentalists have also personalized their politics. One example is the anti-heterosexist activism that some lesbian and gay activists articulated in the early and mid-1990s. Groups reappropriating the term "queer" practiced the same sort of personalized commitment to participatory democracy and cultural change that characterized the Green movement. They created egalitarian groups emphasizing intensive participation. They aimed to resist heterosexism through public education campaigns and "direct action" protests against conservative public officials, and by making their own lives into "signposts" demanding free sexual expression and a freer construction of gender identity than conventional norms would dictate. They demanded a more participatory politics from professionalized lesbian and gay organizations, and from society at large, insisting that new voices get a hearing on questions of sexual rights and sexual representation. Other lesbians and gay men have practiced a personalized politics in professional settings by identifying themselves in their classrooms or pursuing research and teaching agendas devoted to lesbian and gay themes, even if they do not participate in sexual minority organizations. Like the movements in this study, this recent politics of sexual identity promotes a cultural radicalism that finds too little space for public expression in established forums. These sexual minority activists criticized the established institutions in their communities for marginalizing their claims in the same way that Greens criticized professional environmentalists for eschewing difficult solutions and broad agendas of social change.[6]

Personalized politics has had a far broader reach than the Green movement and its movement predecessors. As culturally radical ideologies continue to percolate through the movement arena, it is likely that their supporters will find their voice at least partly through personalized politics. These activists may continue to revisit the difficulties and limitations Greens experienced in maintaining organizations. But activists with diverse political identities and varied politicization experiences like those of the Greens or ACES members will not construct the tightly bound communities of the sort that support groups like Hillviewers Against Toxics. If these activists self-consciously try to "build community," as the Greens tried to do in their multicultural organizing workshop, they would most likely envision and try to create a community of empowered individuals, not one that would highlight unity and shared standards over individuality. We cannot expect them to "go home again" to traditional forms of political community. For activist groups whose members do not publicly share many cultural standards, personalism has provided a common ground for a politics of the public good. Personalism suits their position as public-spirited individuals navigating a sea of small culturally radical groups, community organizing efforts and "alternative" service organizations, with national, professionalized organizations such as the Sierra Club seemingly distant on the horizon. It is hard to identify some tradition other than personalism that is widely familiar in the post-1960s US and flexible enough to sustain activism that is not closely identified with established communities or institutions.

A personalized sense of public commitment has made cultural sense for some activists, then, in a way that other forms of commitment have not. How does this form of activism illuminate the possibilities and limits of radically democratic political communities like those Habermas and Mouffe have envisioned? Could personalized commitments get practiced in organizations that avoid the frustration and exhaustion experienced by Greens, anti-nuclear activists, radical feminists, and others, without restricting opportunities for democratic participation? I want to use the case material now to speak back to both theoretical and practical questions.

PRACTICE MEETS THEORY

A focus on commitment

The communitarian terms of debate about commitment provided little language for understanding personalized political commitments. But the basic question of commitment that communitarians have asked contributes much to how we think about grassroots movements. Much recent writing about social movements emphasizes the new identities and new perspectives on social reality that movements construct. We learn that it takes much cultural work for activists to define themselves as "Greens", for instance, and to establish their difference from other movements and from the wider public. The ideologies or "frames" that these activists use to define their grievances and their proposals for change are also products of interaction, negotiation, and conflict, rather than self-evident reflections of a "reality" that presents itself immediately to activists. This scholarship asks how activists define social and political reality, how they define themselves in relation to allies and antagonists. It has greatly advanced our understanding that movements are purposive, interactive creations rather than logical responses to self-evident social problems, much less socially deficient responses to activists' own lack of integration into a polity. The question asked less often is what it means to be an activist to begin with – what it means to be committed. Contemporary research on social movements views activists as negotiators of social reality, processors of information, seekers after identity. We need to add that activists are "connectors" too. Activism implies a sense of connectedness to others, a sense of obligation, and the cultural means activists have to connect themselves into political communities constitutes an important subject of inquiry in itself.

We need this focus on commitment to fully understand the frustrations as well as the achievements of personalized politics. It is easy to wonder why someone like Carl of the Ridge Greens would let himself feel so "guilty," as he put it, about resisting new group responsibilities in a group that emphasized individual initiative and choice. If the Green movement existed primarily to announce a new, "Green" way of living life and finding fulfillment, as some new social movement theory would suggest, then it becomes all the more difficult to understand why these cultural pioneers would allow themselves to feel constricted by group ties. And why would some continue activist involvements so quickly after having fled a frustrating, ultimately failing group? These patterns of involvement resist explanation – or else invite reductive psychological diagnoses – unless we understand personalized politics as a cultural form of commitment rather than mainly a means to announcing an identity.

Cultures of commitment provide the taken-for-granted ground on which activists would build democratic political communities. Activists talk far more about the ideologies they are formulating, the identities they want to represent, or the routine administrative tasks they need to carry out, than about modes of commitment that they take for granted most of the time. Likewise, these often taken-for-granted practices have gone little noticed in the radical democratic theories introduced in Chapter 1. By focusing on commitment, this study offers insights on the everyday practice of democratic political community, and suggests some challenges to which neither theorists nor activists have given much attention. By viewing the experiences of the Greens, the anti-toxics activists, and other grassroots movements examined in this study through radical democratic perspectives, I will also suggest a response to those challenges.

A communication ethic in the professional middle class

The democratic political community Habermas envisioned relied on a shared dedication to free debate about the public good amongst individuals. Habermas implied there could be a kind of rational individualism in the public interest, a common respect for individual expression among fellow citizens. Rational communication would depend on free, knowledgeable use of language. Clear communication itself would set the standard for good deliberations, rather than the word of specific authoritative persons, or rules or beliefs taken without question. In this ideal, rational communication scenario,

language no longer serves merely to *transmit* and actualize prelinguistically guaranteed agreements, but more and more to *bring about* rationally motivated agreements as well (Habermas 1987: 107; emphases are the author's).

In other words, communication in a fully democratic, post-traditional community would build upon itself, not upon unspoken assumptions or ideological taboos. Habermas thought that the possibilities for rational, critical communication develop in tandem with individuals' capacities to act in a reflective, self-directed way.[7] Critical, self-reflective communication would, ideally, make possible a democratic political community guided by a "communication ethic" that recognizes the value of open-mindedness and mutual respect among individuals seeking to discover the common good.

Habermas' communication ethic is a theoretical model for assessing actually existing forms of democracy. Actually existing forms of course draw on existing cultural practices, not on ideal theoretical categories themselves. This study has focused on actual repertoires of democratic practice which are available to contemporary activists who might try to live out a communication ethic in their movements. Personalism is one repertoire of practice that has made a folk-ethic of communication possible for some activists. The US Greens' emphasis on personal expression and on discussion itself, the anti-nuclear activists' insistence on planning protest tactics through a highly participatory democracy, the feminist peace activists' mission to name unspoken relations between male domination and war-making: each of these collective practices embodies a strong will to replace uncritical habits of thought or unquestioned authorities with explicit agreements ratified through discussion.

These movements tried to practice a highly communicative politics through the shared understanding that each member is a unique *person* whose feelings and opinions matter to any collective decison. These movements have practiced democratic "communicative action" as democratic personal expression – the way Seaview Greens did at their general meetings (see also Lichterman 1995a).

The Greens and the ACES may well represent a substantial number of Americans who, if finding themselves together in a citizen group, would not share the same publicly acknowledged cultural standards, and so would not know how to talk with one another as mutually respecting equals. For some of these citizens, personalism has provided a basis for togetherness – a way of talking and listening and creating group routines – that enables them to sustain a political community with a dedication to free discussion. From examining personalized politics, we learn that at least some public-spirited activists will face a dilemma that goes unremarked in Habermas' theory – the dilemma of practicing commitments that will create sufficient unity from diversity. Highly participatory political communities need a cultural basis that can invite sufficiently diverse, individual participation while eliciting sufficient allegiance to their survival as a stable collectivity. Abstract appeals to rationality and mutual regard do not by themselves supply this culture.

Habermas has conceptualized a particular kind of social site for the communication ethic he envisions. He locates this ethic in the "public sphere," a collective term for those sites in which citizens might freely discuss issues of the day in order to discover their opinions, and debate them in a spirit of mutual respect for rational arguments.[8] Habermas developed the concept to describe the growing social space for citizen deliberation in eighteenth-century England. Historically, there have been many sites for the kind of interaction that might potentially characterize the public sphere – the coffeehouses of eighteenth-century London, the agrarian cooperatives of the nineteenth-century US populist movement, the talk-radio shows of the 1990s. Grassroots movements have been sites for broad discussion and opinion-formation as well as for tactical campaigns and organization-building.[9] Activists not only strategize and mobilize resources together, they also converse and learn together. Critical studies of specific public spheres point out that some of these sites of the public sphere are "counterpublics," or "insurgent" publics, or "parallel publics" that have developed because of systematic class, race, or gender discrimination, or institutionalized differences in power, that limit access to the largest (often mass-mediated) forums for public debate.[10] We could conceive the US Green or anti-toxics movements as sponsoring insurgent publics or counterpublics because these movements create opinions on issues that are shut out of or marginalized within mainstream political debate.

Different kinds of public spheres rely on different cultural practices. Habermas referred (1987: 391–396, 1979, 1975, 1970) to highly educated professionals or college students as those people whose social and cultural backgrounds would make them most able to realize something approaching a democratic communication ethic. Chapter 5 revealed that Greens, and other "new social movement" activists like them, have tended to come from just such backgrounds. Many of these activists have had the cultural skills to personalize their politics. And at least in the case of Greens, they have shared personalism without sharing a lot of other traditions or communal identities in common. But other activists, such as those in the anti-toxics movement, followed a different cultural logic of commitment, and seemed less likely to have either the affinity for or the need for a personalized politics. Does that mean that their own everyday cultural repertoires are less valid or less valuable means for establishing democratic public spheres?

At this point, we must identify the limits in Habermas' vision of a democratic political community. Habermas theorized clear communication in "the" public sphere without reference to the specific cultural underpinnings of actual public spheres. While personalism clearly has limits as a basis for an ongoing public sphere, it allows groups to maintain a degree of individual autonomy that approximates the ideal, rationally debating individual of Habermas' theory. The communitarian-style culture of HAT highlighted individual autonomy and responsibility much less, opening HAT up to the danger that members might too easily or uncritically accommodate their leaders. This was in fact a challenge that HAT members did not always meet successfully. Yet HAT, too, developed group opinions that members mostly shared as willing volunteers, not as puppets or dupes. Public spheres in a highly differentiated, multicultural society will have varied cultural bases. To appreciate their strengths and limits we must move beyond the biases and blind spots in Habermas' thinking about political community.

A grammar of democracy for progressive movements

Habermas theorized how reason might replace either unquestioned tradition or coercion as the basis for political wills. He continued the quest of Enlightenment philosophers to understand how individuals might become truly free by becoming fully rational. To this quest he brought theories of moral and psychological evolution that could validate at least some of this quest in scientific terms.[11] Habermas' theories could scarcely avoid limitations in the philosophical and scientific categories upon which they relied. Critics have taken those categories to task for confusing a specifically male, intellectually oriented, or over-idealized notion of rationality with human reasoning capacities in general.[12] Rather than start from the quest for reason, Chantal Mouffe's thinking about political community started from a quest for democracy. And rather than focus on the public sphere of society in general, Mouffe directed her theoretical efforts toward the prospects for contemporary, progressive social movements such as environmentalism. Of course for Habermas, reason and democracy resulted as closely connected, and social movements might play a role in reversing the shrinkage of a democratic public sphere. By making democracy rather than human reason her central principle, though, Mouffe's thinking could be more attuned at the outset to basic political and cultural differences – different kinds of reason – that a fully democratic community would have to negotiate. Still, Mouffe's project is not so different from Habermas' in basic terms. Like Habermas, she wanted to understand how free, critically-thinking individuals could sustain a public-spirited community of citizens:

Our only choice is not one between an aggregate of individuals without common public concern and a pre-modern community organized around a single substantive idea of the common good. Envisaging the modern democratic political community outside of this dichotomy is the crucial challenge (Mouffe 1992b: 231).

Like Habermas, then, Mouffe tried to envision a political community beyond the communitarian imagery introduced in Chapter 1, without reducing public-spirited commitment to purely private or selfish motivation.

Mouffe's vision of political community diverges most importantly from Habermas' with her proviso that such a community cannot expect to arrive at a single set of common priorities. Habermas conceived an ideal scenario in which reasoning individuals with good will might arrive at a consensus, even if a changing one, about the common good. Mouffe, in contrast, insisted that there would always be communities with diverse, incommensurable notions of what political activity should achieve. In practical terms, this means that there would be no democratic way for a single movement or community to prioritize some of the competing political claims made by, say, women and racial minority groups. In Mouffe's view, any single, over-arching political will, even one developed amongst progressive activists, would slight the autonomy or the aspirations of some groups. It would limit democracy by limiting those group's rights to self-determination and self-representation.

Then how would diverse political communities ever work together? Mouffe's solution was to imagine a greater, public-spirited community made up of progressive movement communities. In this broader community, activists from a wide range of movements could share a loyalty to democracy itself, to self-determination in a context of mutual respect for any other group aspirations that do not infringe on opportunities for public expression in the wider community. In place of Habermas' single public sphere of reasoning individuals, Mouffe proposed a network of autonomous communities – feminist groups, environmental efforts, projects of racial and ethnic self-expression – in which individual activists might maintain multiple allegiances to diverse priorities.

Mouffe's community of progressive communities would hold together because its members would identify themselves, their grievances and projects, in relation to a common quest for democracy. Clearly, those groups whose identities relied on the domination of other groups would have to reformulate their own identities. In fact, Mouffe emphasized (1992a, 1992b) the necessity for members of disparate social change movements to adopt a common identity as "radical democratic citizens" who would abide by the principle of ongoing, limitless democratization. In public forums, these citizens would talk about their own collective identities and their claims in a democratic way that respects all democratic aspirations of others. They would speak and organize together through a grammar of democracy. Mouffe held out the hope that participants in diverse activist efforts might agree on public rules of democratic action – a democratic grammar – so that various movements of women, environmentalists, workers, lesbians and gays, and others could make common cause through a common dedication to expanding democracy – whether at work sites, in state agencies, or in private life.

In contrast with Habermas' communication ethic, Mouffe's grammar of democracy seems to invite more diverse notions of how public-spirited activism could look and sound. We more easily imagine a complex public arena that includes both the highly verbal, intensively personal activism of highly educated Greens or anti-nuclear activists, and the locally grounded populist struggles of some anti-toxics activists and other community efforts before them. Mouffe's view suggests that there are different, perhaps incommensurable routes to participatory democracy, none of which ought to be privileged over others as activists engage in many democratization projects. Mouffe concerned herself most with the differences expressed by collective identities that speak up for public recognition: workers, women, or racial minority groups, for instance. Mouffe's attentiveness to different identities is important for highlighting the complexity of cultural difference and cultural domination within any body of citizens or any public sphere. At the same time, I want to suggest that a perspective on commitment adds a needed dimension to any picture of a radical democratic citizenry.

Activists produce democracy in differing ways, not only because they make different claims as women, environmentalists, or African-Americans, but because they practice different kinds of commitment. Activists in this study not only created somewhat different collective identities, they also drew on specific, only partially complementary traditions – personalism, populism, African-American Christianity, among others – in attempting a democratic, citizen activism. A focus on identity does not by itself bring to view the different *ways* in which activists obligate themselves, relate themselves to their identities. Mouffe imagined that a democratic network of activist communities could cohere if activists shared ways of speaking and representing others democratically in public. The question remains: How would activists work together if, even within the same movement, they practice democratic citizenship in different ways? How would activists who practice "democracy" as a personalized life project and activists who practice democracy as a communal accomplishment create common grounds?

The question of differing commitment styles is not an insuperable one for Mouffe's multicultural vision. Mouffe advocated that many forms of citizenship could co-exist under a democratic aegis (1992b: 237) and this variety could extend to commitment styles as well as to different group identities. But I want to suggest that the question of commitment leads us to appreciate other grounds for shared political community than the grammar of democracy Mouffe offers. Activists who recognize these grounds could make personalized politics less frustrating than it has been for some. First, it is important to review that differing commitment styles could indeed affect the quest for a broad community of activists.

Green and anti-toxics activists committed themselves to different kinds of community, and the differences contributed to difficulties in alliance-building. During this study, Seaview Greens established some contacts with local people-of-color groups, but their efforts did not broaden social or cultural diversity within their own ranks, and they did not add up to a strong, sustained program for multicultural alliances either. The Green movement at the national level likewise attracted little cultural diversity and produced relatively minimal contacts with non-white organizations during that time. Greens in this study made some sincere alliance-building efforts, and the Green movement adopted anti-toxics activists' claims about both "environmental justice" and about racism in the environmental movement as their own. I suggest that different ways of building political community contributed to alliance-building difficulties, even apart from differences in political ideology, by producing different, taken-for-granted expectations about how "activism" should get practiced.[13] Greens assumed individuals mattered a great deal as carriers of social responsibility, and they overestimated the importance of personalized commitment in other movements. Anti-toxics activists assumed that other activists would represent the will of their own local "communities," and did not understand from where exactly Greens came. Some Greens in turn wondered whether locally oriented activists were committed to changing cultural patterns and personal lifestyles that Greens held partly responsible for environmental degradation. It may not be coincidence that other movements characterized by personalized commitments have also met frustration in attempting multicultural contacts.[14]

A broad, democratic community of progressive activists would have to negotiate these different forms of commitment and community. The personalized form of commitment is no mere matter of taste that could simply be changed like clothing. It emerged out of and sustained specific social and institutional contexts for activism, the contexts we saw in Chapters 5 and 6. The more communitarian-style political commitments work within different contexts. A shared grammar of democracy may not provide enough common ground for activists who have built their lives around different cultural skills, social identities and institutional affiliations, even if these activists support the same program for democratization.

Scenes from Green and anti-toxics activism suggest that a sense of obligation itself offers additional grounds for a broad community of public-spirited activists. In fact it makes sense to picture culturally radical Greens, culturally conventional anti-toxics activists and many others as potential members of a broad political community, rather than simply a network or coalition, only because these activists share a sense of obligation. Greens in this study wanted to do more than announce new Green values or new, democratic aspirations for environmental policy-making; through their personalized commitments they wanted to practice *obligation* to a broader public. The fragmented grassroots activist arena and their own cultural radicalism made the "public" to which they directed their efforts vague and abstract, while making their own personal efforts carry special urgency and moral weight. Still, the conflicts over organization and direction among Greens and similar activists before them become hard to understand if we lose sight of the sense of obligation to a broader public in their efforts.

Members of ACES and HAT of course maintained a sense of obligation too. They most often practiced obligation to localized communities, but sometimes their moral horizons expanded beyond their specific locales. Activists in ACES felt obligated not only to Airdale but to the surrounding region, and to a society whose military apparatus endangered its own people with toxic waste. Recall that Laura had characterized ACES as taking a broad social agenda "down to the local level." And members of HAT spoke of obligations not only to Hillview but to the cause of justice for African Americans. These activists shared with Greens a sense of obligation, though they enacted obligation in different ways.

This sense of obligation could help unite a broad, interdependent community of activists if that community shared ways to talk about public commitment itself, ways that would honor different forms of commitment. Such a community might ground personalized politics more firmly in specific communities, giving it more stability so that activists like Greens could invest themselves more in specific organizations and institutions. This community of public-spirited activists might also broaden the purview of those pursuing struggles defined mainly in local terms.

A democratic, public-spirited citizen arena needs both the critical reflection Habermas emphasized and the explicit openness to diverse cultures and diverse democratization projects upon which Mouffe insisted. I argue that it will also need shared ways of talking about obligation. Here, we return to the central, indispensable theme that communitarian thinkers have contributed to the debate about political community. But we need to think of public-spirited obligation in terms of multiple traditions and sources of commitment, including personalized ones. I propose a translation ethic.

INTERDEPENDENT ACTIVISM: A TRANSLATION ETHIC

A good translator has an obligation to the languages being translated and the cultures those languages articulate. A good translator practices a kind of universalistic obligation, but one grounded in specific cultures. A democratic community of diverse activists needs to translate not only diverse political ideologies, as Mouffe implies, but also definitions and practices of commitment itself. By taking on a role of translator between political cultures, activists could learn the different ways that movements maintain commitment and community. Like sociological participant-observers, they would become familiar with everyday group routines in order to understand what "participation" or "self-interest" mean in different political cultures. With this understanding they could help explain to some activists what they were doing and why. Greens could learn why intensive, egalitarian participation did not matter to anti-toxics activists in Hillview as much as it did to them. Locally oriented activists could learn why Greens and other cultural radicals insisted on making personal acts subject to a political imagination, and why they so valued individually held ideological stances.

Acting as cultural translators, activists could foster ties between different movements that may take the same sides on issues or ideologies and still have difficulties working together because their different definitions of commitment lead them to prioritize issues differently: while agreeing on a number of basic issues, Greens wanted to do more than "put out fires" in the terrain of single-issue politics. Hillviewers Against Toxics in turn had little use for abstract ideological discussion because their own local "fire" threatened to engulf their community. While Greens adopted anti-toxics ideologies, neither movement was likely to adopt the specific tactical priorities of the other because these arose out of different kinds of public commitment to begin with. Translation would encourage a broader sense of membership in a political community whose activists engage in different but complementary and worthwhile projects.

Translation might facilitate more broadly-based and long-term political wills than those now held together by the mutual aid principle of anti-toxics coalition-builders. The mutual aid principle allows activists in different locales to maintain themselves as local constituencies trying to solve problems often national or global in scope. Appeals to a broader political imagination too easily run the risk of appearing as extra-local domination or co-optation. This is an issue of commitment as well as one of defining issues. If local community activists learned to see their locally grounded commitments in relation to the broader moral and political horizon maintained by activists like Greens, they would less easily take local forms of authority for granted. They might replace a sometimes uncritical sense of commitment to an organic community with a sense of membership in a more complex locale and a complex society in which their own cultural authorities – civic and religious leaders – must co-exist with others. A more nuanced, reflective sense of local belonging would make it easier for community activists like Mrs. Davis to ask critical questions of their own leaders and to develop a more complicated picture of the "community's" interests and of their own interests as well. A critical, democratic citizenship could evolve more easily than it does when citizens assume that respected local leaders will tell them all they need to know.

The metaphor of translation has special import for activists who now practice personalized politics. It might replace some of the psychologisms, such as "personal empowerment," or "consciousness-raising," that ended up limiting groups like the Greens and ACES. A vocabulary of commitment inspired by the translator metaphor could orient individualized morality toward a broader public, just as "translation" implies a broader constituency than does "personal empowerment." Activists who now create highly individualized activist lifestyles might cast more of their political identity with an interdependent, multicultural arena, instead of relying so heavily on their separate political imaginations for validation as activists.

A greater interdependence would have great implications for the sometimes frustrating, always intensive kind of commitment that goes with personalized politics. The Greens' political imaginations gave them enormous burdens. Carl, for instance, spent months helping keep the tenuous Ridge Greens afloat, fighting off anxieties about defaulting on feminist parenting principles at home, while also wanting to find a socially responsible career. As long as activists like Carl personalize their politics, they would each assume that they need to carry their social responsibility as individual, twenty-four-hour-a-day agents of social change. A Green once told me that activists like him needed to be full-time agents of social change because they had the burden of accomplishing 95 percent of the social change efforts in the US while the rest of the population contributed 5 percent. A translation ethic might encourage activists like this one to take some of the political and moral weight off their actions in private life because they would feel like members of a community that practices public-spirited commitment with more interdependence and less reliance on highly individualized and sometimes crushing obligations.

I am not suggesting activists like Greens should stop honoring individuals as equals, or stop valuing private relationships like parenting instead of devaluing them as "women's work." Nor is it likely that activists like Greens would suddenly adopt communally grounded identities and lose their emphasis on individual responsibility. But they might feel less defensive about choosing professional pursuits that pay relatively well, and may more easily choose occupations that do not usually get considered pro-active for social change. A good society that is a complex society needs critical college instructors and women's health counsellors to be sure, but it will also need electricians and administrators.

A translation ethic might also make personalized politics more amenable to a manageable division of labor in organizations. With somewhat less emphasis on individual efficacy and more emphasis on a collective sense of responsibility in a broader activist community, activists like Greens might more willingly empower and trust organizational leaders. A translation ethic might also encourage them to thread part of their commitment through concrete, localized political projects with larger constituencies, projects like anti-toxics activism, rather than burrowing too deep into an ideologically abstract politics with long-term goals and relatively small constituencies. Activists with highly personalized commitments could make their individualized callings work more effectively for diverse political communities, and for a broader public, if they had more language for orienting those commitments outward to others who understand them. But it should be clear that we cannot simply expect them to orient themselves "outward" through appeals to shared, traditional cultural reference points.

News of the demise of public commitment at the hands of personalism has been misleading. A multicultural society needs to honor diverse sources of public commitment, rather than accepting only those traditional sources that sustained a less complex society than the US at the close of the century. "Seesaw" thinking about personalism and commitment keeps us from recognizing, let alone honoring, the personalized commitments of many Americans whose sense of self resonates only partially, if at all, with long-established communities, political or religious traditions. No force of moral will enables these Americans to reconnect with such sources of commitment on command. In a time when many political leaders and some wary citizens speak as if the greatest good is a private good, we must recognize and cultivate the wellsprings of public commitment where we find them.

Appendix I

Choosing and studying the organizations

When I began this study in 1989, *Time* magazine had just placed Earth on its year-end issue's cover as "planet of the year." Dire reports of a greenhouse effect in the atmosphere cast new doubts on the wisdom of indefinite industrial expansion. As in previous years, most spectators of 1989 Earth Day events would have their consciousness temporarily "raised," reminding themselves about recycling and growing native plants in their backyards. And a few people would carry on their commitments to participating in movements for environmental change. It has been popular to define action for a common good – the environment in this case – in terms of largely private deeds, like garbage recycling. I was intrigued by those relatively few people who define themselves as publicly engaged activists; this study focuses on them.

CHOOSING THE MOVEMENTS AND THE ORGANIZATIONS

Why environmentalists?

I wanted to find out how personalism has shaped the way people become politicized in the name of a broad public good. Many forms of environmentalism propose broad public goods – clean air and water, safe working conditions, ecologically sound technology – and appeal in theory to all people in a given environment. And communitarian and some radical democracy theorists have noted affinities between personalism and the cultural milieux of the educated middle-class strata. Environmentalist attitudes and environmental activism have been tied to highly schooled middle-class backgrounds as well (Kriesi 1989; Kitschelt 1985; Scaminaci and Dunlap 1986; Cotgrove and Duff 1980; Ladd,

Hood, and Van Liere 1980), although prior to this study, there has been little demographic evidence on grassroots environmental activists in the US (see Scaminaci and Dunlap 1986). So on theoretical grounds, environmentalism was a good candidate for this study.

Historical chance strengthened the case. If the communitarians were right that personalism had weakened political commitment among ordinary citizens in the 1970s and 1980s, then the consequences would surface in what was becoming an upsurge of grassroots environmental activism. The celebrations, denunciations, community fairs, and media glare associated with Earth Day 1990 rivaled only those of the first Earth Day in 1970. And by 1990, new "environmentalist" constituencies had begun to identify themselves. Blue-collar workers, housewives, and other culturally non-"hip" people were clamoring for protection from or cleanup of thousands of toxic waste sites which, like the highly publicized Love Canal contamination, had intruded into previously unpoliticized lives.

These anti-toxics activists have brought a new racial and class diversity to a movement usually associated with white, upper-middle-class people with expensive camping equipment, for whom environmentalism means caring about the wilderness. Very recently, activists and scholars have begun to challenge this image of environmentalism itself as the conceit of a dominant culture's definitions. Nonwhite activists are increasingly using environmentalist discourse to articulate long-standing grievances about the physical and economic health of their locales (Bullard 1993). These changes resulted in the opportunity to compare political community-building in the same general arena of "environmental" issues, but across class and culture. For the sake of simplicity, I have called each of the organizations in this study "environmental." But ACES had begun as a self-acknowledged "peace group" and continued to consider itself such even after most of its activities focused on specific toxics issues. As the US peace movement contracted during the 1980s,[1] peace activists increasingly became environmental activists, though without losing their commitment to world peace. The form of political community enacted in ACES endured largely unchanged even though their specific issues changed and their ideologies expanded.

Why grassroots movement organizations?

Candidates for this study needed to do more than recycle garbage, donate money annually to the Sierra Club or Greenpeace, or score as "environmentalists" in attitude surveys. The point was to find people actively advocating a public cause by participating in a social movement.

What would happen when individuals came together to enact a common will and work in the public interest, outside of large well-established organizations? Communitarian and radical democracy theories have both suggested that grassroots social movements would be sites for understanding how personalism may shape political commitment.

The four movement organizations in this study easily qualified as "grassroots": each was open to active volunteer participation by anyone who subscribed to the group's purpose as stated in pamphlets or by-laws. HAT included professional environmentalists in its steering committee, but there were no credential requirements for membership in any of the groups. The organizations in this study arose in part through dissatisfaction with well-established environmental interest groups – the Sierra Club, the Audubon Society, and the others that make up the "Group of Ten" (FitzSimons and Gottlieb 1988). They qualify as social movement organizations under widely known definitions: they and groups like them are "challengers" and not routine contenders in environmental policy-making (Gamson 1975). They also "represent preferences for changing some elements of the social structure and/or reward distribution" in the US (McCarthy and Zald 1977: 1217–1218).

Why these particular organizations?

As explained in Chapter 1, I chose organizations in which participants created different relationships between selfhood and political commitment. But I also wanted organizations from which I might make tentative generalizations to other grassroots movement organizations. Both Green organizations and both anti-toxics organizations were associated with national and regional Green or anti-toxics networks. Each organization received some of the same advice, newsletters, organizing pamphlets, traveling speakers or videos as other groups in its loose network. HAT belonged to the American Communities Fighting Toxics network while ACES did not. But both sent a representative to the Citizen's Clearinghouse for Hazardous Wastes 1989 national conference, and both belonged to the California Environmental League pictured briefly at the end of Chapter 4. Each of the four organizations in the study was based in California. To supplement the field work in these organizations, I observed and interviewed at regional and national conferences, and surveyed two national samples of activists. I have substantial evidence, then, for my claim that these organizations do not differ significantly from corresponding groups in other parts of the US. California activists are not nearly as singular as some of the popular lore about the state would have it.

GAINING ACCESS

Becoming a participant-observer

Initiating participant-observation meant negotiating a role as participant in each of the organizations. I introduced myself and my project to a regular meeting of each organization, and I told each that I wanted to do what regular members did. Subsequently I introduced myself to new members as I met them. I pointed out that I was broadly sympathetic to environmentalism, and wanted to understand how people became committed and stayed committed in different kinds of movement organizations. I made it clear that I would not be making purely token appearances at meetings. I sought a participatory, non-leadership role in each organization – preferably a role the organization already recognized. In HAT this meant being a student helper. In the Green groups it meant being an "active" member but not a task group leader. ACES already had a term for the role I wanted – "worker bee."

The highly participatory character of Green groups made it especially difficult not to take a leading decision-making role at some point. Taking a position as a task coordinator or vocal member may have risked altering the "natural" group dynamic. Avoiding such a position definitely risked arousing mistrust, and confusion, in a participatory group whose solidarity would have been threatened by someone who insisted on being less personally expressive than others. In the end, psychological survival resolved the dilemma: I simply could not become a leading figure in one organization, even if I had wanted to, while studying three other organizations as well. I explained this predicament to various Greens on several occasions.

Carrying out a survey as a participant-observer

Participant-observation made me recognize the extra challenges I would meet in obtaining valid and reliable survey information from grassroots social movement organizations. Being a participant-observer also helped me in formulating responses to those challenges. Here I explain the survey procedures I developed.

One of the difficulties in tapping national samples of activists is that their oppositional politics can make them wary of research interventions. Green and anti-toxics activists seemed to be no exception. Prior to the anti-toxics conference, a CCHW worker helping organize the conference informed me that a researcher had been refused permission to conduct a survey at a prior CCHW-sponsored conference. And two years after my survey of the US Green conference, a researcher with prior personal experience in the Green movement informed me of being denied permission by national-level Green organizers to conduct a mail survey of local chapters of the Greens.

Another challenge for surveying in this milieu involves the informal nature of "membership." In the case of this study, one of the four local organizations did not have an official "member" status at all, one counted among its members people who rarely if ever attended meetings, and two included active, core participants who were not paid-up "members." The survey needed to navigate these vagaries of "membership" status. The goal was to sample participants in the Green or anti-toxics movements that were the most actively involved, those who were most likely to be frequent participants in their local groups, regardless of whether they had happened to pay dues or appear on membership lists. These "core" members would be the most influential in sustaining the norms of the dominant commitment style within their local movement organizations. Participant-observation easily revealed the standards that would be appropriate for identifying core members in each group.[2] The Green voting plenary and the keynote address at the anti-toxics conference reasonably sampled the "core members" crucial to this study. These were activists who put out the effort to attend an hours-long plenary with complicated rules of order, or else a morning speakers' session after a late evening of festivities in the case of the anti-toxics activists.

With the survey sites chosen, the task was to secure compliance from busy conference participants. Activists at a final voting plenary (Greens) or keynote address assembly (anti-toxics activists) could not be expected to allow distracting interruptions or specific time set aside for filling out a researcher's survey questionnaire. To request that conference organizers allot even a brief period for participants to fill out the survey would have risked compromising the necessarily *voluntary* nature of participation in the survey; it could have given the misleading impression that conference organizers either sponsored or else expected participation in the survey. It could also have chilled free expression of viewpoints, giving activists the sense that I had been granted permission to scrutinize them without their invitation. Both research ethics and a desire to secure compliance pointed toward a less intrusive sampling procedure: at each of the two assemblies I distributed questionnaires on the seats that participants would occupy, and included an introductory statement that described the study and specified the voluntary nature of participation.[3]

In the case of both Greens and anti-toxics activists, there are no clear reasons why activists who declined the survey and those who participated would differ in a way that would systematically bias results relevent to the arguments I make. Some activists may not have had time to complete the surveys and deposit them as directed. Or, the oppositionalism mentioned above may have been operating in the Green or anti-toxics surveys: some activists in either movement may have defined a researcher's survey questionnaire as an unsympathetic, technocratic intrusion. But if these political stances were effective in inhibiting survey participation, it is not clear they would correlate with social backgrounds in a way that would systematically bias the data I used to make my arguments about class culture, group affiliations, and commitment.

These limitations must be kept in mind when interpreting the data on differences between Greens and anti-toxics activists. Given the challenges in surveying grassroots movements, it may be that few if any surveying procedures would produce results more reliable or generalizable than those provided here. Considering the small amount of systematic demographic data on American grassroots activists of the 1970s, 1980s, and 1990s, these data warrant consideration for their potentially large implications.

Appendix II

Why participant-observation was necessary

WHY INTERVIEWS WERE NOT ENOUGH

One way to discover how and why activists have committed themselves to a cause is to ask them. During an interview with Barb, a member of ACES, I learned that a lot of people she knew at work and on her softball team would have ridiculed her anti-toxics activism had they known about it. Barb preferred to be known as a good baseball player, not an activist. The portion of the county that she lived in relied on Microtech, the military contractor located there, for a significant number of jobs. The company had polluted local groundwater, and had emitted toxic smoke and gasses into the air in several documented and an unknown number of undocumented incidents. Barb's group focused on these issues with the goal of drawing more local residents into discussion about Microtech. But to many area residents, it was not polite to question the contractor; to some, it was irrational.

So during the interview, I asked how she knew that her activism was the right thing to do.

Well, it's my nursing background. I'm able to read some of the technical books that come out – I'm able to understand some of the chemistry of groundwater pollution ... having taken care of cancer patients, having been there when they come out of surgery ... having learned what I've learned about them (the company) and how they operate and how they hide things, I don't trust them.

But this did not strike Barb as a completely satisfactory answer. Her answer trailed off, "'How do I know?' I don't know ..." I observed that a lot of nurses have seen cancer patients without joining anti-toxics groups. Barb reasoned her way tentatively through another answer:

Well I think – I don't know. When you believe that something might cause a problem, and you don't do anything about that something, you might feel bad.

So therefore some people may not make the connection so therefore they don't have to do anything about it.

She corroborated this answer with another group member's claim that their community was in a state of "denial" about problems with Microtech. They were cutting themselves off from potentially troubling feelings. She concluded with her own briefer version of this feelings-oriented rationale:

Barb: "I don't know. I tend not to think about why I'm doing it – it just feels right so I do it." (chuckles nervously)
PL: "I'm not criticizing you."
Barb: "I know – I feel like a space cadet that I can't explain why I'm doing what I'm doing."

When pushed on the point, Barb adduced a strongly personalist rationale for her activism. Did she have a durable basis for commitment, or did her commitment turn on the caprice of personal feelings that might change unpredictably as communitarian theorists have worried? Could other members of her group trust her to remain committed?

Barb was a member of ACES almost from its inception. In the above interview, she said that she and other core members were "in it for the long haul." Their ultimate goal was to pressure Microtech to end highly toxic work altogether and to pursue contracts that would not depend on a military economy. Though she did not have a ready rationale, her commitment showed through nonetheless in her willingness to spend some of her weekends preparing technical briefs for public hearings, and especially in her statements at public hearings about how ACES wanted to pull ordinary Airdale citizens into policy-making about environmental hazards. At a public meeting on groundwater contamination, for instance, Barb reminded a timid audience of local residents,

We have a responsibility to provide input … to request information when we don't know it … it doesn't take superhuman ability to go to the library and call people up.

In the everyday rounds of activist life, Barb spoke and acted, then, as a "responsible" citizen of a local community. It would have been difficult to arrive at this from interview material alone. Barb used a popular-psychological idiom that other people in grassroots movements have used to talk about their activism, but Barb's social identity was based more on local community membership than on personalized cultural dissent. She contributed to a group that defined its role as a "community conscience" more than as a laboratory for new values.

When I interviewed Carl of the Ridge Greens about why he thought his activism was the right thing to do, he did not use personalist discourse at all. He explained his own activism as a product of independent-minded parents who had once fought racial discrimination at the college where they taught. Carl avoided the self-discovery talk of some of the other Greens, and satirized it when it took on spiritual overtones. During our interview he even used the word "duty" to describe the Greens' commitment to a larger citizenry.

Yet in the previous two years Carl had expressed a lot of ambivalence about leadership of any kind. He had shied away from enforcing a hierarchy of responsibility in his Green group: visible divisions of rights and responsibilities would "push people's buttons." In the first months of the new Green Party of California, in front of new Green Party volunteers without a well-formed opinion of the organization, he laid bare the sparse party infrastructure: "Some feel like we're rushing ahead without an organizational structure – and we are." He downplayed his own instrumental role too: "It's just me and my word processor." Carl did not like taking on an institutional political identity – it did not fit comfortably. Since the Green Party's beginnings, he had become more reconciled to a need for some structure in political organizations. But his heart was still in minimally planned political salvos, like his project to plaster grocery store chickens with printed stickers alerting customers to the new methods of preserving fowl: "Do you know you're eating radioactive chicken?" In Green organizational settings, Carl often spoke and acted so as to imply that people should participate in politics as empowered selves more than as obligated members of a community. And at crisis points, he had joined other Greens in blaming his group's problems on a lack of "personal empowerment," a lack of respect amongst members as personal selves.

To understand what different moral or political traditions are available to people who "go public," it is best to see how they present themselves in everyday movement settings, and not rely on interviews alone. The personalist tradition, for instance, provides an everyday basis for commitment even if it does not always show itself in the way activists talk in interviews. It would not suffice for activists to name all their prior organizational affiliations on a survey sheet so a researcher might deduce the cultural sources of their commitments. Barb was raised a Catholic, married in a Catholic ceremony towards the close of this study, and identified herself on a survey form as a "mildly Catholic" person who attended church a few times a year. Barb's Catholic upbringing, even if only "mildly" significant to her as an adult, may well have contributed an unacknowledged part to her development as a publicly involved person. But she did not make her religious upbringing a part of her commitment account during our interview, and she never mentioned it in everyday situations involving her anti-toxics group.

For these reasons, intensive participant-observation needed to be the primary source of evidence for my arguments about commitment. Some researchers have suspected that participant-observers choose their method because of a too-easy humanism, a skittishness about assembling "hard" data, or a romanticized understanding of the insights we can reap from getting "up close and personal" with the researched. The examples of Carl and Barb should help clarify that participant-observation is the only method for deriving some kinds of "social facts." Practices of commitment and everyday enactments of social identity are just such social facts.[1] Social and political identities are not simply given; people must construct themselves as political actors – in interaction with others – to organize social movements. Only through participant-observation can we find out how people construct these identities in everyday milieux and create bonds of political community.

Sociologists of culture have increasingly argued that if people cannot talk coherently about their own commitments, then those commitments are weak, or in jeopardy.[2] I uphold their underlying idea that public speech is a force that gives privately held beliefs their social efficacy. My point is that we need to understand speech in the context of everyday action and interaction if we want to see how commitments translate into group solidarities. Interviews can produce valuable narratives that teach us a lot about how an interviewee images community. Interviews also tell us what kind of political or moral conversation an interviewee can sustain; that in itself is an important thing to find out. That is different, however, from finding out how people's talk produces, and develops out of, collective action. Barb may have turned into a "space cadet" when I prodded her during an interview about the moral basis for her activism, but she was also a long-term member of an organization that wanted to expand the local space for down-to-earth political debate.

FINDING OUT WHAT "EVERYBODY KNOWS"

Participant-observation reveals the common sense people are working from when they use words like "community," or "participation," slippery words with diverse meanings. In the Green movement groups I studied, for instance, "everybody knew" that "participation" meant taking individual initiative without the constraint of any strong, centralized leadership. Members took for granted that orientation meetings needed to be evaluated according to whether newcomers had participated a lot or not. And this remained the case even though some of the questions I heard newcomers ask at these meetings implied that what they wanted was more information about the Greens' goals and projects, not more or better participation. "Participation" meant sharing political ideas among activists who act as equal, personal selves.

Participant-observation also made clear that even with this highly personalized definition of participation, none of the Greens thought they were in the movement just for personal growth. After only a short amount of field work I saw that though Greens appreciated their egalitarian, participation-oriented groups in theory, they were sometimes frustrated in practice and would have found it laughable that anyone might join the movement in search of personal growth alone. The Seaview Greens wanted to include personal introductions and some personal "sharing" at meetings so that new recruits "can connect with us." But they also agreed with one of its members that "if we want to do group therapy – fine, we can do it somewhere else." The Greens, like other grassroots movements before them, used personal, self-expressive language in pursuit of political ends.

Members of the African-American anti-toxics groups in the study valued "participation" too but meant by it something different. The board members of the organization insisted on participating in local environmental policy-making as a "community." This was not the same kind of community Greens had in mind when they used the term. The anti-toxics group depended on skilled speakers with more than a little demagogic appeal to articulate the identity of the community as a whole and its interests. And "everybody knew" that depending on the circumstances, "community" could mean either local African-American neighborhoods in particular, or any residents in general who did not benefit from the large chemical industries in their area. Sometimes it meant both. Finding out this complex bit of common knowledge made it easier for me to understand why the activists articulated race as an explicit part of their political agenda in some settings, while insisting on a color-blind ideology in others. In any case, "community" did not mean a network of people with similar, politicized lifestyles and commitments as it did for Greens. To the black anti-toxics activists, community was a basis for a common identity, not a site for individualized, political experimentation.

Finding out what everybody knows makes good sense on theoretical, as well as experiential, grounds. Sociologically oriented linguistics research[3] supports the point that words – "community" and "participation" for instance – take on regular meanings in routine group contexts that differ from the ways people may use them outside of their everyday milieux. Reviewing the technicalities of recent linguistics would go beyond what is necessary to make that point here. But as a recent essay makes clear (Cicourel 1991), linguistic studies of "background knowledge" in everyday conversation can help us understand how groups give vague phrases regular, specific meanings. Different bodies of background knowledge have been passed down in the communitarian and personalized politics of recent grassroots movements.

Notes

1 Personalism and political commitment

1 A recent book (1993) by Amitai Etzioni, leading US sociologist and a major figure in the intellectual "communitarian" movement has popularized some of this cultural criticism. This call to re-build "community" was heard frequently in President Bill Clinton's speeches and those of many US public figures of both liberal and conservative persuasions during the later 1980s and 1990s.

2 I have used pseudonyms for names of all locations and all people who were not widely known public figures. My decision to use a surname or first name follows the customary form of address in a person's everyday social contexts: some individuals in HAT went by surname, while most of those in the other groups in this study went by first name.

3 Personalism here describes the orientation that others have variously conceived as "expressive individualism" (Bellah et al. 1985), "therapeutic ideology" (Lasch 1979), or "the culture of self-fulfillment" (Taylor 1991). Other accounts frequently treat personalism from a critical standpoint at the outset (as when it is named an "ideology"), while the aim here is to understand the uses and limits of personalism without casting it pejoratively from the start. The definition and discussion of personalism here benefits much from Taylor's (1991, 1989) treatments of individualism and the self.

4 The personalism I am discussing has certainly influenced contemporary Protestant notions of faith communities (see for instance Swanson 1979). Still, I want to distinguish between selves defined ultimately in allegiance to a specific "outside" authority, and the self of contemporary personalism whose definition does not depend on one specific outside authority or inspiration.

5 See, for instance, Potter's work (1988) on the cultural construction of self in rural China.

6 It is debatable whether nineteenth-century writers and educators articulated their visions of personal fulfillment and expression with as tenuous a relationship to communal or institutional authorities as some champions of

personal development do today. Walt Whitman, for instance, celebrated the unique, self-expressive individual but also upheld a notion of citizenly community bound by republican virtues (Bellah *et al.* 1985; Lasch 1991).

7 I focus on theorists strongly identified with sociological theory and research or else widely read by sociologists. The term "communitarian" has been used to name positions within moral and political philosophy as well as sociology, and differences in discourse between disciplines can lead to somewhat different referents for the term. For instance, the philosopher Charles Taylor has been called a communitarian, but he has criticized some of the theses that communitarian sociologists advance (Taylor 1991, 1989), and he articulates positions similar in some ways to those of the "radical democracy" theorists treated here.

8 Many would agree that a growth in the culture of self-fulfillment is related to a society's increasing social and technological complexity, and an increase in the numbers of highly-schooled professional workers. Statements of this thesis are available in works from a variety of sociological and political positions, including: Bellah *et al.* (1985); Bernstein (1975); Inglehart (1981); Melucci (1989); Swanson (1979).

9 See, for instance, Clecak (1983), and Gans (1988).

10 This is a brief summary of the main argument in Clecak (1983), which influenced Skolnick's (1991) treatment of US family life, Cancian's (1987) work on the changing meanings of love, and Flacks' (1988) treatment of recent changes in radical political culture. Flacks' work, however, concerns itself a great deal with public commitment. While he notes that many Americans have entered public life to secure the means for private fulfillment, he emphasizes differences between this majority and a "tradition of the left" that has valued public engagement as an end in itself.

11 I do not want to overestimate the similarities between a theorist such as Habermas who grounds his ideal political community in reasoned interaction between individuals, and one such as Chantal Mouffe who "belongs to another philosophical universe" (Mouffe 1992a: 13) and finds that appeals to "reason" only obscure or silence cultural difference and oppression. Mouffe and others also refuse the "naive" view Habermas implicitly upholds that we can speak of a "real" essential individual rather than of subject positions which we know only through different discourses (Mouffe 1992b: 237). For my purposes it is fair to place these theorists with such differing operating assumptions in the same general camp because they all advocate an extension of democratic freedoms into realms of life otherwise bound by uncritically accepted communal standards, unequal relations, or assumptions about a consensus that may not exist. They all emphasize the conditions for participation in a democratic community.

12 Again, I do not want to overstate some rough affinities between Mouffe and Habermas as radical democracy theorists. Habermas draws on G. H. Mead (Habermas 1987) and Kohlberg (Habermas 1979) among others to theoretically ground his individuated, communicative actor in developmental and social psychology, and in a larger scheme of moral evolution. Mouffe rejects

evolutionary schemes, and her advocacy for individual autonomy within a public-spirited community draws not on evidence from developmental psychologies, but on reinterpretations of diverse political theories.

13 They would share this observation as well with a number of researchers who study or theorize what have come to be called "new social movements," which include the movements named here. Following chapters will introduce and critically engage with theses about new social movements.

14 See in particular Bellah *et al.* (1985).

15 For instance, Rieff hoped that "the movement of negro non-violent protest" (1966: 23) might "save" the US from a soft "barbarism" and rejuvenate a sense of collective moral purpose. Lasch wrote as a critic disenchanted with the way that 1960s political radicalism had unraveled. Bell addressed what he considered the cultural explosions of the 1960s. Bellah *et al.* wrote with reference to liberal community activism in California (1985: 74) and upheld a "citizens' movement" organization in Pennsylvania (1985: 214–218) as a moral exemplar.

16 Lasch's understanding of culture was much indebted to Frankfurt School critical theory, especially work by Horkheimer and Adorno (Horkheimer 1936; Horkheimer and Adorno 1944). Bell (1976) defined culture as the overriding values that answer life's largest questions about existence and meaning and placed those values in an analytic trio of "spheres" that included the "political" and "economic" spheres of social life. Rieff derived his theory of culture from Freudian psychoanalysis.

17 In Wuthnow's succinct statement, commitment is not just raw behavior itself but the "cultural understandings that transform [these acts] from physical motions into human action" (1991: 45).

18 Social identity is an ongoing "effort made by ordinary people to make sense of themselves in relation to community and culture (Hewitt 1989: 172). I wanted to understand what kind of "relation to community and culture" activists constructed through their political commitments – how much of their personal selves they related to political change, and what kinds of affiliations outside of the personal self inspired their practice of activism. I am concerned, then, with *activist social identity* in particular, and not other aspects of social identity that the activists created in settings they do not relate to activism. Faye Ginsburg (1989) similarly focused on activist social identities, in this case the social identities of pro-choice and pro-life activists. She reconstructed these from interviews, while I derived them from participant-observation. See also Andrews (1991).

19 While the names of all local organizations – "Ridge Greens," "ACES," etc. – are pseudonyms, names of national groups and nationally known figures are real unless otherwise noted. To preserve the anonymity of local participants, I changed descriptive details of their social backgrounds, and some details of the geographical setting, without giving a distorted picture of their class, family status, or cultural milieu.

20 CCHW leaders have referred to their grassroots constituency in these terms. See also Szasz (1994).

2   Personalized politics: the case of the US Greens

1 Unless noted otherwise, dialogue extracts are excerpts from field notes.
2 This information about other Green local chapters comes from the Summer 1989 and Winter 1989 issues of the US Green movement's combined journal of record at the time, *Green Letter/In Search of Greener Times*.
3 This type of activist commitment gets suggested particularly in arguments by Lasch (1979), Bellah *et al.* (1985), Rieff (1966), and Bell (1976). The transcendentalist-inspired search for cosmic truths within the self gets mentioned as a variant of "expressive individualism" by Bellah *et al.* (1985).
4 Supporting literature for placement of these examples includes Barkan (1979); Breines (1982); Echols (1989); Epstein (1991, 1988); Evans (1979); Freeman (1972–73); Gitlin (1987); Hannon (1990); Lichterman (1989a); Marx (1979); Sperling (1988); Vogel (1980).
5 The Seaview and Ridge Greens shared the same movement culture, had roughly the same number of members, were demographically similar, and were representative of the social backgrounds of Greens nationally in 1989.
6 The principles received endorsements from a number of well-known writers and activists, including: Harry Boyte, activist and writer of several books on American community activism, who also attended the meeting; Lawrence Goodwyn, historian of American populism; Grace Paley, writer; Cornel West, theologian and writer; Jeff Escoffier, writer and former editor of *Socialist Review*.
7 Quotes and descriptions of this founding meeting come from "Proceedings of the Green Organizing Planning Meeting" (4pp., n.d.).
8 During this study, Green activists argued strenuously with one another over the party option and its timing. Green Party organizers I met understood party organizing not so much as preparation for winning immediate power but as a "tool" that would get more publicity and more involvement than the US Green movement had previously. Given this, and given that establishing state Green parties was very much an unsure gambit at the time of writing, I treat the US Greens as a *movement* with some electoral organizing, and not as an incipient nationwide political party.
9 This insight has been the basis for much recent academic writing about social movements. For representative statements on the point, see Melucci (1989, 1988); Offe (1985); Giddens (1991); Epstein (1991).
10 See Habermas' (1975, 1970) critique of technocratic policy-making that excludes or trivializes citizen participation. For complementary accounts, see Bellah *et al* (1985); Eliasoph (forthcoming).
11 The core of the new Ridge electoral politics collective, the Ridge Green Party, was comprised almost entirely of core members along with one other member from the old Ridge Greens.
12 See, for instance Wuthnow (1991).
13 The storytellers could have mentioned organizations like the Sierra Club or Greenpeace – either identifying themselves with or distancing themselves from these groups – as they recounted their entry into the Greens. But these organizations occurred only to Donald, the former employee of Greenpeace

and Citizens for a Better Environment. The Greens could have mentioned hiking and camping trips, or "love of the outdoors" as springboards to concern for the environment; all of those present had enjoyed such activities.

14 Most women in the Greens would agree with (and no doubt some had read) the ample research findings that men and women tend toward different kinds of roles and communication styles in organizations, with men tending toward the instrumental roles, which are often the more prestigious and rewarded ones.

15 By calling the centrifugal dynamic a main cause of gender inequities in the organization, I reject the "essentialist" position that women and men carry propensities which directly or inexorably affect how organizations work. If centrifugal organizations like those of the Greens (and other recent movements) exaggerate gender differences, other organizational arrangements might *to some degree* lessen their effects.

16 While grassroots environmentalists may have learned "personal process" from activists in the feminist movement, there are enough "feminist men" in activist circles that it is not accurate to assume that advocates for process are always women. One male participant in early Green Party organizing criticized the Ridge Green party organization for having scared away most of the women participants at the first few meetings. He vowed that if the Green Party was going to be "a bunch of men wagging their dicks in politics, then I don't want any part of it."

17 Starhawk's writings have combined radical feminism, mysticism, and notions of participatory democracy. She was read widely in peace, anti-nuclear, environmental, and feminist groups that favored consensus governance and intensive individual participation.

18 The facilitators produced for Seaview a booklet of quotes they had taken from members about Seaview's "mission and vision" and other topics. These statements come from the booklet.

19 For instance, publicized environmental hazards less than two miles from the Ridge Green office spurred a new local anti-toxics group to action during this study, and anti-toxics groups in other locales joined with them in a loose coalition. Ridge Greens did not have contact with them.

20 See, for instance, Cohen (1985), Eder (1985, 1982), Habermas (1987), Melucci (1989, 1988, 1985, 1981), Touraine (1981), Touraine *et al.* (1983), Epstein (1991). For cogent criticisms of the NSM category, see Calhoun (1993), Tarrow (1989), or Tucker (1991).

3 Speaking out in suburbia

1 This quote is taken from a 1984 newsletter. A nearly identical statement was being used as an introductory flyer on the group in 1990.

2 For the sake of simplicity, "member" will refer to any regular participant in ACES. ACES did not have a formal membership. Laura used the phrase "members and friends of ACES" to refer to participants. During my field work, the group had a stable core of seven, with roughly eight others who attended meetings at least twice a year. "Core" members all recognized each other.

3 And she mentioned it to me only during an interview. The book was Carlos Castaneda's *The Teachings of Don Juan.*

4 Sandy was a supportive liaison from metropolitan groups; she was not a local member of ACES.

5 "Sunshine" was a natural foods market popular with activists and others living in the metropolitan "alternative" cultural milieu.

6 One ACES volunteer described Airdale as "20 years behind" Salton, a sprawling commuter town with a reputation among local activists as being "backward."

7 It is easy to point out that opposing the policies of a town's major employer is a different political enterprise from promoting Green values through diffuse educational projects and a long-term Green electoral strategy. And yet, Greens *could* have become more involved in the controversies around Microtech than they did. It is too simple to assume that the Greens' style came from a lack of concrete, pressing issues.

8 I have deduced this figure from other statistics. In 1984, roughly 4,400 of Microtech's regular employees resided in Airdale ("Microtechnologies Limited Commuter Characteristics 1984," author's file). Airdale had a population of almost 54,000 ("County General Plan 1986," author's file), about 23,000 of which were workers over age 16. The latter figure is a rough extrapolation from 1980 census figures (Bureau of the Census 1983) and errs on the low side. So the estimated proportion of one to five is probably too high. I have used pseudonyms for the two statistical reports in order to preserve activists' anonymity.

9 "Urban Development in Airdale," 1986, Ph.D. Dissertation, again given a pseudonym to preserve anonymity.

10 This would be true even if the military contractor loomed still larger than it does in Airdale's economic picture. First, opposition to Microtech's way of dealing with its wastes did not necessarily translate into a strident anti-military politics. Opponents of Microtech policies expressed a wide variety of stances toward Microtech as a whole. Some metropolitan activists expressed a "shut-it-down" bravado toward the firm. Some ACES members and other metropolitan activists advocated that the firm work only on peacetime projects. And some ACES members and local residents opposed only a particular waste management plan. Second, there is no easy correspondence between participation in debate about the contractor and economic or political interests on the part of residents not employed by the contractor. No doubt some local residents declined to sign the ACES petition against the proposed incinerator because they did not want to abet any initiative that could even remotely threaten jobs. On the other hand, some residents at public hearings opposed the same incinerator on the economic grounds that it threatened property values.

11 A precise sociological definition of "suburb" for this study is less important than a clear description of a local, privatistic culture that may also characterize some more urban or rural areas. Following Baumgartner, I want to highlight the culture of suburbia rather than its commuting patterns or social networks. For dated but insightful field studies that emphasize the informal

socializing in suburban culture rather than privatism or avoidance of conflict, see Seeley *et al.* (1956); Dobriner (1963). For an ecological definition of suburb, see Fischer and Jackson (1976: 280). Airdale did meet most of Fischer and Jackson's criteria for a suburb, including distance from a major city center and low housing density.

12 Suburban patterns of commerce and civic life are so common in the US that they are easy to take for granted. So it is worth reminding the reader that an activist might "go to the people" in other ways. In Hillview, for instance (Chapter 4), activists included visits to various churches in their organizing drives as a matter of course. In Airdale, churches became sites for publicizing ACES largely to the extent that two individual members happened to be involved in two particular churches.

13 For instance, Gaventa (1980) described the Appalachian coal-mining valley he studied as sharing a fundamentalist Protestantism and a traditional "mountain culture." While these supported quiescence in the valley, they may also have provided resources for solidarity when valley residents organized to demand concessions from the company controlling most of the valley's land. Gaventa did not directly study the role of cultural institutions in the protests he surveyed at the end of his study. But we can see elements of both religious and regional culture in one mountaineer's grievances about strip-mining, which Gaventa quoted at length (1980: 223): " ... I wouldn't want to touch God's work ... God created ... this timber and created our wildlife and it's torn it all ... I wouldn't work in the strip mines, I wouldn't destroy this earth."

14 ACES entered a float most years in the Airdale "Wild West Days" parade. That year, the float was a cardboard mock toxic incinerator with bright orange and gray fiberglass material representing toxic fumes bellowing out of a smokestack. ACES members dressed in white lab coats to accompany it, and Laura blew bubbles from behind the "incinerator" to represent the diffusion of toxic substances from burning wastes. Inside the float was a tape-recorder set on high volume, playing "Don't Worry, Be Happy."

15 The "empowerment" theory with its emphasis on a personal "consciousness" may sound like unquestionable common sense. But activists portrayed in the next chapter never talked about recruiting members in terms of developing individual "consciousness," and rarely if ever talked about local residents in terms of a "mindset." They spoke of "empowerment" as an attribute of a whole community, not separate individuals.

4 Imagining community, organizing community

1 Door-knocking is a strategy from the community-organizing tradition. Door-knockers solicit residents of a neighborhood to join the organization. Failing this, the door-knocker will try to secure an immediate goal – promise of attendance at the forum or special event, or a signature on a petition. Door-knocking is also an opportunity for finding out what local concerns residents have that could be made part of a campaign or organization-building agenda.

2 For instance, see Bellah *et al.*'s characterization of "genuine communities"

(1985: 153). In this usage, community implies social bonds based on interdependence and a shared sense of cultural authority; it is not simply another term for "group" or "locale." Not all students of community would distinguish between "genuine" communities and other aggregations the way some communitarian theorists have. I want to understand different forms of interdependence that people accomplish, without designating some as more deserving of the term "community" than others. But I do want to limit my use of the term to designate forms of togetherness based on some sense of shared obligation. This study resists the common, loose usage of "community" which often has little to do with imagined or practiced obligations, and at times becomes meaningless – as when television newscasters or public administrators talk about "the world community," or "the heterosexual community." When simply referring to a local population, I will use "locale" or some similar term, and not "community."

3 These constructions have "real" affects on action, and HAT's construction of community may well represent local ties of interdependence that were older than those of, say, Greens in their own locale. But those ties needed to get represented in words and images; they were not self-evident. For theoretical statements on the construction of groups and communities through naming, see for instance Bourdieu (1985) or Anderson (1991); see also Suttles (1972).

4 Works by Edelstein (1988) and Freudenberg (1984) have treated neighborhood and community environmental groups, but without much empirical attention to questions about commitment or everyday routines in these groups.

5 For highly sympathetic chronicles of community activism in the 1970s and 1980s, see Boyte (1984; 1980). For treatments critical of the populism and lack of class analysis in community organizing networks, see Boggs (1983), and Lustig (1981). Delgado (1986) relates that the majority of ACORN chapters had minority constituencies. Few have been studied in depth (but see Lancourt 1979). HAT's demographics – largely minority and low-to-moderate income – make it likely to be representative of groups in the "Saul Alinsky" tradition, particularly groups in the largest US community organizing network, ACORN.

6 Supporting literature for this list includes Delgado (1986); Boyte (1989, 1980); Reitzes and Reitzes (1987); Szasz (1994); Castells (1983).

7 A white ex-mayor of a small neighboring city positioned herself as a spokesperson for the concerns of African-American Hillviewers, making common cause with black members on HAT's board without claiming to be rooted in Hillview herself.

8 Demographic information comes from the 1980 census (Bureau of the Census 1980) as reprinted in "Hillview Demographic Study" – a pseudonym for a major research report completed by one of the organizations represented on HAT's executive board.

9 For examples of the self-interest themes in the organizing materials, see Gibbs and Collette (1983); Collette (n.d., "Best of 'Organizing Toolbox'").

10 Some might say it was simply rational for most Hillviewers not to get involved in collective action with HAT, especially if they could enjoy what-

ever benefits HAT won while pursuing their own legal cases against polluters for damages. In Olson's (1965) famous analysis, they would be "free riders," and would need extra incentives to become involved in HAT. While those "extra incentives," to use Olson's economic language, *could* have been phrased in terms of individual honor or power, or an individual sense of altruism, they were not. HAT appealed to black Hillviewers as already members of a solidary "community" whose common good was of the highest concern.

11 CCHW organizing manuals and pamphlets are thick with anti-bureaucracy and anti-corporate themes that its loose network of grassroots groups shares with earlier community activist organizations (see Delgado 1986; Gaventa 1980).

12 A comprehensive study done by one of the environmental organizations assisting HAT found its targeted "toxic hot spot" neighborhoods between 72 and 94 percent African-American. The study is not cited here to preserve anonymity ("Hillview Demographic Study," author's file).

13 A rough "measure" of participation confirms that HAT meetings tended to be much less "participatory" than those of Greens, if we take participatory to mean extent of participation by individual members. During typical HAT meetings in 1990–91, the chair, executive director, and advisor from Environmental Advocates did the lion's share of talking. The more active, non-officer board members – Mrs. Davis and James Shaver in particular – would take a turn with a question, suggestion, or comment an average of two or three times in a meeting (not counting comments following up or elaborating upon responses to their initial turn). Members at typical Ridge Green spokescouncil meetings occupied the floor six to eight times in one meeting (same definition of turn-taking), and the facilitator would often need to establish a queue of participants waiting to take their turn to speak.

14 Laura of ACES attended "toxics boot camp," a set of organizer training workshops sponsored by CCHW. Lester of HAT had attended the workshops too.

15 Perhaps low-income members of African-American urban locales have ample reason for disenfranchisement in civic groups. Yet the board included some of the most civically involved residents in black Hillview, several of whom had been awarded for their efforts.

16 It is interesting, too, that De Rose did not phrase her desire for greater participation in terms of political principles, but instead said that meetings had become "stultifying," and were too rushed to be genuinely informative. To a HAT leader, these could sound more like matters of style or otherwise secondary to the overriding priority of forging an effective, common will. The Greens might have considered this evaluation a serious indictment of group process.

17 For instance, at Shaver's behest, HAT included a short "Acknowledgment of the Elders of the Community" on the agenda for one of its public forums. He explained to me the honorific, vernacular titles "mother" and "sister" that blacks have used for women considered to be local sages or opinion leaders, and affirmed their worth.

18 During my interview with Liz, she asked semi-rhetorically why the resources devoted to military-related research couldn't be diverted to developing cheap building materials for housing the homeless, or to public works projects for the unemployed "the way F.D.R. did."

19 "General significance" is of course a matter of degree. Mrs. Sherman, Mrs. Davis, and other HAT members certainly thought that helping blacks in one locale had some meaning as assisting an historically oppressed people in general. Mrs. Davis placed some wider significance for blacks on her decision to run for city council, as when she announced to HAT members that "as a black woman, I may run for city council." But we could say that she interpreted her activism with less significance for national movements or nationwide structures of power than Norton, who spoke many times about his involvements in multistate coalitions of grassroots activists and encouraged HAT to become involved in these.

20 For more detail on the ideologies underlying this and similar workshops presented in Green circles, see Adair and Howell 1988.

21 We might assume this to be the particular conceit of white, middle-class activists. In HAT, perhaps only James Shaver would have strongly valorized this approach to coalition- and community-building. But at a forum on multicultural alliance-building a few days after this workshop, a latina community leader advocated a similar sort of personalism as the royal route to a multicultural, environmental coalition. "We should look to our private lives" for models of culture contact, she advocated. And though the white cultural cast to much early feminism put her off, she cited approvingly the slogan "the personal is political" as a watchphrase for would-be coalition-builders. "Notice I didn't say building institutions," she concluded, "because institutions are *people*" (emphasis hers). Minority group activists with typically middle-class educational experiences or backgrounds might be just as adept at, and interested in, this individualized approach to community-building as white environmentalists.

22 During this study, the Greens' multicultural alliance-building efforts with anti-toxics groups produced relatively little, despite good intentions and a willingness to adopt the anti-toxics activists' terms of debate about the environment. For extended examples of these efforts and further analysis, see Lichterman (1995b).

23 Tensions and failed communication between majority and minority group cultures within the women's movement, for instance, could be exacerbated by well-meaning white women who wanted to will themselves out of their position as whites. See Anzaldua and Moraga (1982).

24 In 1986, CCHW counted 1,000 local groups that it had served in some way (CCHW 1986: 42) At its 1989 national conference it claimed to have had contact with over 8,000 local groups, many of which did not exist three years earlier.

25 Obviously other factors also influence the breadth of issues and constituencies a grassroots movement will take on. My emphasis is on the cultural bases for movement solidarity.

5   Culture, class, and life-ways of activism

1 Different theories and studies of political ideology agree that expressing one's own, articulate political ideology is easier, more "natural"-seeming, for those of higher class standing, or those with a lot of "cultural capital." See, for instance, Bourdieu (1985, 1984); Gramsci (1971); Lichterman (1989b); Mansbridge (1983).

2 Freudenberg's (1984) survey of citizen "environmental health" organizations largely preceded the phenomenal growth of anti-toxics groups in the US during the 1980s.

3 Given that anti-toxics leaders have portrayed theirs as a "working people's" movement, it could be objected that this survey oversampled those participants in the anti-toxics movement who were affluent enough to attend a national conference. But two factors militate against this possibility. First, conference organizers offered financial assistance for activists of limited means to attend. Second, surveys asked respondents to choose one of several categories to describe their affiliation with the anti-toxics movement. Of the surveys returned, I analyzed only those that included the identification "member or leader of local or grassroots anti-toxics group" among responses checked in the question on affiliation. For many, this was their only affiliation with the movement. These and other categories of affiliation in the survey were derived from the conference announcement issued in CCHW's newsletter *Everyone's Backyard* 7(2), Summer 1989.

4 The Green response rate figure is based on the high estimate that 140 Green members or delegates were active plenary participants; this estimate is corroborated by vote tallies recorded during the plenary. At the anti-toxics keynote address, 50 percent of attendees returned their surveys. Of those, I analyzed only members in or leaders of grassroots groups. There are no figures available on the proportion of keynote address attendees who were grassroots activists, rather than purely professional environmentalist staffers, public officials, or others, but participant-observation throughout the conference gave me no reason to think I had undersampled grassroots activists in relation to others in the conference room.

5 Ladd *et al.* (1983) obtained a response rate of about 42 percent for their survey of protesters at an anti-nuclear demonstration. Scaminaci and Dunlap (1986) received around 28 percent of their surveys back from demonstrators at a San Francisco protest. Neither of these studies differentiated active movement organization members from others present at these demonstrations.

6 I use "life-way" to denote an individual's or group's typical way of juggling and matriculating through institutionalized relationships over time, in private and public life. We can see life-ways operating in everday practice. The term may be applied to an individual, a group, or a society; an individual has a particular life-way, and a society might have a dominant type of life-way and subordinate or subcultural ones. Life-ways arise out of taken-for-granted assumptions, skills, and priorities shared in at least part of a culture. They are not purely individual inventions; the "rugged individualist" has been a predominant life-way in US history.

7 The Greens at both national and local levels have been almost entirely white (Moses and Spretnak 1989); no minority activists responded in my survey. At the 1989 national conference, almost all of the (very few) people of color present had been invited by a Green ideologue and activist. They were not officially voting delegates and probably for that reason did not register in the survey.

8 Ben Norton, board member of HAT, personal communication.

9 Bourdieu uses the term "habitus" to refer to a taken-for-granted way of perceiving and presenting oneself. Those with high amounts of cultural capital share a certain kind of habitus. I do not use the term here because it is relatively obscure, and because its use presupposes a dense theoretical framework that ties habitus problematically to cultural capital (Bourdieu 1984). For a fuller treatment of habitus, cultural capital, and their uses and limitations in studying politicization, see Lichterman (1989b).

10 Michele Lamont argued from her cross-national research (1992) that the ability to speak and act in an individualized way is especially valued in the US.

11 He pointed out, for instance (1973), that in newer teaching styles, a child's "play" mattered almost as much as her schoolwork in evaluating her "development." In almost Foucaultian tones Bernstein described the kind of family culture that complements the newer pedagogy:

> In person-centered families, the insides of the members are made public through the communication structure, and thus more of the person has been invaded and subject to control (1973: 185).

Bernstein's oeuvre abounds with categories and typologies; its most important contribution here is its distinction between a more and a less individuated group culture.

12 See Hochschild (1983).

13 While the surveys were anonymous, participant-observation made clear that Left Greens had an age distribution very similar to that of other participants in the conference. Informal interviews with several revealed similar educational experiences as well.

14 Kriesi explained the differences between his categories and those in other work on the new class in 1989: 1082–1085.

15 For a survey of differing definitions of "new class" see Brint 1984. For a variety of positions in the debates over the rise of a new class, see Bruce-Briggs (1979). Accounts of the opposition between the new class and "older" classes vary: for Inglehart (1990), the opposition is one between those with "post-materialist values" and those with a more traditional materialist worldview; for Lamont (1986) the core opposition is between public sector knowledge workers and workers whose jobs are directly tied to profit maximization; for Kriesi, the opposition between technocratic managers of large-scale organizations and professional specialists (1989: 1085) is most important.

16 To minimize the complexity of the survey and therefore maximize the response rate, respondents were not asked to place themselves in a standard census category. Instead they were asked to write in their occupation if they

had one. A closed-response question was included to determine whether the respondent worked full- or part-time, as an employee or self-employed. The unit of analysis for occupational status here is the individual, not households via breadwinners.

17 One hypothesis has it that activists with relatively low incomes like the Greens in this study are always trying to compensate for economic loss by "showing off" their individuality or displaying resentment against the power of money or property. See Kitschelt's (1988) debate with Bürklin (1988).

18 I was surprised at the number of Greens who actually wrote onto their survey that they did not watch TV at all, and in some cases did not own one. Chastened by my survey's insensitivity to Greens' ideas about television viewing, I decided to add the category "I do not watch television" to the anti-toxics survey. The 17 percent in parenthesis stands for the number of Greens who wrote in that they do not watch TV. Most of these people also ticked "3 hours or less." The 77 percent represents all those who either ticked that category or wrote in an answer that would fit the category.

19 Though I did not systematically survey core members of the Seaview Greens, discussions with several intensively involved members revealed that they, too, wanted work that would complement self-consciously held values or at least not contradict them.

20 We should be careful, though, about using "counter-cultural" to describe either Greens or the more committed student radicals of twenty years ago, since "counter-culture" has often connoted hedonism, degeneration, or generally a lack of commitment. Whalen and Flacks' (1989) follow-up study of student activists suggests that a significant proportion of student radicals retained political commitments in some form over the next twenty years.

21 In his visit to a Hillview church, Rev. Jesse Jackson skillfully weaved environmentalist messages in with themes from African-American Christianity, recreating the "black community" and its moral standards as accountable to Nature as well as to a human society under God.

22 HAT's paid staff person described his role in black Hillview in terms of "service" and compared it with the role he thought church leaders should take in rallying Hillviewers to stand up for themselves.

23 Apparently unbeknownst to Carl, Beyond War was a small peace organization made up of people who eschewed most forms of collective mobilization and taught that each individual can contribute to peace by reducing conflict in his or her own life, regardless of livelihood. Or, to paraphrase a popular motto, the personal is global.

24 This paragraph paraphrases, and adds examples for, a particularly abstract discussion of "individualization" (Melucci 1989: 45–48). Examining problems with this thesis goes beyond the bounds of this chapter. Melucci presented the thesis largely as an orienting hypothesis without confirming evidence.

25 Thanks to Todd Gitlin for pointing out this possibility, one advocated in some Frankfurt School writings.

6 Personalized politics and cultural radicalism since the 1960s

1 This short sketch comes from the account in Gitlin (1987).

2 See, for instance, Lasch (1966) on the cultural radicalism of intellectual American reformers, or Dellinger's (1993) story of a life of personalized politics.

3 This describes some of the "new age" spiritualisms of the 1970s, 1980s, and 1990s. Some of these promote "personal growth" or personal spirituality to bring individuals into direct harmony with the earth. They leave established religious or political institutions mostly out of this picture of social evolution as they focus on the efficacy of the pure, totally actualized or cleansed self.

4 See, for instance, Breines (1982); Carson (1981); Gitlin (1987); McAdam (1988b); Miller (1987); Whalen and Flacks (1989).

5 The tendencies co-existed not only within the same movements but within the same activists. As Gitlin writes: "Strategy and expression, far from being pure alternatives, are coordinates like latitude and longitude; any action partakes of both, in degrees hard to measure" (1987: 135).

6 While I focus on personalized politics in grassroots movements, it can on rare occasions enter institutionalized policy-making directly. A prime example is California State Assemblyman John Vasconcellos, who actually assigns more political significance to personal growth than most of the activists in this study. In his study of commitment and cultural change, Tipton (1982) noted Vasconcellos' "human-potential" politics. A decade later Vasconcellos was still offering a "new human politics." Pushing many elements of a liberal-democratic agenda, his new politics truly envisions a statewide polity of selves. The mobilized citizenry promoting his program would "come together in small local 'self-esteem and responsibility circles' ... for the purposes of personal growth *and* social action – to heal and rebuild ourselves ... " They would require a therapeutic leader, too: "Such a leader must be somebody of integrity, enough grown whole, as a person, with/in her/himself." Meantime, Vasconcellos points to a precursor in the national "self-esteem" movement, which has resulted in "self-esteem task forces" in several states, and programs in California schools and workplaces. "Self-esteeming" as he calls it is his version of civics education in a polity of selves. (Quotes from "A Proposal for Generating Leadership and an Effective National Political Campaign," J. Vasconcellos, 1991).

7 Of course one other duality, that of male and female essences, was a defining one for these activists. For a succinct review of the contradictions entailed in this version of feminism, see Brenner (1988).

8 The main author of the Ridge Green's 1989 revised by-laws had said he interpreted "consensus" and borrowed the affinity group structure from material at a regional peace center. The peace center in turn claimed that the material had come through the Livermore Action Group. LAG was a contemporary of the Seneca activists.

9 Earth First! spells its name with an exclamation point. An abbreviation used here is "EF!"

10 I had prepared for a relatively short amount of participant-observation with

Earth First!, similar to my field work with the Seaview Green comparison group. As I was about to enter EF!'s "field," two of its most important organizers were injured by a bomb that exploded in their car. Earth First! had already gained a very controversial reputation through association with acts of sabotage against logging companies, and allegedly, against power companies. Its participants and sympathizers had aroused considerable, sometimes violent antipathies among loggers. To EF!'s chagrin, federal investigators defined the bomb case as one of thwarted bomb-throwers, not injured bomb-victims. One EF!-associated contact told me that the casual spirit in the network had suffered since the bomb incident. A publicly identified EF! participant would not return my phone calls. In all, it was a most inauspicious time to introduce myself as a field worker. Covert study was ethically unacceptable, and in the context of high police suspicions and high explosives, unacceptably risky for a secondary comparison case. Instead, I captured some of EF! participants' everyday understandings of political commitment by encountering the activists at Green meetings and sociable gatherings at activists' houses. Hearing EF! participants in Green meetings was in fact a wonderful way to find out what political culture they shared with Greens, as well as what differences divided them. I also interviewed three activists who had participated or were still participating in EF!-sponsored pubic demonstrations.

Participants in EF! actions did not necessarily support or condone what has been alleged as industrial sabotage by people who identify with EF! Organizers of Redwood Summer insisted that all participants in civil disobedience as well as legal demonstrations adhere to a code of nonviolence.

11 See Appendix II.
12 Linda of the Ridge Greens, who introduced self-exploration exercises to a less than wholly enthusiastic coordinating council, complained "we never do anything." Borrowing a native American phrase (suitably distant from Western/instrumental images of political organizing) Linda declared, "You have to talk your walk, but you also have to walk your talk."
13 On the lecture circuit with his new book *Green Rage*, Earth First! activist Christopher Manes explained EF!'s public mission in just exactly these terms.
14 Out of 72 respondents, 6 wrote "none" under the survey question about organizational affiliations, and another 12 did not fill in any response. Out of the range of political, environmental, community, religious, and spiritual group affiliations respondents named, I did not identify any as "conservative" on the political spectrum. No one mentioned affiliations with anti-abortion or anti-drug groups, for instance.
15 Chapter 4 explained how HAT officially organized itself as a coalition of local Hillview leaders, residents, and environmental organization representatives under sponsorship of American Communities Fighting Toxics. The ACFT had responded to calls for assistance from Hillview activists who were already interested in mobilizing Hillview residents around toxics issues.
16 The promotional video began with a brief statement by a Greenpeace founder who was not interested in being "left or right, or in the center" and wanted no connections between the organization and political parties.

17 The hippie milieu in Greenpeace is not specific to California. At the national anti-toxics conference, a keynote speaker (from Vermont) spoke of the need for anti-toxics activists to maintain and broaden their political outreach in their locales. She asked rhetorically, "And where are the unions? And where are the churches? And where are the Grateful Dead hippies?!" Amid chuckles of recognition, Greenpeace staffers scattered across the conference hall raised their hands.

18 These meetings presented for the broader "peace and environmental community" a lot of the same news and decisions discussed at monthly ACES meetings. The regional coalition meetings also streamlined contacts between ACES and supportive allies headquartered outside of Airdale – the Sierra Club, an older women's peace group, a Greenpeace chapter, an environmental illness survivor's organization, the Ridge Greens, among others.

19 See for instance the conservative critics cited in chapter 1 of Breines (1982).

7 The search for political community

1 See for instance Evans (1979) on the intimidating, intellectual male debating style that still characterized early personalized politics in the new left. See Epstein (1991) on the space for female voices in anti-nuclear gatherings.

2 See, for instance, the argument about a "spill-over" from feminist to anti-nuclear movements in Meyer and Whittier (1994).

3 After the time I conducted the field work for this study, some US Green movement organizations transformed into party organizations with more conventionalized, less personalized, and less culturally radical group routines. Others remained "movement" organizations. As of this writing, it was a very open question whether a "personalized" form of Green politics would continue for a long time in the US.

4 For instance, Delgado (1986) relates that the community-organizing movements of the 1970s and 1980s were influenced by the student new left. It is likely that at least some of the younger participants in "community activism" after the 1960s carried personalized commitments even as they adoped the communal identity of a specific locale. They would have related to local communities as individual agents of social change selecting arenas for action, rather than as long-time community members who take their local milieu for granted. See Gitlin's (1987) description of local projects begun by Students for a Democratic Society for evidence of this commitment style in a community-organizing context. On alternative schools, alternative counselling agencies, and cooperatives, see Swidler (1979), Mansbridge (1983), Lichterman (1989a), Case and Taylor (1979).

5 Some new left activists became professionals in the national public service organizations that grew during the 1970s. Some of these activists, too, may have carried personalized political commitments into their new work. On the growth of public service professions and non-profit organizations with a liberal-left agenda, see McCann (1986).

6 For a treatment of personalized politics among gay social science professionals, see Taylor and Raeburn (1995). The short descriptions of "queer"

activism here borrow from ongoing field research I was conducting for a project on cultural radicalism and cultural conservatism in the contemporary US.

7 Habermas' ideas about relations between language, social responsibility, and individuality draw on the thinking of, among others, George Herbert Mead. In short, Mead theorized that increasing individuation and an increasing sense of social responsibility develop together through language use. As Habermas reiterates, the maturing (and ideal) individual learns to talk more and more with reference to universalistic standards instead of particular ones tied to particular people. Through that same process the individual creates an increasingly specific sense of personal identity in relation to the universal. Taking full responsibility for one's own life (through speaking and acting) means taking a generalized other's standpoint on one's life history. It means evaluating oneself by universalistic moral standards. So a universalistic outlook and a highly individualized personal identity develop together (Habermas 1987: 96–100).

8 See Habermas (1974) for a brief description and historical sketch of the public sphere. For a much more detailed treatment, see Habermas (1989).

9 For historical studies of specific public spheres in different societies, see Calhoun (1992), Eagleton (1984), and Herbst (1994). For studies that show activists dedicated to democratic interaction as a good in itself, see Goodwyn (1978), Boyte and Evans (1986), or Epstein (1991). The Seaview Greens' general meetings were forums for discussion that would characterize the public sphere conceptualized by Habermas.

10 See, for instance, Fraser (1992), Boyte (1992), Ryan (1992), Herbst (1994).

11 See, for instance, his work on the stages of personal, moral development (1979), as well as his extensive synthesis and expansion (1987, 1984) of some earlier work.

12 See, for instance, Fraser (1992, 1985), Benhabib and Cornell (1987), and Schudson (1992).

13 I emphasize that different modes of commitment *contributed* to difficulties in building alliances. Certainly there were other important factors as well, including varying longterm agendas.

14 See Lichterman (1995b) for an extensive development of these observations. For observations of multicultural relations in movements characterized by personalized politics, see Epstein (1991); Anzaldua and Moraga (1982); Mansbridge (1983).

Appendix I

1 For a variety of accounts of the rise and decline of the 1980s peace movement, see Marullo and Lofland (1990).

2 "Core" designated the members who considered themselves and were considered by others to be regular contributors to the group, ones who could be counted upon to volunteer for tasks and who demonstrated active interest in routine group decisions.

3 At the Green assembly I briefly announced the study. At the anti-toxics assembly, a conference organizer briefly introduced the study. Activists were then free to consider the invitation to participate, and to fill out the questionnaires, whenever they had time to do so before the end of their assembly.

Appendix II

1 Or in Paul Rabinow's (1986) parsimonious statement, "representations are social facts."
2 See Wuthnow (1991); Bellah *et al.* (1985).
3 See, for instance Cicourel's work (1991, 1981, 1973). Cicourel has been a consistent proponent of analyzing talk in relation to specific social contexts in which talk occurs.

References

The primary sources listed are only those cited in the text. In addition to those, I examined:

Ridge Green (semi-monthly newsletter), most issues, 1986–1991.

Green Letter/In Search of Greener Times (national newsletter of US Green movement), 1989–1991; some issues 1987–1989.

Preliminary drafts of statements for the 1989 Green "SPAKA" document (Strategy and Policy Approaches in Key Areas), roughly 500 pp.

First completed draft of 1989 SPAKA document, provisionally ratified at 1989 Green conference, Eugene, Oregon, 22 pp.

"Green Committees of Correspondence Program," consisting of further revised SPAKA statements, as ratified at third national Green conference, 1990, 23 pp.

Airdale Citizens for Environmental Sanity (newsletter, monthly since 1990, occasional 1983–1989), 1990–1991; scattered issues as available 1983–1989.

Everyone's Backyard (quarterly journal of Citizens' Clearinghouse for Hazardous Wastes, Inc.), "Spring" issue 1989–"April" issue 1991.

Primary sources

Adair, Margo and Howell, Sharon. 1988. *The Subjective Side of Politics*. San Francisco: Tools for Change.

Citizens' Clearinghouse for Hazardous Wastes (CCHW). 1986. *Five Years of Progress, 1981–1986*. Arlington, VA: CCHW.

Collette, Will. n.d. "Best of 'Organizing Toolbox'." A collection of reprints originally published in *Everyone's Backyard*. Arlington, VA: CCHW.

Gibbs, Lois. 1989. "The Movement on the Move." *Everyone's Backyard* 7(2): 1, 3.

Gibbs, Lois and Collette, Will. 1983. *Leadership Handbook on Hazardous Waste*. Arlington, VA: CCHW.

Kelly, Petra. 1988. "Toward a Green Europe! Toward a Green World!" *Green Letter/In Search of Greener Times* 4(3).

Moses, Daniel and Spretnak, Charlene. 1989. "A Consideration of GCoC History." *Green Letter/In Search of Green Times* 5(1) (Spring).

Moyer, Bill. 1987. "The Movement Action Plan." Cambridge, MA: Movement for a New Society.

Newman, Penny. 1991. "Organizing Toolbox: National vs. Nationwide." *Everyone's Backyard* 9(1): 9.

"Proceedings of the Green Organizing Planning Meeting," 4 pp., n.d.

Ridge Greens Handbook. Draft, n.d. (1989).

Russell, Dick. 1989. "Environmental Racism." *The Amicus Journal* (Spring).

Solnit, David. 1990. "Notes on a Dysfunctional Pattern in the Greens: Power and Process." *Green Letter/In Search of Greener Times* Vol. 6(3) (Autumn).

Stults, Karen. 1989. "Women Movers: Reflections on a Movement by Some of its Leaders." *Everyone's Backyard* 7(1) (Spring).

Tokar, Brian. 1989. "Toward a More Vital Grass-Roots Green Politics." *Green Letter/In Search of Greener Times*, 5(2) (Summer).

"Women's Encampment Resource Handbook." Produced for the Women's Encampment for a Future of Peace and Justice, Seneca Army Depot, New York, Summer 1983.

Zeff, Robbin Lee, Love, M. and Stults, K. 1989. *Empowering Ourselves: Women and Toxics Organizing*. Arlington, VA: CCHW.

Secondary sources

Abbey, Edward. 1975. *The Monkey Wrench Gang*. New York: Avon.

Anderson, Benedict. 1991. *Imagined Communities: Reflections on the Origins and Spread of Nationalism*. London: Verso.

Andrews, Molly. 1991. *Lifetimes of Commitment*. New York: Cambridge University Press.

Anzaldua, Gloria and Moraga, Cherrie (eds.) 1982. *This Bridge Called My Back: Writings of Radical Women of Color*. New York: Kitchen Table, Women of Color Press.

Barkan, Steve. 1979. "Strategic, Tactical and Organizational Dilemmas of the Protest Movement Against Nuclear Power." *Social Problems* 27(1): 19–37.

Baumgartner, M. 1988. *The Moral Order of a Suburb*. New York: Oxford University Press.

Bell, Daniel. 1976. *The Cultural Contradictions of Capitalism*. New York: Basic Books.

Bellah, Robert. 1988. "The Idea of Practices in *Habits*: A Response." In C. Reynolds and R. Norman (eds.), *Community in America: The Challenge of Habits of the Heart*. Berkeley: University of California Press, pp. 269–288.

Bellah, Robert (ed.) 1973. *Emile Durkheim: On Morality and Society*. Chicago: University of Chicago Press.

Bellah, Robert, Madsen, R., Sullivan, W., Swidler, A., and Tipton, S. 1985. *Habits of the Heart*. Berkeley: University of California Press.

Benhabib, Seyla and Cornell, Drucilla. 1987. "Introduction: Beyond the Politics of Gender." In S. Benhabib and D. Cornell (eds.), *Feminism as Critique*. Minneapolis: University of Minnesota Press, pp. 1–15.

Bernstein, Basil. [1971, 1973] 1975, 1976. *Class, Codes, and Control*, vols. i and iii. New York: Schocken.

Boggs, Carl. 1983. "The New Populism and the Limits of Structural Reforms." *Theory and Society* 12: 343–373.

Bourdieu, Pierre. 1977. *Outline of a Theory of Practice*. Cambridge: Cambridge University Press.

1984. *Distinction*. Cambridge, MA: Harvard University Press.

1985. "The Social Space and the Genesis of Groups." *Theory and Society* 14(6): 723–743.

1986. "The Forms of Capital." In J. G. Richardson (ed.), *Handbook of Theory and Research for the Sociology of Education*. New York: Greenwood, pp. 240–258.

1990. *The Logic of Practice*. Stanford: Stanford University Press.

Bourdieu, Pierre and Passeron, J. C. 1977. *Reproduction in Education, Society and Culture*. Beverly Hills: Sage.

Bowles, Samuel and Gintis, Herbert. 1976. *Schooling in Capitalist America*. New York: Basic Books.

Boyte, Harry. 1980. *The Backyard Revolution: Understanding the New Citizen Movement*. Philadelphia: Temple University Press.

1981. "Populism and the Left." *democracy* 1(2): 53–66.

1984. *Community is Possible: Repairing America's Roots*. New York: Harper and Row.

1989. *CommonWealth: A Return to Citizen Politics*. New York: Free Press.

1992. "The Pragmatic Ends of Popular Politics." In C. Calhoun (ed.), *Habermas and the Public Sphere*. Cambridge, MA: MIT Press, pp. 340–355.

Boyte, Harry and Evans, Sara. 1986. *Free Spaces: The Sources of Democratic Change in America*. First edn. New York: Harper and Row.

Breines, Wini. 1982. *Community and Organization in the New Left: 1962–1968*. New York: Praeger.

Brenner, Johanna. 1988. "Beyond Essentialism: Feminist Theory and Strategy in the Peace Movement." In M. Davis and M. Sprinker (eds.), *Reshaping the US Left: Popular Struggles in the 1980s*. London: Verso, pp. 93–113.

Brint, Steven. 1984. "'New Class' and Cumulative Trend Explanations of the Liberal Political Attitudes of Professionals." *American Journal of Sociology* 90: 30–71.

Bruce-Briggs, B. 1979. *The New Class?*. New Brunswick: Transaction Books.

Bryant, Bunyan and Mohai, Paul. 1992. *Race and the Incidence of Environmental Hazards*. Boulder: Westview Press.

Buechler, Steven. 1990. *Women's Movements in the United States: Woman Suffrage, Equal Rights, and Beyond*. New Brunswick: Rutgers University Press.

Bürklin, Wilhelm. 1988. "A Politico-Economic Model Instead of Sour Grapes Logic: A Reply to Herbert Kitschelt's Critique." *European Sociological Review* 4(2): 161–166.

Bullard, Robert. 1989. "The New Environmental-Equity Movement: Black Mobilization Against the Toxic Threat." Presented at Society for the Study of Social Problems annual meeting, Chicago, IL, 1987.

1990. *Dumping in Dixie: Race, Class, and Environmental Quality*. Boulder: Westview.

Bullard, Robert (ed.). 1993. *Confronting Environmental Racism: Voices from the Grassroots*. Boston: South End Press.

Bullard, Robert and Wright, B. 1987. "Environmentalism and the Politics of Equity: Emergent Trends in the Black Community." *Mid-American Review of Sociology* 12(2): 21–38.

Calhoun, Craig. 1993. "Postmodernism as Pseudohistory." *Theory, Culture and Society* 10: 75–96.

Calhoun, Craig (ed.). 1992. *Habermas and the Public Sphere*. Cambridge, MA: MIT Press.

Cancian, Francesca. 1987. *Love in America*. Cambridge: Cambridge University Press.

Capek, Stella. 1993 "The 'Environmental Justice' Frame: A Conceptual Discussion and an Application." *Social Problems* 40(1): 5–24.

Capra, Fritjof and Spretnak, Charlene. 1984. *Green Politics*. New York: E. P. Dutton.

Carson, Clayborne. 1981. *In Struggle: SNCC and the Black Awakening of the 1960s*. Cambridge, MA: Harvard University Press.

Case, John and Taylor, Rosemary. 1979. *Co-ops, Communes and Collectives*. New York: Pantheon.

Castells, Manuel. 1983. *The City and the Grassroots*. Berkeley: University of California Press.

Cicourel, Aaron. 1973. *Cognitive Sociology: Language and Meaning in Social Interaction*. Harmondsworth and Baltimore: Penguin Books.

1981. "Notes on the Integration of Micro- and Macro-Levels of Analysis." In K. Knorr-Cetina and A. Cicourel (eds.), *Advances in Social Theory: Toward an Integration of Micro- and Macro- Sociologies*. Boston: Routledge and Kegan Paul, pp. 51–80.

1991. "Semantics, Pragmatics, and Situated Meaning." Forthcoming in Jef Verschueren (ed.), *Pragmatics at Issue*, Vol. i. Amsterdam and Philadelphia: John Benjamins, pp. 37–66.

Clecak, Peter. 1983. *America's Quest for the Ideal Self*. New York: Oxford University Press.

Cohen, Jean. 1985. "Strategy or Identity: New Theoretical Paradigms and Contemporary Social Movements." *Social Research* 52(4): 663–716.

Commission on Racial Justice, United Church of Christ. 1987. "Toxic Wastes and Race in the United Sates: A National Report on the Racial and Socio-Economic Characteristics of Communities with Hazardous Waste Sites."

Comstock, George. 1978. *Television and Human Behavior*. New York: Columbia University Press.

Cotgrove, Stephen and Duff, A. 1980. "Environmentalism, Middle Class Radicalism, and Politics." *Sociological Review* 28: 333–351.

Delgado, Gary. 1986. *Organizing the Movement: The Roots and Growth of ACORN*. Philadephia: Temple University Press.

Dellinger, David. 1993. *From Yale to Jail: The Life Story of a Moral Dissenter*. New York: Pantheon Books.

Dietz, Mary. 1992. "Context is All: Feminism and Theories of Citizenship." In C. Mouffe (ed.), *Dimensions of Radical Democracy*. London: Verso, pp. 63–85.

Dobriner, William. 1963. *Class in Suburbia*. Englewood Cliffs, NJ: Prentice-Hall.

Eagleton, Terry. 1984. *The Function of Criticism: From "The Spectator" to Post-Structuralism*. London: Verso.

Echols, Alice. 1989. *Daring to Be Bad: Radical Feminism in America: 1967–1975*. Minneapolis: University of Minnesota Press.

Edelstein, Michael. 1988. *Contaminated Communities*. Boulder: Westview Press.

Eder, Klaus. 1982. "A New Social Movement?" *Telos* 52: 5–20 (Summer).

1985. "The 'New Social Movements': Moral Crusades, Political Pressure Groups, or Social Movements?" *Social Research* 52(4): 869–890.

Ehrenreich, John and Ehrenreich, B. 1977. "The Professional-Managerial Class." *Radical America* 11: 7–31.

Eliasoph, Nina. 1990. "The Presentation of the Political Self: A Study of the Public Sphere in the Spirit of Erving Goffman." *Theory and Society* 19: 465–495.

Epstein, Barbara. 1988. "The Politics of Prefigurative Community: The Non-Violent Direct Action Movement." In Mike Davis and M. Sprinker (eds.), *Reshaping the US Left*. New York and London: Verso, pp. 63–92.

1991. *Political Protest and Cultural Revolution*. Berkeley: University of California Press.

Etzioni, Amitai. 1993. *The Spirit of Community: Rights, Responsibilities, and the Communitarian Agenda*. New York: Crown Publishers.

Evans, Sara. 1979. *Personal Politics*. New York: Knopf.

Eyerman, Ron and Jamison, A. 1989. "Environmental Knowledge as an Organizational Weapon: The Case of Greenpeace." *Social Science Information* 28(1): 99–119.

Fischer, Claude and Jackson, R. M. 1976. "Suburbs, Networks, and Attitudes." In B. Schwartz (ed.), *The Changing Face of the Suburbs*. Chicago: University of Chicago Press, pp. 279–308.

FitzSimmons, M. and Gottlieb, R. 1988. "A New Environmental Politics." In Mike Davis and M. Sprinker (eds.), *Reshaping the US Left*. New York and London: Verso, pp. 114–130.

Flacks, Richard. 1976. "Making History vs. Making Life: Dilemmas of an American Left." *Sociological Inquiry* 46: 263–280.

1988. *Making History*. New York: Columbia University Press.

Foglia, Gina and Wolffberg, D. 1981. "Spiritual Dimensions of Feminist Anti-Nuclear Activism." In C. Spretnak (ed.), *The Politics of Women's Spirituality*. New York: Doubleday, 1982, pp. 446–461.

Fraser, Nancy. 1985. "What's Critical About Critical Theory? The Case of Habermas and Gender." *New German Critique* 35: 97–133.

1992. "Rethinking the Public Sphere: A Contribution to the Critique of Actually Existing Democracy." In C. Calhoun (ed.), *Habermas and the Public Sphere*. Boston: MIT Press, pp. 109–142.

Freeman, Jo. 1972–1973. "The Tyranny of Structurelessness." *Berkeley Journal of Sociology* 17: 151–164.

1975. *The Politics of Women's Liberation*. New York: Longman.

Freudenberg, Nicholas. 1984. "Citizen Action for Environmental Health: Report on a Survey of Community Organizations." *American Journal of Public Health* 74: 444–448.

Gamson, William. 1975. *The Strategy of Social Protest*. Homerwood: Dorsey Press.

1992. "The Social Psychology of Collective Action." In Aldon Morris and Carol Mueller (eds.), *Frontiers in Social Movement Theory*. New Haven: Yale University Press.

Gans, Herbert. 1988. *Middle American Individualism*. New York: The Free Press.

Gaventa, John. 1980. *Power and Powerlessness*. Urbana: University of Illinois Press.

Gerbner, George, Gross, Larry, Morgan, Michael and Signorielli, Nancy. 1982. "Charting the Mainstream: Television's Contributions to Political Orientations." *Journal of Communication* 32(2): 100–127.

Giddens, Anthony. 1991. *Modernity and Self-Identity: Self and Society in the Late Modern Age*. Stanford: Stanford University Press.

Ginsburg, Faye. 1989. *Contested Lives: The Abortion Debate in an American Community*. Berkeley: University of California Press.

Gitlin, Todd. 1987. *The Sixties: Years of Hope, Days of Rage*. New York: Bantam.

Goodwyn, Lawrence. 1978. *The Populist Moment*. New York: Oxford University Press.

Gouldner, Alvin. 1979. *The Future of Intellectuals and the Rise of the New Class*. New York: Seabury.

Gramsci, Antonio. 1971. *Selections from the Prison Notebooks*. Ed. and trans. Quintin Hoare and Geoffrey N. Smith. New York: International Publishers.

Habermas, Jürgen. 1970. *Toward a Rational Society*. Boston: Beacon Press.

1974. "The Public Sphere: An Encyclopedia Article." *New German Critique* no. 3: 49–55.

1975. *Legitimation Crisis*. Boston: Beacon Press.

1979. "Moral Development and Ego Identity." In *Communication and the Evolution of Society*. Boston: Beacon Press, pp. 69–94.

1984. *Theory of Communicative Action*, Vol. i. Boston: Beacon Press.

1986. *Autonomy and Solidarity*, Interviews edited and introduced by Peter Dews. London: Verso.

1987. *Theory of Communicative Action*, Vol. ii. Boston: Beacon Press.

1989. *The Structural Transformation of the Public Sphere*. Trans. Thomas Burgle. Cambridge, MA: MIT Press.

Hannon, James. 1990. "Becoming a Peace Activist: A Life Course Perspective." In Sam Marullo and J. Lofland (eds.), *Peace Action in the Eighties*. New Brunswick: Rutgers University Press, pp. 217–232.

Henry, Charles. 1990. *Culture and African American Politics*. Bloomington: Indiana University Press.

Herbst, Susan. 1994. *Politics at the Margin*. New York: Cambridge University Press.

Hewitt, John. 1989. *Dilemmas of the American Self.* Philadelphia: Temple University Press.

Hochschild, Arlie. 1983. *The Managed Heart.* Berkeley: University of California Press.

Horkheimer, Max. [1936] 1972. "Authority and the Family." In *Critical Theory.* New York: Herder and Herder, pp. 47–128.

Horkheimer, Max and Adorno, Theodor. [1944] 1972. "The Culture Industry: Enlightenment as Mass Deception." In *Dialectic of Enlightenment.* New York: Herder and Herder, pp. 120–167.

Hunt, Scott, Benford, Robert and Snow, David. 1994. "Identity Fields: Framing Processes and the Social Construction of Movement Identities." In Enrique Larana, H. Johnston and J. Gusfield (eds.), *New Social Movements: From Ideology to Identity.* Philadelphia: Temple University Press, pp. 185–208.

Inglehart, Richard. 1981. "Post-Materialism in an Environment of Insecurity." *American Political Science Review* 75: 880–900.

1990. *Culture Shift in Advanced Industrial Society.* Princeton: Princeton University Press.

Isserman, Maurice. 1987. *If I Had a Hammer: The Death of the Old Left and the Birth of the New.* New York: Basic Books.

Kaminstein, Dana. 1988. "Toxic Talk." *Social Policy* 19(2): 5–10.

Kazin, Michael. 1995. *The Populist Persuasion.* New York: Basic Books.

Kitschelt, Herbert. 1985. "New Social Movements in West Germany and the United States." *Political Power and Social Theory* 5: 273–324.

1988. "The Life Expectancy of Left-Libertarian Parties. Does Structural Transformation or Economic Decline Explain Party Innovation? A Response to Wilhelm Bürklin." *European Sociological Review* 4(2): 155–160.

Kriesi, Hanspeter. 1989. "New Social Movements and the New Class in the Netherlands." *American Journal of Sociology* 94(5): 1078–1116.

Kulka, R., Veroff, J. and Douvan, E. 1979. "Social Class and the Use of Professional Help for Personal Problems: 1957 and 1976." *Journal of Health and Social Behavior* 20: 2–17.

Ladd, A., Hood, T. and Van Liere, K. 1980. "Ideological Themes in the Antinuclear Movement: Consensus and Diversity." *Sociological Inquiry* 53: 252–272.

Ladd, E., Jr. 1978. "The New Lines Are Drawn: Class and Ideology in America, Part I." *Public Opinion* 3:48–53.

Lamont, Michele. 1986. "Cultural Capital and the Liberal Political Attitudes of Professionals: Comment on Brint." *American Journal of Sociology* 92(6): 1501–1515.

1992. *Money, Morals, and Manners.* Chicago: University of Chicago Press.

Lamont, Michele, and Lareau, Annette. 1988. "Cultural Capital: Allusions, Gaps, and Glissandos in Recent Theoretical Developments." *Sociological Theory* 6: 153–168.

Lancourt, Jane. 1979. *Confront or Concede: The Alinsky Citizen-Action Organizations.* Lexington, MA: D. C. Heath.

Lasch, Christopher. 1966. *The New Radicalism in America, 1889–1963: The*

Intellectual as a Social Type. New York: A. Knopf.

1979. *The Culture of Narcissism.* New York: W. W. Norton and Co.,Warner edition.

1991. *The True and Only Heaven: Progress and its Critics.* New York: Norton.

Lears, T. J. Jackson. 1981. *No Place of Grace.* New York: Pantheon.

Lichterman, Paul. 1989a. "Making a Politics of Masculinity." In C. Calhoun (ed.), *Comparative Social Research*, Volume xi. Greenwich, CT: JAI Press, pp. 185–208.

1989b. "Revisiting a Gramscian Dilemma: Problems and Possibilities in Bourdieu's Analysis of Culture and Politics." Paper presented at American Sociological Association meeting, San Francisco.

1992. "Self-Help Reading as a Thin Culture." *Media, Culture and Society* 14(3): 421–447.

1995a. "Beyond the Seesaw Model: Public Commitment in a Culture of Self-Fulfillment." *Sociological Theory* 13(3).

1995b. "Piecing Together Multicultural Community: Cultural Differences in Community-Building among Grassroots Environmentalists." *Social Problems* 42 (4): 513–534.

Lincoln, C. Eric and Mamiya, L. 1990. *The Black Church in the African American Experience.* Durham: Duke University Press.

Lustig, Jeff. 1981. "Community and Social Class." Review of Boyte, *The Backyard Revolution* and Piven and Cloward, *Poor People's Movements: Why They Succeed, How They Fail. democracy* 1(2): 96–111.

Lynch, Barbara. 1993. "The Garden and the Sea: US Latino Environmental Discourses and Mainstream Environmentalism." *Social Problems* 40(1): 108–124.

MacIntyre, Alasdair. 1981. *After Virtue.* Notre Dame, IN: University of Notre Dame Press.

Macy, Joanna Rogers. 1983. *Despair and Personal Power in the Nuclear Age.* Philadelphia: New Society Publishers.

Manes, Christopher. 1990. *Green Rage: Environmentalism and the Unmaking of Civilization.* Boston: Little, Brown.

Mansbridge, Jane. 1983. *Beyond Adversary Democracy.* Chicago: University of Chicago Press.

Marullo, Sam and Lofland, John (eds.). 1990. *Peace Action in the Eighties: Social Science Perspectives.* New Brunswick: Rutgers University Press.

Marx, John. 1979. "The Ideological Construction of Post-Modern Identity Models in Contemporary Cultural Movements." In R. Robertson and B. Holzner, (eds.), *Identity and Authority.* Oxford: Basil Blackwell, pp. 145–189.

McAdam, Doug. 1988a. "Micromobilization Contexts and Recruitment to Activism." In *International Social Movement Research*, Vol. i. Greenwich, CT: JAI Press, pp. 125–154.

1988b. *Freedom Summer.* New York: Oxford University Press.

McCann, Michael. 1986. *Taking Reform Seriously: Perspectives on Public Interest Liberalism.* Ithaca: Cornell University Press.

McCarthy, John and Zald, M. 1977. "Resource Mobilization and Social

Movements: A Partial Theory." *American Journal of Sociology* 82(6): 1212–1241.

Melucci, Alberto. 1981. "Ten Hypotheses for the Analysis of New Movements." In D. Pinto (ed.), *Contemporary Italian Sociology*. Cambridge: Cambridge University Press, pp. 173–194.

1985. "The Symbolic Challenge of Contemporary Movements." *Social Research* 52(4): 789–815.

1988. "Getting Involved: Identity and Mobilization in Social Movements." In *International Social Movement Research*, Vol. i. Greenwich, CT: JAI Press, pp. 329–348.

1989. *Nomads of the Present: Social Movements and Individual Needs in Contemporary Society*. Philadelphia: Temple University Press.

1991. "The Global Planet and the Internal Planet. New Frontiers for Collective Action and Individual Transformation." Paper presented at the conference "Social Movements and Cultural Politics," University of California, Santa Cruz.

Meyer, David and Whittier, Nancy. 1994. "Social Movement Spillover." *Social Problems* 41: 277–298.

Miller, James. 1987. *"Democracy is in the Streets": From Port Huron to the Siege of Chicago*. New York: Simon and Schuster.

Morris, Aldon. 1984. *The Origins of the Civil Rights Movement*. New York: The Free Press.

Mouffe, Chantal. 1992a. "Preface: Democratic Politics Today." In C. Mouffe (ed.), *Dimensions of Radical Democracy*. London: Verso, pp. 1–14.

1992b. "Democratic Citizenship and the Political Community." In C. Mouffe (ed.), *Dimensions of Radical Democracy*. London: Verso, pp. 225– 240.

1993. "Feminism, Citizenship, and Radical Democratic Politics." In *The Return of the Political*. London: Verso, pp. 74–89.

Offe, Claus. 1985. "New Social Movements: Challenging the Boundaries of Institutional Politics." *Social Research* 52(4): 817–869.

Olson, Mancur. 1965. *The Logic of Collective Action*. Cambridge, MA: Harvard University Press.

Parkin, Frank. 1968. *Middle Class Radicalism*. Manchester: Manchester University Press.

Potter, Sulamith H. 1988. "The Cultural Construction of Emotion in Rural Chinese Social Life." *Ethos* 16(2): 181–208.

Rabinow, Paul. 1986. "Representations Are Social Facts: Modernity and Post-Modernity in Anthropology." In J. Clifford and G. Marcus (eds.), *Writing Culture: The Poetics and Politics of Ethnography*. Berkeley: University of Calfornia Press, pp. 234–261.

Rabinow, Paul and Sullivan, W. 1979. *Interpretive Social Science: A Reader*. Berkeley: University of California Press.

Reitzes, Donald and Reitzes, Dietrich. 1987. *The Alinsky Legacy: Alive and Kicking*. (*Research in Social Movements, Conflict, and Change*, Supplement 1). Greenwich, CT: JAI Press.

Rieff, Philip. 1959. *Freud: The Mind of the Moralist*. New York: Viking Press.

1966. *The Triumph of the Therapeutic: The Uses of Faith After Freud*. London: Chatto and Windus.

1987. "For the Last Time Psychology: Thoughts on the Therapeutic Twenty Years After." *Salmagundi* 74–75.

Ryan, Mary. 1992. "Gender and Public Access: Women's Politics in Nineteenth-Century America." In Craig Calhoun (ed.), *Habermas and the Public Sphere.* Cambridge, MA: MIT Press, pp. 259–288.

Scaminaci, John and Dunlap, R. 1986. "No Nukes! A Comparison of Participants in Two National Antinuclear Demonstrations." *Sociological Inquiry* 56(2): 272–282.

Schudson, Michael. 1992. "Was there ever a public sphere? If so, when? Reflecting on the American case." In Craig Calhoun (ed.), *Habermas and the Public Sphere.* Cambridge, MA: MIT Press, pp. 143–163.

Seeley, J., Sim, R. and Loosley, E. 1956. *Crestwood Heights: A Study of the Culture of Suburban Life.* New York: Basic Books.

Sennett, Richard. 1977. *The Fall of Public Man.* New York: Vintage Books.

Skolnick, Arlene. 1991. *Embattled Paradise.* New York: Basic Books.

Snow, David and Benford, Robert. 1988. "Ideology, Frame Resonance and Participant Mobilization." In Bert Klandermans, Hanspeter Kriesi and Sidney Tarrow (eds.), *International Social Movement Research* 1. Greenwich, CT: JAI Press, pp. 197–217.

Snow, D., Rochford, E., Worden, S., and Benford, R. 1986. "Frame Alignment Processes, Micromobilization, and Movement Participation." *American Sociological Review* 51: 464–481.

Sperling, Susan. 1988. *Animal Liberators.* Berkeley: University of California Press.

Spretnak, Charlene. 1986. "Postmodern Populism: The Greening of Technocratic Society." In H. Boyte and F. Riessman (eds.), *The New Populism.* Philadelphia: Temple University Press, pp. 156–164.

Staggenborg, Suzanne. 1988. "The Consequences of Professionalization and Formalization in the Pro-Choice Movement." *American Sociological Review* 53: 585–606.

Suttles, Gerald. 1972. *The Social Construction of Communities.* Chicago: University of Chicago Press.

Swanson, Guy E. 1979. "A Basis of Authority and Identity in Post-Industrial Society." In R. Robertson and B. Holzner (eds.), *Identity and Authority.* Oxford: Basil Blackwell, pp. 190–217.

Swidler, Ann. 1979. *Organization Without Authority.* Cambridge, MA: Harvard University Press.

1986. "Culture in Action: Symbols and Strategies." *American Sociological Review* 51: 273–286.

Szasz, Andrew. 1994. *Ecopopulism: Toxic Waste and the Movement for Environmental Justice.* Minneapolis: University of Minnesota Press.

Tarrow, Sidney. 1988. "National Politics and Collective Action: Recent Theory and Research in Western Europe and the United States." In *Annual Review of Sociology* 14: 421–440.

1989. *Struggle, Politics and Reform: Collective Action, Social Movements and Cycles of Protest.* Cornell Western Societies Paper no. 21. Ithaca: Cornell University Press.

1992a. "Mentalities, Political Cultures, and Collective Action Frames: Constructing Meanings through Action." In Aldon Morris and Carol Mueller (eds.), *Frontiers in Social Movement Theory.* New Haven: Yale University Press, pp. 174–202.

1992b. "Costumes of Revolt: The Political Culture of Collective Action." Unpublished manuscript.

Taylor, Charles. 1989. *Sources of the Self: the Making of the Modern Identity.* Cambridge, MA: Harvard University Press.

1991. *The Ethics of Authenticity.* Cambridge, MA: Harvard University Press.

Tilly, Charles. 1978. *From Mobilization to Revolution.* Englewood Cliffs: Prentice-Hall.

Tipton, Steven. 1982. *Getting Saved from the Sixties.* Berkeley: University of California Press.

de Tocqueville, Alexis. 1945. *Democracy in America,* 2 vols. Ed. Phillips Bradley. New York: A. Knopf.

Touraine, Alain. 1981. *The Voice and the Eye.* Cambridge: Cambridge University Press.

Touraine, Alain, Hegedus, Z., Dubet, F. and Wieviorka, M. 1983. *Anti-Nuclear Protest.* Cambridge: Cambridge University Press.

Tucker, Ken. 1991. "How New are the New Social Movements?" *Theory, Culture and Society* 8: 75–98.

US Bureau of the Census. 1980. *Neighborhood Statistics Program.* Washington, DC.

1983. *Census of Population and Housing.* Washington, D.C.

Verba, Sidney and Nie, Norman. 1972. *Participation in America.* New York: Harper and Row.

Veroff, J., Douvan, E. and Kulka, R. 1981. *The Inner American: A Self-Portrait from 1957 to 1976.* New York: Basic Books.

Vogel, Stephen. 1980. "The Limits of Protest: A Critique of the Anti-Nuclear Movement." *Socialist Review* 54 (vol. 10, no. 6): 125–134.

Whalen, Jack and Flacks, R. 1989. *Beyond the Barricades: The Sixties Generation Grows Up.* Philadelphia: Temple University Press.

Wuthnow, Robert. 1991. *Acts of Compassion: Caring for Others and Helping Ourselves.* Princeton: Princeton University Press.

1994. *Sharing the Journey.* New York: Free Press.

Yankelovich, Daniel. 1981. *New Rules: Searching for Self-Fulfillment in a World Turned Upside Down.* New York: Random House.

Young, Iris. 1987. "Impartiality and the Civic Public: Some Implications of Feminist Critiques of Moral and Political Theory." In Seyla Benhabib and Drucilla Cornell (eds.), *Feminism as Critique.* Minneapolis: University of Minnesota Press, pp. 56–76.

Index

272